ZEN TEXTS

BDK English Tripiṭaka 73-III, 98-VIII, 98-IX, 104-I

ZEN TEXTS

Essentials of the Transmission of Mind

(Taishō Volume 48, Number 2012-A)

Translated from the Chinese by

John R. McRae

A Treatise on Letting Zen Flourish to Protect the State

(Taishō Volume 80, Number 2543)

Translated from the Japanese by

Gishin Tokiwa

A Universal Recommendation for True Zazen

(Taishō Volume 82, Number 2580)

Translated from the Japanese by

Osamu Yoshida

Advice on the Practice of Zazen

(Taishō Volume 82, Number 2586)

Translated from the Japanese by

Steven Heine

Numata Center for Buddhist Translation and Research
2005

First Printing, 2005
ISBN: 1-886439-28-1
Library of Congress Catalog Card Number: 2004116544

Published by
Numata Center for Buddhist Translation and Research
2620 Warring Street
Berkeley, California 94704

Printed in the United States of America

A Message on the Publication of the English Tripiṭaka

The Buddhist canon is said to contain eighty-four thousand different teachings. I believe that this is because the Buddha's basic approach was to prescribe a different treatment for every spiritual ailment, much as a doctor prescribes a different medicine for every medical ailment. Thus his teachings were always appropriate for the particular suffering individual and for the time at which the teaching was given, and over the ages not one of his prescriptions has failed to relieve the suffering to which it was addressed.

Ever since the Buddha's Great Demise over twenty-five hundred years ago, his message of wisdom and compassion has spread throughout the world. Yet no one has ever attempted to translate the entire Buddhist canon into English throughout the history of Japan. It is my greatest wish to see this done and to make the translations available to the many English-speaking people who have never had the opportunity to learn about the Buddha's teachings.

Of course, it would be impossible to translate all of the Buddha's eighty-four thousand teachings in a few years. I have, therefore, had one hundred thirty-nine of the scriptural texts in the prodigious Taishō edition of the Chinese Buddhist canon selected for inclusion in the First Series of this translation project.

It is in the nature of this undertaking that the results are bound to be criticized. Nonetheless, I am convinced that unless someone takes it upon himself or herself to initiate this project, it will never be done. At the same time, I hope that an improved, revised edition will appear in the future.

It is most gratifying that, thanks to the efforts of more than a hundred Buddhist scholars from the East and the West, this monumental project has finally gotten off the ground. May the rays of the Wisdom of the Compassionate One reach each and every person in the world.

NUMATA Yehan
Founder of the English
Tripiṭaka Project

August 7, 1991

Editorial Foreword

In January 1982, Dr. NUMATA Yehan, the founder of the Bukkyō Dendō Kyōkai (Society for the Promotion of Buddhism), decided to begin the monumental task of translating the complete Taishō edition of the Chinese Tripiṭaka (Buddhist canon) into the English language. Under his leadership, a special preparatory committee was organized in April 1982. By July of the same year, the Translation Committee of the English Tripiṭaka was officially convened.

The initial Committee consisted of the following members: (late) HANAYAMA Shōyū (Chairperson), (late) BANDŌ Shōjun, ISHIGAMI Zennō, (late) KAMATA Shigeo, KANAOKA Shūyū, MAYEDA Sengaku, NARA Yasuaki, (late) SAYEKI Shinkō, (late) SHIOIRI Ryōtatsu, TAMARU Noriyoshi, (late) TAMURA Kwansei, URYŪZU Ryūshin, and YUYAMA Akira. Assistant members of the Committee were as follows: KANAZAWA Atsushi, WATANABE Shōgo, Rolf Giebel of New Zealand, and Rudy Smet of Belgium.

After holding planning meetings on a monthly basis, the Committee selected one hundred thirty-nine texts for the First Series of translations, an estimated one hundred printed volumes in all. The texts selected are not necessarily limited to those originally written in India but also include works written or composed in China and Japan. While the publication of the First Series proceeds, the texts for the Second Series will be selected from among the remaining works; this process will continue until all the texts, in Japanese as well as in Chinese, have been published.

Frankly speaking, it will take perhaps one hundred years or more to accomplish the English translation of the complete Chinese and Japanese texts, for they consist of thousands of works. Nevertheless, as Dr. NUMATA wished, it is the sincere hope of the Committee that this project will continue unto completion, even after all its present members have passed away.

It must be mentioned here that the final object of this project is not academic fulfillment but the transmission of the teaching of the Buddha to the whole world in order to create harmony and peace among humankind. To that end, the translators have been asked to minimize the use of explanatory notes of the kind that are indispensable in academic texts, so that the attention of general readers will not be unduly distracted from the primary text. Also, a glossary of selected terms is appended to aid in understanding the text.

To my great regret, however, Dr. NUMATA passed away on May 5, 1994, at the age of ninety-seven, entrusting his son, Mr. NUMATA Toshihide, with the continuation and completion of the Translation Project. The Committee also lost its able and devoted Chairperson, Professor HANAYAMA Shōyū, on June 16, 1995, at the age of sixty-three. After these severe blows, the Committee elected me, then Vice President of Musashino Women's College, to be the Chair in October 1995. The Committee has renewed its determination to carry out the noble intention of Dr. NUMATA, under the leadership of Mr. NUMATA Toshihide.

The present members of the Committee are MAYEDA Sengaku (Chairperson), ISHIGAMI Zennō, ICHISHIMA Shōshin, KANAOKA Shūyū, NARA Yasuaki, TAMARU Noriyoshi, URYŪZU Ryūshin, YUYAMA Akira, Kenneth K. Tanaka, WATANABE Shōgo, and assistant member YONEZAWA Yoshiyasu.

The Numata Center for Buddhist Translation and Research was established in November 1984, in Berkeley, California, U.S.A., to assist in the publication of the BDK English Tripiṭaka First Series. In December 1991, the Publication Committee was organized at the Numata Center, with Professor Philip Yampolsky as the Chairperson. To our sorrow, Professor Yampolsky passed away in July 1996. In February 1997, Dr. Kenneth K. Inada became Chair and served in that capacity until August 1999. The current Chair, Dr. Francis H. Cook, has been continuing the work since October 1999. All of the remaining texts will be published under the supervision of this Committee, in close cooperation with the Editorial Committee in Tokyo.

MAYEDA Sengaku
Chairperson
Editorial Committee of
the BDK English Tripiṭaka

Publisher's Foreword

The Publication Committee shares with the Editorial Committee the responsibility of realizing the vision of Dr. Yehan Numata, founder of Bukkyō Dendō Kyōkai, the Society for the Promotion of Buddhism. This vision is no less than to make the Buddha's teaching better known throughout the world, through the translation and publication in English of the entire collection of Buddhist texts compiled in the *Taishō Shinshū Daizōkyō,* published in Tokyo in the early part of the twentieth century. This huge task is expected to be carried out by several generations of translators and may take as long as a hundred years to complete. Ultimately, the entire canon will be available to anyone who can read English and who wishes to learn more about the teaching of the Buddha.

The present generation of staff members of the Publication Committee includes Marianne Dresser; Reverend Brian Nagata, president of the Numata Center for Buddhist Translation and Research, Berkeley, California; Eisho Nasu; and Reverend Kiyoshi Yamashita. The Publication Committee is headquartered at the Numata Center and, working in close cooperation with the Editorial Committee, is responsible for the usual tasks associated with preparing translations for publication.

In October 1999, I became the third chairperson of the Publication Committee, on the retirement of its very capable former chair, Dr. Kenneth K. Inada. The Committee is devoted to the advancement of the Buddha's teaching through the publication of excellent translations of the thousands of texts that make up the Buddhist canon.

Francis H. Cook
Chairperson
Publication Committee

Contents

ESSENTIALS OF THE TRANSMISSION OF MIND

Contents

Translator's Introduction

The *Essentials of the Transmission of Mind* (*Chuanxinfayao*) is a brilliantly insistent work. From beginning to end it repeatedly espouses a single vision of religious training: one's own mind, just as it is and without any qualification whatsoever, is the Buddha. And to be a Buddha is to act in constant recognition of that fact, without ever generating any thoughts, intentions, or inclinations based on selfish dualistic conceptualization. The text explains this simple doctrine in various different ways, concatenating iteration upon iteration in relentless exhortation: the one and only task of true religious practice is to simply cease discriminating between ordinary person and sage, between sentient being and Buddha. The preface to the text describes the mind by means of the following image:

> The essence of the mind is empty, and the myriad conditions are all serene. It is like the great orb of the sun climbing into space—the refulgent brilliance gleams in illumination, purity without a single speck of dust. . . . Right now, and that's it! To activate thoughts is to go against it!

The use of the sun as a metaphor for the enlightened mind is known from the formative early stage of Chan or Zen Buddhism, the East Mountain teaching and Northern school phases of the late seventh and early eighth centuries. A text attributed retrospectively to Hongren (600–74), the Fifth Patriarch of the traditional lineage and the teacher of the legendary Sixth Patriarch, Huineng, contains the image of an eternally radiant sun whose illumination is not destroyed but only adventitiously intercepted by the clouds and mists of this world. Just as the sun is always in the sky, even on cloudy and stormy days, so is Buddha-nature always immanent within us.

The admonition to avoid "activating thoughts" is also a hallmark of the early Chan tradition. The ideal was to avoid even the slightest trace of mental activity predicated on the ignorant conception of the self, the notion that "I" and "mine" somehow represent a domain cut off from the rest of the universe, a domain isolated and protected by the self-defense mechanisms of the ignorant ego. As the *Essentials of the Transmission of Mind* says,

> Just do not generate conceptual interpretations on the basis of those perceptive faculties, do not activate thoughts on the basis of those perceptive faculties, do not look for the mind apart from the perceptive faculties, and do not reject the perceptive faculties in order to grasp the *dharma*s.

Yet this is not an early Chan text. On the contrary, it is perhaps the earliest reliable doctrinal treatise of the classical phase of Chan that began with Mazu Daoyi (709–88). The central element of "classical" Chan was the use of oral dialogue between teacher and students as the primary mode of spiritual cultivation. We may be sure that trainees in Mazu's school still engaged in seated meditation (*dhyāna*), but there was a palpable taboo against even referring to this subject, let alone considering it the quintessential feature of Buddhist spiritual discipline. Instead, the real locus of self-cultivation was to be found in the intimate interaction between teacher and student known as "encounter dialogue." Some excellent examples of encounter dialogue occur in the *Essentials of the Transmission of Mind,* but there are also admonitions against being overly attached to the words and sounds of the teachings of the Buddhas and patriarchs. Presumably, by the time this text was compiled there was already a need to warn against excessive dependence on the oral medium.

The *Essentials of the Transmission of Mind* is based on the teachings of Huangbo Xiyun, who is identified in the title of the *Taishō shinshū daizōkyō* text as Chan Master Duanji. Huangbo's dates are unknown (he probably died in the mid-850s), but he was a disciple of Baizhang Huaihai (749–814), who was in turn a student of Mazu. Although not necessarily Mazu's most important disciple, Baizhang

Huaihai's retrospective status became higher after his death. Huangbo spent part of his career teaching in Hongzhou, and Zongmi's use of the term "Hongzhou school" with regard to the teachings of Mazu seems to refer to Huangbo. Hence during his own lifetime Huangbo may well have represented the dominant Mazu lineage.

In later years Huangbo is remembered chiefly through his connection with the great Linji Yixuan (d. 867), who is regarded as the founder of the Linji (Rinzai) school. Although there is no substantial difference between the teachings attributed to Huangbo in the *Essentials of the Transmission of Mind* and the *Recorded Sayings of Linji* (*Linji lu;* translated by J. C. Cleary and published in *Three Chan Classics,* Numata Center, 1999), in the latter work he appears solely in his status as Linji's teacher.

The nucleus of the *Essentials of the Transmission of Mind* was recorded by the literati Pei Xiu (797–870). Pei Xiu came from a family of devout Buddhists with long connections to the Chan tradition, and he was closely associated with the great Huayan and Chan scholar-monk Zongmi (780–848). It is interesting to note that Pei Xiu's evaluation of Huangbo would have been quite unacceptable to Zongmi, who posited sharp distinctions between mainstream and splinter interpretations of the Chan religious message. Zongmi was unready or unable to accept the novel spirit of Mazu's Hongzhou school, and it is intriguing to wonder whether Huangbo was responding to Pei Xiu's previous spiritual compatriot in some of the dialogues found in the *Essentials of the Transmission of Mind.*

Pei Xiu records in his preface that the teachings contained in the *Essentials of the Transmission of Mind* derive from discussions between him and Huangbo in 842 and 848, and that he sent the transcript of those discussions—as he had done his best to transcribe them—back to Huangbo's religious community in 857. It is unknown precisely what editorial forces may have been at work after this, but it is certain that material has been added to Pei Xiu's initial recension. The air of dogged insistence that pervades the text may be due in part to the inclusion of variant renditions of the original (or extremely similar) dialogues.

This translation was originally prepared on the basis of the critical edition and modern Japanese translation in Yoshitaka Iriya's *Denshin hōyō—Enryōroku,* Zen no goroku, no. 8 (Tokyo: Chikuma shobō, 1969). This was actually a group project headed by Professor Iriya, under whom I worked briefly in the past and who I know to have been a consummate authority on Chinese literature. I have rendered Iriya's headings into English and have included them in the text for the convenience of the reader; these divisions differ from those of the traditional text only in that the first three sections here represent one overly long section in the traditional version. For the purposes of this translation I have generally followed the text found in the *Taishō shinshū daizōkyō* where this differs from Iriya's edition. However, the punctuation of the Taishō edition is frequently in error, and I have almost always followed Iriya's lead in the grammatical interpretation of the text. Except at the very early stages of this project, I have not consulted the only extant English translation, John Blofeld's *The Zen Teaching of Huang Po on the Transmission of Mind* (New York: Grove Press, 1958). This is not to imply any undue criticism: Blofeld's sensitive renditions of the classics of Chinese religious literature have proved to be extremely valuable over the years, but the intervening decades of development in Chan and Zen studies mandate the appearance of new translations.

Given the widespread efforts toward the international dissemination of Buddhism as a modern message of peace and spiritual well-being, I am honored to be able to offer this contribution to the Bukkyō Dendō Kyōkai for inclusion in its English Tripiṭaka series. May it serve as a catalyst for the enlightenment of all sentient beings!

ESSENTIALS OF THE TRANSMISSION OF MIND

by

Duanji

Compiled with a Preface by Pei Xiu of Hedong

[Preface]

There was a great Chan master of the religious name Xiyun, who lived beneath the Eagle Promontory of Mount Huangbo in Gao'an County in Hongzhou. He was a direct successor to the Sixth Patriarch of Caoqi and the religious nephew of Baizhang [Huaihai] and Xitang [Zhizang]. Alone did he gird himself with the ineffable seal of the supreme vehicle. He transmitted only the One Mind, other than which there are no other *dharma*s. 379b26

The essence of the mind is empty, and the myriad conditions are all serene. It is like the great orb of the sun climbing into space—the refulgent brilliance gleams in illumination, purity without a single speck of dust. The realization [of this mind] is without new or old, without shallow or deep. Its explanation depends neither on doctrinal understanding, on teachers, nor on opening up the doors and windows [of one's house to let in students]. Right now, and that's it! To activate thoughts is to go against it! Afterward, [you'll realize] this is the fundamental Buddha. 379c

Therefore, his words were simple, his principles direct, his path steep, and his practice unique. Students from the four directions raced to his mountain, where they looked on his countenance and became enlightened. The sea of followers who came and went always numbered more than a thousand.

In the second year of the Huichang [period] (842), when I (Pei Xiu) was stationed in Zhongling (Hongzhou), I invited [Chan Master Huangbo] down from his mountain to the prefectural city. He reposed at Longxingsi, where I inquired of him regarding the path morning and night. In the second year of the Dazhong [period] (848), when I was stationed in Yuanling, I again respectfully welcomed him to my offices. He resided at Kaiyuansi, and I received the teachings morning and night. After leaving his company I noted down [his teachings], although I managed to get [down in writing] only one or two of every ten things he said. I have girded myself [with these teachings] as my mind-seal, but I have not dared circulate them. Now, fearing that these inspired ideas might not be known in the future, I have finally copied them out and am giving them to [Huangbo's] disciples Taizhou and Fajian. They will return to Guangtangsi on Mount Huangbo, where they will inquire of the congregation of elders as to whether [what I have written] is in accord with what they formerly heard themselves.

Preface done this eighth day of the tenth month of the eleventh year of the Dazhong [*period*] (857) *of the Great Tang*

1. Mind Is Buddha

The master said to [Pei] Xiu: The Buddhas and all the sentient beings are only the One Mind—there are no other *dharmas*. Since beginningless time, this mind has never been generated and has never been extinguished, is neither blue nor yellow, is without shape and without characteristic, does not belong to being and nonbeing, does not consider new or old, is neither long nor short, and is neither large nor small. It transcends all limitations, names, traces, and correlations. It in itself—that's it! To activate thoughts is to go against it! It is like space, which is boundless and immeasurable.

It is only this One Mind that is Buddha; there is no distinction between Buddhas and sentient beings. However, sentient beings are attached to characteristics and seek outside themselves. Seeking it, they lose it even more. Sending the Buddha in search of the Buddha, grasping the mind with the mind, they may exhaust themselves in striving for an entire eon but will never get it. They do not understand that if they cease their thoughts and end their thinking, the Buddha will automatically be present.

This mind is the Buddha; the Buddha is the sentient being. When it is sentient being, the mind is not lessened; and when it is [one of] the Buddhas, the mind is not increased. And as for the six perfections (*pāramitās*) and the myriad practices, and the types of merit as numerous as the [sands of the] Ganges River—[every sentient being is] fundamentally sufficient in these and requires no further cultivation. If the conditions occur then give forth [one's spiritual charity]; when the conditions cease then be silent.

If you are not able to believe resolutely that this [mind] is the
Buddha but attempt spiritual training while attached to charac- 380a
teristics, your quest for spiritual efficacy will be entirely based on false thoughts and contrary to the enlightenment [of Buddhahood]. This mind is the Buddha; there is neither any separate Buddha nor any separate mind.

This mind is bright and pure and like unto space, without a single bit of characteristic. To rouse the mind and activate thoughts is to go against the essence of the Dharma and to be attached to characteristics. Since beginningless time, there has never been any Buddha attached to characteristics (i.e., any Buddha associated with or defined by phenomenal characteristics). [The teaching that one can] cultivate the six perfections and the myriad practices in order to achieve Buddhahood—this is the progressive [approach to Buddhahood]. Since beginningless time, there has never been a Buddha [who achieved that state] progressively. Just be enlightened to the One Mind and there will not be the slightest *dharma* that can be attained—this is the true Buddha.

The One Mind is undifferentiated in Buddhas and sentient beings. It is like space, with no heterogeneity and no deterioration. It is like the great orb of the sun that illuminates all beneath the four heavens: when the sun rises its brightness extends throughout all the heavens, but space itself does not become bright; when the sun sets darkness extends throughout all the heavens, but space itself does not become dark. The realms of bright and dark besiege each other but the nature of space is expansive and unchanging. The mind of Buddhas and sentient beings is also like this.

If you conceive of the Buddha in terms of the characteristics of purity, brilliance, and liberation, and if you conceive of sentient beings in terms of the characteristics of impurity, darkness, and samsara—if your understanding is such as this, then you will never attain *bodhi* even after passing through eons [of religious practice] as numerous as the sands of the Ganges River. This is because you are attached to characteristics. There is only this One Mind and not the least bit of *dharma* that can be attained.

This mind is Buddha. Trainees these days are unenlightened to this essence of the mind, and they generate mind on top of mind, looking outward in search of the Buddha, and undertaking spiritual cultivation in attachment to characteristics. These are all bad methods (*dharma*s) and not the path to *bodhi*.

2. No-mind

To make offerings to all the Buddhas of the ten directions is inferior to making offerings to a single religious person with no-mind. Why? No-mind refers to the absence of all [states of] mind. The essence of suchness is unmoving like wood or stone within and unhindered like space without. It is without subject and object, without location, without characteristic, and without gain or loss. Those who would proceed [to enlightenment] are unwilling to enter this Dharma, fearing that they will fall into the void with nowhere to alight. Therefore they gaze upon the precipice and retreat, then they all seek widely after conceptual knowledge. Therefore those who seek after conceptual knowledge are as [numerous as strands of] hair while those who are enlightened are as [uncommon as] horns.

Mañjuśrī stands for principle and Samantabhadra stands for practice. "Principle" refers to the principle of unhindered true emptiness, while "practice" refers to the practice of the inexhaustible transcendence of characteristics. Avalokiteśvara stands for great compassion, and Mahāsthāmaprāpta stands for great wisdom. Vimalakīrti means "pure name." "Pure" is [essential] nature, and "name" is characteristic; he is called Pure Name because of the nondifferentiation of nature and characteristic.

[The virtues] typified by the various great bodhisattvas are possessed by all people; they do not transcend the One Mind, so if you are enlightened to that then you've got it. Trainees nowadays do not look within their own minds for enlightenment but become attached to characteristics and grasp realms outside the mind. This is totally contrary to the enlightenment [of Buddhahood].

[Take the] sands of the Ganges River: the Buddha has preached that when the Buddhas and bodhisattvas, Indras, Brahmās, and the various gods walk on them, the sands are not happy. And when cattle, sheep, worms, and ants step on them, the sands are not angry. When there is the fragrance of precious treasures, the sands 380b
do not lust after them. And when there is the stench of excrement and urine, the sands are not displeased.

This mind is the mind of no-mind. Transcending all characteristics, there is yet no difference between sentient beings and Buddhas. If you can just [attain] no-mind, then that is the ultimate [state of enlightenment]. If a trainee does not instantly [attain] no-mind but spends successive eons in cultivation, he will never achieve enlightenment. He will be fettered by the meritorious practices of the three vehicles and will not attain liberation.

However, there is fast and slow in realizing this mind: there are those who attain no-mind in a single moment of thought after hearing the Dharma; those who attain no-mind after [passing through] the ten faiths, the ten abodes, the ten practices, and the ten conversions; and those who attain no-mind after [passing through] the ten stages [of the bodhisattva]. In spite of the length of time it takes them to [attain it, once they] reside in no-mind there is nothing else to be cultivated or realized. Truly without anything to be attained, true and not false [is no-mind]. Whether it is attained in a single moment of thought or at the tenth stage [of the bodhisattva], its efficacy is identical. There are no further gradations of profundity, only the useless striving of successive eons. The performance of good and evil is entirely [within the domain of] characteristics. Being attached to characteristics and doing evil, one uselessly experiences samsara. Being attached to characteristics and doing good, one uselessly experiences laborious suffering. Neither alternative is equal to recognizing the fundamental Dharma at a word [from a true teacher].

These *dharmas* are the mind; there are no *dharmas* outside of the mind. This mind is the *dharmas*; outside of the *dharmas* there is no mind. The mind is of itself no-mind, yet it is without no-mind. If you take the mind as no-mind, you make the mind into something that exists. Just conform with it in silence, ceasing the various [types of] conceptualization. Therefore it is said, "the way of words is cut off, and the activities of the mind cease."

This mind is the fundamentally pure Buddha, which is possessed by both the Buddhas and [ordinary] people. The wriggling insects and all that has life, the Buddhas and bodhisattvas—these are identical and not different. It is only through false thoughts and discrimination that [sentient beings] create various types of karmic fruits.

3. The Fundamentally Pure Mind

There is truly not a single thing in this fundamental Buddha. It is transparent and serene, brilliantly wondrous, at ease, and nothing more. To become profoundly enlightened into [this truth]—right now, and that's it! Perfect and sufficient, nothing is lacking.

One may cultivate energetically for three eons, passing through the various stages. Then in a single moment of realization one realizes only that originally one was oneself a Buddha, with not a single thing that could possibly be added. Looking back on the efforts of those successive eons, [one realizes] they are all false activities of the dream [of delusion]. Therefore, the Tathāgata has said, "I am really without anything that is attained in the ultimate *bodhi.* If there were something that was attained, then Dīpaṃkara Buddha would not have conferred the prediction [of future Buddhahood] on me." He has also said, "These *dharma*s are universally 'same,' with neither high nor low; this is called *bodhi.*"

This fundamentally pure mind—whether in sentient beings or Buddha, in world-systems or the mountains and rivers, in that with characteristics and that without characteristics—throughout all the realms of the ten directions, it is always universally same, without the characteristics of self and other.

This fundamentally pure mind is always perfectly bright and uniformly radiant. People of the world are not enlightened and only recognize their perceptive faculties as mind. Since their [understanding] is obscured by their perceptive faculties, they therefore do not witness the pure and bright fundamental essence. If one can only right now achieve no-mind, the fundamental essence will appear of itelf. It is like the great orb of the sun risen in the sky, which illuminates uniformly throughout the ten directions without being hindered at all.

380c Therefore, trainees only recognize their perceptive faculties and act [accordingly]. But if they render those perceptive faculties void, so that the pathways of the mind are eliminated, they will be without any way to enter [into enlightenment]. They should simply recognize the fundamental mind within their perceptive faculties. Although the fundamental mind does not belong to those perceptive faculties, neither is it separate from the perceptive faculties. Just do not generate conceptual interpretations on the basis of those perceptive faculties, do not activate thoughts on the basis of those perceptive faculties, do not look for the mind apart from the perceptive faculties, and do not reject the perceptive faculties in order to grasp the *dharmas*. Neither identical nor separate, neither abiding nor attached, it is universally autonomous, and there is nowhere that is not the place of enlightenment (*bodhimaṇḍa*).

People of the world hear it said that the Buddhas all transmit the Dharma of mind, and they take it that there is a Dharma apart from the mind that can be realized and grasped. They search for the Dharma with the mind, not understanding that the mind is the Dharma and the Dharma is the mind. You cannot search for the mind with the mind—you will pass through a thousand and ten thousand eons [trying] and never get it. [Such useless efforts] are not equal to right now achieving no-mind—this is the fundamental Dharma.

It is like the warrior who was deluded regarding the pearl within his forehead and who searched for it elsewhere. He traveled about all the ten directions but was ultimately unable to recover it, whereupon a wise person pointed it out and he [then] saw for himself that the pearl [was on his forehead] as it had always been. Thus it is that students of the Way are deluded as to their own fundamental mind, not recognizing it as Buddha. They search for it outside [of their own minds], generating effortful practices and depending on graduated increases in realization. They pass through eons of diligent seeking but never achieve enlightenment. This is not equal to right now achieving no-mind.

If one definitively understands that all *dharma*s are fundamentally nonexistent and that there is nothing that can be attained, with no reliance and no abiding, no subject and no object, without activating false thoughts—this is to realize *bodhi*. And when one realizes enlightenment, this is only to realize the fundamental Buddha of the mind. To pass through eons of effort is nothing but useless cultivation. Just as when the warrior attained his pearl he merely attained the pearl that was originally on his forehead, and this had nothing to do with his ability to seek elsewhere. Therefore the Buddha has said, "I have truly not attained anything in the ultimate *bodhi*." Out of the fear that people will not believe does he (i.e., the Buddha) invoke that which is seen with the five eyes and that which is said in the five [types of] speech. This is true and not false; this is the cardinal meaning.

4. This Mind Is Buddha

You trainees should have no doubts. It is the four elements that make up your bodies, but the four elements are without a self and the self is without a master. Therefore you should understand that this [human] body is without self and without master.

It is the five *skandha*s that make up the mind, but the five *skandha*s are without a self and without a master. Therefore you should understand that the mind is without self and without master. The six senses, six types of sense objects, and the six consciousnesses, which combine together in generation and extinction, are also like this. These eighteen realms are empty, they are all empty. There is only the fundamental mind, which is expansive and pure.

[*Gloss:*] There is consciousness eating and wisdom eating. To consider the hunger and decay (lit., "boils") of the body of the four elements as [personal] disasters and to nourish it as appropriate, without generating greed or attachment—this is called wisdom eating. To willfully grasp at flavors and falsely generate discrimination, only seeking to please the palate and never generating [feelings of] revulsion and detachment—this is called consciousness eating.

*Śrāvaka*s attain enlightenment on the basis of [the Buddha's] voice, and so they are called "auditors." They simply fail to comprehend that their own minds generate [conceptual] interpretations on the basis of the oral teaching. Whether through [the
381a Buddha's demonstration of] supramundane powers or through his supernatural characteristics, words, or actions, they hear about *bodhi* and nirvana, cultivate over three immeasurable eons, and achieve the enlightenment of Buddhahood. All such people belong to the path of *śrāvaka*s, and so they are called *śrāvaka*-Buddhas.

To simply right now suddenly comprehend that one's own mind is fundamentally Buddha, without there being a single *dharma* one can attain and without there being a single practice one can cultivate—this is the insurpassable enlightenment, this is the Buddha of suchness. The only thing trainees should fear is having a single thought that [such things] exist, which is to be alienated from enlightenment (the Way). For each successive moment of thought to be without characteristics, for each successive moment of thought to be unconditioned—this is Buddha.

Trainees who wish to achieve Buddhahood [should understand that] it is completely useless to study any of the Buddhist teachings—just study nonseeking and nonattachment. Nonseeking is for the mind (i.e., moments of thought) not to be generated, and nonattachment is for the mind not to be extinguished. Neither generating nor extinguishing—this is Buddhahood. The eighty-four thousand teachings are directed at the eighty-four thousand afflictions and are only ways to convert and entice [sentient beings into true religious practice]. Fundamentally all the teachings are nonexistent; transcendence is the Dharma, and those who understand transcendence are Buddhas. By simply transcending all the afflictions, there is no *dharma* that can be attained.

5. The Teaching of the Mind-ground

Trainees who want to understand the essential determination [of the teaching] should simply not be attached to a single thing in the mind. To say that the true Dharma body (*dharmakāya*) of the Buddha is like space is to say metaphorically that the Dharma body is space and space the Dharma body. Ordinary people say that the Dharma body pervades space and that space contains the Dharma body, not understanding that space is the Dharma body and the Dharma body is space.

If you say definitively that space exists, then space is not the Dharma body. If you say definitively that the Dharma body exists, then the Dharma body is not space. Simply refrain from creating an interpretation [of the existence] of space, and space will be the Dharma body. Refrain from creating an interpretation [of the existence] of the Dharma body, and the Dharma body will be space.

Space and the Dharma body are without any dissimilar characteristics (lit., "characteristics of differentiation"). The Buddhas and sentient beings are without any dissimilar characteristics, samsara and nirvana are without any dissimilar characteristics, and the afflictions and *bodhi* are without any dissimilar characteristics.

To transcend all characteristics is to be a Buddha. Ordinary people grasp at [their sensory] realms, while religious persons grasp at the mind. For the mind and the realms to both be forgotten is the True Dharma. To forget the realms is relatively easy, but to forget the mind is extremely difficult. People do not dare to forget the mind, fearing that they will fall into the void (i.e., the emptiness of space) with nowhere to grab hold. They do not understand that the void is without void, that there is only one true Dharma body.

This numinous awareness nature has since beginningless time been of the same lifespan as space. It has never been generated and never extinguished, never existent and never nonexistent, never defiled and never pure, never disquieted and never serene, and never young and never old. It is without location, without interior and exterior, without enumeration, without shape, without form, and without sound. It cannot be seen and cannot be sought after. It cannot be recognized with wisdom, cannot be grasped with words, cannot be conformed to realms or things, and cannot be arrived at with [religious] effort.

The Buddhas and bodhisattvas and all beings that harbor life, [even down to] the wriggling insects, all share this same great nirvana nature. This nature is the mind, mind is the Buddha, and
381b the Buddha is the Dharma.

If you depart from the true for a single moment, all is false thoughts.

You cannot seek the mind with the mind, you cannot seek the Buddha with the Buddha, and you cannot seek the Dharma with the Dharma. Therefore, trainees should achieve no-mind right now. Simply conform with [the mind] in silence—if you try to use the mind you will miss it.

To transmit the mind with the mind—this is the correct view. I warn you, do not look outward and chase after realms but recognize that the realms are the mind. [To commit this error would be] to accept the thief as one's own child.

Due to the existence of greed, anger, and delusion there are established morality (*śīla*), meditation (*samādhi*), and wisdom (*prajñā*). Fundamentally there are no afflictions, so how can there be *bodhi*? Therefore the patriarch has said, "The Buddha has preached all the *dharma*s in order to eliminate all [states of] mind. If I am without all [the states of] mind, what use is there for all the *dharma*s?"

The fundamentally pure Buddha has not a single thing attached to it. It is likened to space, and even if one [attempted to] adorn it with immeasurable precious treasures, there would never be any place to make them stay. Buddha-nature is identical to space, and even if one [attempted to] adorn it with limitless [feats of] merit and wisdom, there would never be any place to make them stay.

It is only that if one is deluded as to the fundamental nature one will become increasingly unable to see.

The so-called teaching of the mind-ground is that the myriad *dharmas* are all established in dependence on the mind. If a [sensory] realm is encountered they exist, and if there is no realm then they do not exist. You must not jump to the conclusion that the pure nature is a [type of] realm. Sayings such as, "the functions of meditation and wisdom are mirrored in explicit clarity" and "the perceptive functions are serene and resplendent" are all interpretations of realms and may only be used as provisional teachings for those of mediocre and lesser abilities. If you wish to experience realization yourself, you must not create any of these interpretations.

If all the realms and *dharmas* are to be buried somewhere, bury them in the earth of being. To simply not create views of being and nonbeing with regard to all *dharmas* is to see the [true nature of all] *dharmas*.

6. Forget the Mind

On the first day of the ninth month, the master addressed [Pei] Xiu: Ever since Great Master [Bodhi]dharma came to China, [his followers in the Chan school] have preached only the One Mind and have transmitted only the One Dharma. Transmitting the Buddha with the Buddha, [we] have not preached about any other Buddha. Transmitting the Dharma with the Dharma, [we] have not preached about any other Dharma. This Dharma is the Dharma that cannot be preached about, and this Buddha is the Buddha that cannot be grasped. They are the fundamentally pure mind. There is only this one reality, and any others are not true.

Prajñā is wisdom, and this wisdom is the fundamental mind that is without characteristics.

Ordinary people do not move toward enlightenment solely because they willfully [exercise] the six sensory capabilities and thus pass through the six modes of existence.

If a trainee considers birth and death for but a single moment he will fall into the way of Māra. If he activates the various ascriptive views for a single moment, he will fall into the way of heresy. If he perceives there to be generation [of the elements of reality] and moves toward [a state of] extinction, he will fall into the way of the *śrāvaka*s. If he does not perceive there to be generation but only perceives extinction, he will fall into the way of the solitary enlightened ones (*pratyekabuddha*s).

The *dharma*s were originally not generated, and neither are they now extinguished. Do not activate the two views, and neither detest nor enjoy [things]. All the myriad *dharma*s are only the One Mind, and after [one realizes this] they become the vehicle of the Buddhas. Ordinary people all chase after the [sensory] realms and generate the mind, so that the mind [has feelings of] enjoyment and detestation. If you would have there be no realms, then you should forget the mind. When the mind is forgotten, then the realms are empty, and when the realms are empty the mind is extinguished. If you do not forget the mind but only eliminate the realms, because the realms cannot be eliminated you will only increase your [inner] agitation. Therefore, [you should understand
381c that] the myriad *dharma*s are only the mind. The mind is also imperceptible (lit., "unattainable"), so how can it possibly be sought?

Those who study *prajñā* do not perceive there to be a single *dharma* that can be attained. They eradicate all consideration of the three vehicles—there being only a single truth, which cannot be realized. Those who say they can realize and can attain [enlightenment] are all people of great conceitfulness. All the [five thousand Hinayanists] who brushed off their robes and left the Lotus assembly were devotees such as this. Therefore, the Buddha has said, "I have truly not attained anything in *bodhi.*" There is only silent conforming [with the mind].

When an ordinary person is about to die, he should merely contemplate the five *skandha*s to be all empty and the four elements to be without self. The true mind is without characteristics and neither goes nor comes: when one is born the [mind]-nature does not come [into one], and when one dies neither does the nature go [anywhere]. Peaceful, perfect, and serene, the mind and its realms are identical. If one can only right now suddenly achieve comprehension in this fashion, you will not be fettered by the three periods of time (i.e., past, present, and future) and will be a person who has transcended the world. You must definitely avoid having even the slightest bit of intentionality. If you see Buddhas of excellent characteristics (i.e., in their resplendent superhuman forms) coming to greet [and escort you to the Pure Land], with all the various phenomena [involved in such visions], then have no thought of following them. If you see various phenomena with evil characteristics, neither should you have any thoughts of fear. Simply forget your mind and identify yourself with the *dharmadhātu,* and you will attain autonomy. This is the essential gist [of my teaching].

7. Be Enlightened to the Mind, Not to the *Dharma*(s)

On the eighth day of the tenth month, the master addressed [Pei] Xiu: The "transformation city" refers to the two vehicles, the ten stages, and the [attainments of] equivalent enlightenment and wondrous enlightenment, all of which are teachings established provisionally in order to entice [sentient beings into undertaking spiritual training]. All of these are the transformation city. The "location of the treasure" is the treasure of the true mind, the fundamental Buddha, the self-nature. This treasure does not pertain to mental calculation and it cannot be established [anywhere as a discrete entity]. It is without Buddha and without sentient beings, without subject and without object, so where could there be any [transformation] city? If you ask whether this is not already the transformation city, then where is the location of the treasure? It is impossible to point out the location of the treasure. If it could be pointed out, then it would have a location and would not be the true location of the treasure. Therefore, it is said only that it is close. It cannot definitively be spoken of, but if you just conform with it in your entire being then that is it.

They who are called *icchantika*s are those without faith. All the sentient beings of the six modes of existence, even including those of the two [Hinayana] vehicles (i.e., the paths of the *śrāvaka*s and the *pratyekabuddha*s), have no faith in the existence of the fruit of Buddhahood. They all may be called *icchantika*s who have cut off their good roots. Bodhisattvas are those who have profound faith in the existence of Buddhism and do not perceive the existence of Mahayana and Hinayana, Buddhas and sentient beings, all of whom are of the same identical Dharma-nature. These may be called *icchantika*s of good roots.

In general, those who are enlightened on the basis of the oral teaching are called *śrāvaka*s. Those who are enlightened through their contemplation of causality are called solitary enlightened ones. If one is not enlightened with respect to one's own mind, even if one attains Buddhahood one may be called a *śrāvaka*-Buddha.

Trainees frequently become enlightened to the teachings and are not enlightened to the mind. Although they pass through eons of cultivation, this is never the fundamental Buddha. If one is not enlightened to the mind but is enlightened to the teachings, this is to belittle the mind and emphasize the teachings. Ultimately, this is to chase after a dirt clod [like a dog] because one has forgotten the fundamental mind. Just conform yourself with the fundamental mind and seek not for the *dharma*s, for the mind is the *dharma*s. Ordinary people frequently consider that the [sensory]
382a realms hinder the mind, or [consider] that phenomena hinder the absolute. They always want to escape from the realms in order to pacify the mind, to eliminate phenomena to reify the absolute. They do not understand that it is the mind that hinders the realms and the absolute that hinders phenomena. Simply make the mind empty, and the realms will be empty of themselves. Simply make the absolute serene, and phenomena will be serene of themselves. Do not mistakenly [attempt to] manipulate the mind.

Ordinary people are frequently unwilling to empty their minds, fearing that they will fall into the void. They do not understand that their own minds are fundamentally empty. The foolish person eliminates phenomena without eliminating the mind, whereas the wise person eliminates the mind without eliminating phenomena. The mind of the bodhisattva is like space, which is completely detached from everything.

One should lust after none of the blessings and merit that may be created [through virtuous action]. However, there are three levels of detachment. To be completely detached from everything within and without one's body and mind, so that one is like space in having nothing to which one is attached but henceforth responding to beings in every direction, with subject and object forgotten: this is great detachment.

If on the one hand one undertakes religious practice and dispenses merit and on the other hand dispenses detachment, without any thoughts of longing: this is medium detachment.

If one extensively cultivates the various types of good while having longings but hears the Dharma and understands emptiness and thereby comes to be without attachment: this is small detachment.

Great detachment is like the flame of a candle that is in front of you, there being no further delusion or enlightenment. Medium detachment is like a candle that is off to one side, which may be bright or dark. Small detachment is like a candle that is behind you, so that you cannot see the hole [into which you may fall].

Therefore, the bodhisattva's mind is like space, which is completely detached from everything. "Past mental states are imperceptible": this is detachment from the past. "Present mental states are imperceptible": this is detachment from the present. "Future mental states are imperceptible": this is detachment from the future. This is called complete detachment from the three periods of time.

Ever since the Tathāgata conferred the Dharma on Kāśyapa, [his successors] have used the mind to seal the mind, and the minds [of all those successors] have not differed [from one another]. If an [ordinary] seal were affixed to emptiness (i.e., space), the seal would not create a [written] character. If the seal [of the mind] were affixed to a thing, the seal would not create the Dharma. Therefore, the mind is used to seal the mind, and the minds [of all the successors] have not differed. The conjunction of sealer and sealed (i.e., teacher and student) is difficult, so those who attain [the transmission] are few. However, the mind is without mind, and attainment is without attainment.

The Buddha has three bodies. The Dharma body preaches the Dharma of the transparency of the self-nature, the reward body (*saṃbhogakāya*) preaches the Dharma of the purity of all things, and the transformation body (*nirmāṇakāya*) preaches the Dharma of the six perfections and the myriad practices. The Dharma body's preaching of the Dharma cannot be sought with word, voice, shape, or [written] character. It is without anything that is preached and without anything that is realized, but is only the transparency of the self-nature. Therefore it is said, "To be without any Dharma that can be preached is called to preach the Dharma."

The reward body and transformation body both respond [to beings] and manifest [their teachings] in accordance with [the abilities of the] persons they teach. The Dharmas that they preach are also responses to the [differing] roots [of sentient beings] in accordance with phenomena and are used to convert [people to Buddhism], and none [of these teachings] are the True Dharma. Therefore it is said, "The reward and transformation [bodies] are not the true Buddha and do not preach the Dharma."

In the saying "identically the one vital brilliance, divided into six that combine together," the one vital brilliance is the One Mind and the six that combine together are the six sensory capabilities. These six sensory capabilities each combine with sense objects: the eye combines with forms, the ear combines with sounds, the nose combines with fragrances, the tongue combines with tastes, the body combines with tactile sensations, and the mind combines with *dharma*s. Between [these senses and sensations] are generated the six consciousnesses. These are the eighteen realms. If you com-

prehend that the eighteen realms do not exist, [you will understand that] the six [sensory capabilities] combine together to form 382b
a single vital brilliance. The single vital brilliance is the mind.

Trainees all understand this but they are merely unable to avoid forming the interpretation of the single vital brilliance and the combining together of the six [sensory capabilities]. They are thus fettered by the Dharma and do not conform themselves with the fundamental mind.

When the Tathāgata was in the world he wanted to preach the True Dharma of the One Vehicle. However, sentient beings did not have faith and reviled [the Dharma], thus drowning themselves in the sea of suffering. If [the Buddha] had not preached anything at all he would have fallen into [the transgression of] parsimony and would not have [been able to] dispense entirely his wondrous enlightenment on behalf of sentient beings. Thus he adopted skillful means and preached the existence of three vehicles. These vehicles include [both the] Great [Vehicle] (Mahayana) and Small [Vehicle] (Hinayana) and their attainments are shallow or profound, but they are all other than the fundamental Dharma.

Therefore it is said, "There is only the enlightenment (Way) of the One Vehicle; the other two are not true." However, [the Buddha] was ultimately unable to manifest the Dharma of the One Mind, so he called Kāśyapa to share his Dharma seat and individually conveyed to him the preaching of the Dharma that is of the One Mind and which transcends words. He had this single branch of the Dharma carried out separately [from the rest of Buddhism]. If you are able to achieve conformance with and enlightenment to [the One Mind], then you have attained the stage of Buddhahood.

8. On Cultivating Enlightenment

Question: What is enlightenment, and how should it be cultivated?

The master said: What sort of thing is enlightenment that you would want to cultivate it?

Question: Masters all over China (lit., "in the various locations") have taught that one should practice Chan and study enlightenment. What about this?

The master said: These are sayings to entice those of dull capabilities and are totally unreliable.

[The questioner] said: If these are sayings to entice those of dull capabilities, then I wonder what Dharma would be preached to entice people of superior capabilities?

The master said: If [you are] a person of superior capabilities, why would you seek it through someone else (i.e., through the words of a teacher)? Even the self is unattainable, so how could there possibly be any other Dharma you could figure on? Have you not seen it said within the teachings, "What can the status of the *dharma*s be?"

[The questioner] said: If it is like this, then seeking is entirely unnecessary.

The master said: Since that is the way it is, you can save some energy.

[The questioner] said: If it is like this, is not everything annihilated and [turned into] nonbeing?

The master said: Who has made it into nonbeing? What is it that you would want to seek?

[The questioner] said: If you do not allow me to seek it, why do you then say not to eradicate it?

The master said: If you are not going to seek for it, then stop. But who is making you eradicate [anything]? You see the space right in front of you—how could you eradicate it?

[The questioner] said: Can this Dharma possibly be identical to space?

The master said: When has space said to you that it is identical to and different from [anything]? If I were to preach a bit like that, you would generate a [conceptualized] interpretation about it.

[The questioner] said: Should not one have people generate interpretations?

The master said: I have never caused you difficulties [in the past, so why do you pester me now]? The point is, interpretations pertain to ratiocination, and the generation of ratiocination means departure from wisdom.

[The questioner] said: So one is not to generate ratiocination about this, is that right?

The master said: If no one generates ratiocination, who is to say it is right?

9. Misspoken

Question: When I said something to you just now, why did you say "you've misspoken"?

The master said: You are unable to speak but how could you be at fault?

10. A Monk Is Someone Who has Ceased Thinking

Question: All of your many sayings up to now have been explanations based on relative distinctions, and nowhere have you indicated any True Dharma to us.

The master said: The True Dharma is without confusion but your question itself will generate confusion. What True Dharma 382c
are you seeking?

[The questioner] said: If my question itself will generate confusion, what about your answer?

The master said: You should get something to reflect your face. Don't worry about others.

[The master] also said: You are just like a stupid dog—if you see something moving you bark, not even distinguishing whether it is just the wind blowing the plants and trees.

[The master] also said: In our Chan school, ever since it was transmitted from previous [generations], never have people been taught to seek after knowledge or to seek after [conceptual] interpretations. We have only said that one should study enlightenment, and even this is a phrase that is meant [only] to entice [people into religious practice]. Even though [this phrase is used], enlightenment cannot be studied. The study of [conceptual] interpretations in the context of ratiocination will on the contrary create delusion regarding enlightenment.

Enlightenment is without location and is called the mind of the Mahayana. This mind does not reside within, without, or in an intermediate [location]. It is truly without location. The most important thing is not to form conceptual interpretations and merely speak on the basis of your current ratiocination. When your ratiocination is exhausted, [you will realize that] the mind is without location.

Enlightenment is naturally true and is fundamentally without names. It is only that people of the world do not recognize it and remain deluded within their ratiocination. The Buddhas then appear [in the world] to destroy their misconceptions. I am afraid that you people do not comprehend but provisionally establish the name "enlightenment." You must not generate interpretations so as to maintain this name. Therefore it is said, "attain the fish and forget the trap."

With body and mind as they are, penetrate enlightenment and recognize the mind. It is because you penetrate the fundamental source that you are called a monk. The fruit of monkhood is achieved through stopping thought, not by study. How could you ever succeed in your present [attempts to] seek the mind with the mind, to rely on someone else's teachings, and to try to get [enlightenment] merely by study?

The ancients were astute, so that by hearing just a single word [of the True Dharma] they immediately ceased studying. Therefore they were called "inactive and aimless religious persons who had ceased studying." People nowadays only want to attain great knowledge and many [different] interpretations [of the Dharma], and they seek extensively the meanings of texts. They say they are practicing but they do not understand that great knowledge, and many interpretations will on the contrary form a barrier [to enlightenment]. It is like feeding a child great amounts of milk and yogurt while being completely unaware of whether or not he can digest it. Trainees in the three vehicles are all of this sort—they all may be referred to as people who consume but do not digest [the Dharma]. As it is said, "conceptual interpretations that are undigested turn entirely to poison"—all [such efforts] are to be totally attached to samsara. There is no such [mode of attainment] within true suchness. Therefore it is said, "There is no such sword within my king's storehouses."

All of the interpretations you have [left over] from the past should be completely disposed of and eliminated, so that one is without discrimination: this is the *tathāgatagarbha* of emptiness. In the *tathāgatagarbha* there exists not even a bit of dust—and this is for "the Dharma King Who Destroys Existence to appear in the world."

[Śākyamuni Buddha] has also said, "There was not the slightest Dharma for me to attain from Dīpaṃkara Buddha." These words were aimed solely at eliminating your ratiocination and conceptual interpretations. To simply meld together superficial and intrinsic [aspects of oneself], with ratiocination exhausted and entirely without dependency—this is to be a person beyond all affairs.

The teachings of the three vehicles are only medicines appropriate for [different] individuals, which have been preached as

appropriate [in each situation. These teachings] have been administered as the occasion warrants, and each is different. If you are just able to comprehend, then you will not be deluded by them. The most important thing is not to maintain the text or form an inter-
383a pretation of a single [individual] case or a single teaching. Why? There is truly no definitive Dharma that the Tathāgata can preach. In our school we do not discuss these matters (i.e., the doctrines of Buddhism). You should simply understand that we do nothing else but stop the mind. There is no use in thinking about this and that.

11. The Meaning of "This Mind Is the Buddha"

Question: For some time everyone has been saying "this mind is the Buddha," but I wonder which mind it is that is the Buddha?

The master said: How many minds do you have?

[The questioner] said: Is it that the ordinary mind is the Buddha, or that the sagely mind is the Buddha?

The master said: Where is it that you have these ordinary and sagely minds?

[The questioner] said: At present it is taught that within the three vehicles there are ordinary and sagely [minds]. How can you say these do not exist?

The master said: Within the three vehicles it is clearly said to you that the [concept of] ordinary and sagely minds is false. You misunderstand this now and insist on grasping onto [the mind as something that] exists, making that which is empty into something real. How can this [understanding] be anything but false? And since it is false you are deluded regarding the mind. You should simply eliminate the ratiocination of the ordinary [mind] and the [enlightened] realm of the sage—there is not any separate Buddha outside of the mind. The patriarch [Bodhidharma] came from the west to point out directly that all persons are in their entireties the Buddha. You fail to recognize this now but grasp onto the ordinary and the sagely, racing after the external and in turn being deluded as to your own mind. Therefore, I say to you: this mind is the Buddha.

To generate a single moment of ratiocination is to fall into a different realm. Since beginningless time, [this truth] has been no different from how it is today; there is no other Dharma. Therefore this is called the attainment of [the stages of] equivalent and correct enlightenment.

[The questioner] said: What do you mean when you say "is [identical to]"?

The master said: What meaning are you looking for? If there is the slightest bit of meaning, this is to be different from the mind.

[The questioner] said: You just said "Since beginningless time [this truth] has been no different from how it is today." What did you mean?

The master said: It is only because of your seeking that you differ from it. If you don't seek for it, then how could you be different?

[The questioner] said: Then if it [means] "not different," why do you say "is"?

The master said: If you do not believe in the ordinary and the sagely, who will say "is" to you? If "is" is not "is," then the mind is also not the mind. If the mind and "is" are both forgotten, where will you try to look for them?

12. Transmission of the Mind with the Mind

Question: If the false is able to obstruct one's mind, I wonder how one is then able to expel the false?

The master said: To activate the false in order to expel the false is to create the false. The false is fundamentally without basis, and it only exists because of discrimination. If you simply eliminate your ratiocination regarding ordinary and sagely you will naturally be without the false. Then how could you try to expel it? To be entirely without even the slightest bit of dependency is called "I have cast off both arms and will certainly attain Buddhahood."

[The questioner] said: If one is without dependency, how can [the mind of the patriarchs] be transmitted?

The master said: The mind is transmitted with the mind.

[The questioner] said: If the mind is transmitted, how can you say that the mind is also nonexistent?

The master said: To not attain a single *dharma* is called the transmission of the mind. If you comprehend this mind, then there is no mind and no *dharma*.

[The questioner] said: If there is no mind and no *dharma*, why do you call it a transmission?

The master said: You have heard me say "transmission of the mind" and have taken it that there is something that can be attained. It is for this reason that the patriarch said, "When one recognizes the mind-nature, it should be called inconceivable. Clearly and distinctly without anything that is attained, when one attains it one does not speak of it as understanding." If I taught
383b this to you how would you be able to understand it?

13. Mind and Realms, Face and Mirror

Question: But can space, which is right here, be anything but a realm [of the mind]? How could you see the mind without pointing at its realms?

The master said: What mind is it that is causing you to look at the realms? If you are able to see [something], this is only the mind that reflects the realms. If you use a mirror to reflect your face, even if you are able to see your features clearly this is fundamentally only an image. How can it have anything to do with you?

[The questioner] said: If one does not depend on [the process of] reflection, when will one be able to see [one's face]?

The master said: If you are going to depend on causes then you will always be dependent on things, and when will you ever comprehend? Haven't you had anyone say to you, "If I open my hand to show it to you, there is nothing there"? It would be a useless waste of effort to explain it to you several thousand times.

[The questioner] said: If someone recognizes it completely, wouldn't there be no things to reflect?

The master said: If there were no things, then what use would reflection be? Don't talk in your sleep with your eyes open!

14. Not Seeking Anything

[The master] entered the hall and said: Rather than the hundred varieties of erudition, to be without seeking is primary. A religious person is someone who does nothing and is truly without the numerous types of mind. There is also no meaning that can be preached. There's nothing else, so you may go.

15. Worthy of Respect Is the Truth of the Mind

Question: What is the conventional truth?

The master said: Why should I explain the tangled [predicament of this world]? Given fundamental purity, why bother with explanations and dialogues? Just be without all the [states of] mind, and this is called untainted wisdom. In all of your daily actions (lit., "walking, standing, sitting, and lying down") every day and in everything you say, simply do not be attached to conditioned *dharmas*. Every utterance and blink of the eye is identical to the untainted [wisdom].

But now, when everyone is tending toward the final period of the Dharma, all those who study the enlightenment of Chan are attached to every sound and form. Why do they pay no attention to their own minds?

When the mind is identical to space, when it is like a dead tree or a piece of rock, when it is like cold ashes or an extinguished fire—only then will one have the least bit of correspondence [with enlightenment]. If you don't, then someday Old Man Yama (the king of hell) will beat [a confession out of] you!

If you simply transcend the various *dharmas* of being and nonbeing, so that your minds are like the orb of the sun—always in the sky, its brilliance shining naturally, illuminating without [intending to] illuminate—isn't this a matter that requires no effort? When you attain this, there is no place to rest. This is to practice the practice of the Buddhas, and it is to "be without abiding and yet to generate the mind." This is your pure Dharma body, which is called the insurpassable *bodhi*.

If you do not understand this idea, then even if you study to the point of erudition, cultivating with diligent asceticism, robing yourself with grasses and eating trees, [yet] without recognizing your own mind: this is all false practice, and you will definitely become an attendant of Māra.

If you practice like this, what benefit could there be? Baozhi has said, "The Buddha is fundamentally created by one's own mind, so how can he be sought within written words?" Even if you attain the three [stages of] sagehood and the four fruits [of the Hinayana] and complete the ten stages [of the bodhisattva], you will still remain within [the domain of] ordinary and sagely.

Haven't you heard it said, "The myriad processes are imper-
383c manent, these being the *dharmas* of generation and extinction"?

Its energy exhausted, the arrow falls to earth. You bring an untoward future birth [upon yourself]—how could this compare to the teaching of the unconditioned true characteristic, in which with a single leap one enters directly into the stage of the Tathāgata? Because you are not the right kind of person, you must extensively study conceptual interpretations based on the teachings of the ancients. Baozhi has said, "If you do not encounter a teacher of wisdom who is beyond this world, you will uselessly partake of the Dharma medicine of the Mahayana."

Now, at all times and during all your activities you should simply study no-mind, and eventually [your efforts] will bear fruit. It is because your abilities are slight that you are unable to make the sudden leap. If you can just get three years, five years, or ten years, then you will definitely be able to get a foothold (lit., a "place to insert the head") and you will understand naturally. It is because you are unable to do so that you must use the mind to study Chan and study enlightenment, but what connection does this have with the Buddha-Dharma? Therefore it is said, "All that the Tathāgata has preached was [stated] in order to teach people." For example, to say that a yellow leaf was gold stopped the crying of a little child, but it was certainly not true.

If [you think] there is something actually to be attained, then you are not a member of my school. And what relationship will you ever have with the fundamental essence? Therefore, the sutra says, "For there to be truly not the slightest *dharma* that can be attained is called the insurpassable *bodhi*." If you are able to understand the meaning of this, then for the first time you will understand that the way of the Buddha and the way of Māra are both wrong.

Fundamentally it is pure and bright, without square and round, without large and small, and without long and short and other characteristics. It is untainted and inactive, without delusion and without enlightenment. See it clearly and distinctly, without there being a single thing, as well as without people and without Buddhas. The world-systems [as numerous as the] sands [of the Ganges River] are but as foam in the ocean, and all the sages are as [evanescent as] lightning. These are all unequal to the truth of the mind. Your Dharma bodies have been since ancient times until now the same as [those of] the Buddhas and patriarchs; where could they have even the slightest flaw?

If you understand what I mean, then you must make great effort for the rest of this lifetime. Breathing out doesn't mean you'll necessarily breathe back in again.

16. Why Huineng Was Able to Become the Sixth Patriarch

Question: The Sixth Patriarch did not understand written scriptures, so why did he receive the transmission of the [Fifth Patriarch's] robe to become a patriarch? The elder [Shen]xiu was the chief monk among the five hundred [disciples]. He [served as] instructor for them, lecturing on thirty-two sutras and treatises. Why did he not [receive the] transmission of the robe?

The master said: Because he (i.e., Shenxiu) took the mind as extant and considered that there were conditioned *dharmas* to be cultivated and realized. For this reason the Fifth Patriarch transmitted [the Dharma] to the Sixth Patriarch. At the time the Sixth Patriarch simply conformed in silence and received the intimate conferral of the profound meaning of the Tathāgatas. Therefore the Dharma was conferred on him. Haven't you heard it said that

> The Dharma is fundamentally the Dharma as non-Dharma; the non-Dharma is the Dharma and still the Dharma. In the present conferral of the non-Dharma, how can the Dharma ever have been the Dharma?

Only if you understand this idea can you be said to have "left home," and only then is it well that you undertake spiritual training.

If you do not believe me, then why did head monk [Hui]ming

chase after the Sixth Patriarch [all the way] to Mount Dayu? The Sixth Patriarch asked him, "What did you come for? Do you seek the robe or the Dharma?" Head monk [Hui]ming said, "I have not come for the robe but only for the Dharma." The Sixth Patriarch said, "You should concentrate your thoughts for just a short while, without thinking of good and evil." [Hui]ming did as he was told. 384a
The Sixth Patriarch said, "Do not think of good and do not think of evil. When you've got it just right, show me the face you had before your parents were born." At these words, [Hui]ming suddenly [experienced a] silent conformance [with the Dharma]. He then paid obeisance [to the Sixth Patriarch] and said, "When a person drinks he automatically knows [whether the water is] hot or cold. When I was in the assembly of the Fifth Patriarch, I labored pointlessly for thirty years, and only today have I been able to eliminate my previous errors."

The Sixth Patriarch said, "So it is. Only after coming here have you understood the ineffability of [the saying] 'the patriarch [Bodhidharma's] coming from the west, directly pointing at people's minds, and seeing [Buddha]-nature and achieving Buddhahood.' Haven't you heard of Ānanda asking Kāśyapa, 'In addition to the golden-threaded [robe], what Dharma did the World-honored One transmit to you?' Kāśyapa called to Ānanda and Ānanda responded ['Yes?']. Kāśyapa [then] said, 'Knock over the standard-pole in front of the gate!'"

[*Gloss:*] (This was the patriarch's [symbolic] standard.)

[*Question:*] How could Ānanda have served [the Buddha] for thirty years and been scolded by the Buddha for being only erudite in wisdom?

[The master] said: For you to study wisdom for a thousand days is not equal to studying enlightenment for a single day. If you do not study enlightenment, how will you be able to use [even] a single drop of water (i.e., of what is naturally provided for you)?

17. Autonomy

Question: How can one avoid falling into the stages?

The master said: Always eating your meals without ever chewing a single grain of rice, always walking without ever stepping on a single bit of earth—when you [function] like this then there are no characteristics of self. You are never separate from all the affairs [of life], and yet you are not deluded by the various realms. Only then may you be called an autonomous person. Furthermore, at all times and in every moment of thought don't perceive all the characteristics and don't recognize past, [present,] and future, the three periods of time. The past does not go, the present does not abide, and the future does not come. Sitting peacefully upright, letting things happen as they will—only then may you be called liberated.

Make effort! Make effort! Of the thousand or ten thousand people in this school, only three or five [have really understood Buddhism]. If you do not take this seriously then you will suffer for it eventually (lit., "there will be a day when you experience a calamity"). Therefore it is said, "Be diligent in taking care of this life, and how could you suffer misfortune in eons to come?"

End of Chan Master Duanji of Mount Huangbo's
Essentials of the Transmission of Mind

A TREATISE ON LETTING ZEN FLOURISH TO PROTECT THE STATE

Contents

Translator's Introduction

Myōan Eisai (1141–1215) was a Buddhist monk of the Tendai school. He is also known as Yōsai, and it is not clear which reading of his name he himself used. It is said that he had people chant "Eisai Yōsai" loudly as they attempted to raise a heavy temple bell, long sunk in the Kamo River in Kyoto, which was to be installed in Kenninji, the temple newly built for him along the river. In this translation I follow the more common reading of Eisai.

When young, Eisai studied and practiced the esoteric teaching transmitted in the Tendai school and became a ritual leader, an *ajari* (*ācārya*). Later, through two visits to Song China (in 1168 and 1187–91) he became an eager advocate of Zen, declaring himself to be an inheritor of the Huanglong (Ōryō) branch of the Linji (Rinzai) sect of the Chan (Zen) school. In this treatise he furnishes proof of this Chan inheritance.

In 1194, three years after his return to Japan, Emperor Gotoba (r. 1183–97) issued a ban on the propagation of the Zen school by Eisai and others in the country. The next year court officials summoned Eisai to give him a chance to defend himself. On that occasion Eisai almost succeeded in gaining their ear by arguing that Zen was one of the teachings introduced from China by Saichō (765–822), founder of the Tendai school, and thus that rejecting Zen inevitably would mean rejecting Saichō. In 1198 he wrote the present work, *Kōzengokokuron*, or *A Treatise on Letting Zen Flourish to Protect the State,* which he is supposed to have presented to then-emperor Tsuchimikado (r. 1198–1209). Through this work, Eisai received imperial sanction to propagate Zen.

In 1203 the imperial government, by official document, announced to Eisai that the three schools—Tendai, Shingon, and Zen—were to be represented with respective installations in his temple. Eisai immediately had two temples, one Shingon and one Tendai, built in the compound of the Kenninji in Kyoto, the Zen temple that had been built for him the previous year by the second shogun of Kamakura, Minamoto Yoriiye. Beginning around that time, warriors of the Kamakura shogunate tended to become financial supporters of the Zen school.

In 1211 Eisai wrote an article on tea, *Kissayōjōki* ("Notes on Taking Tea for Nourishing Life"), and presented it to the third shogun, Minamoto Sanetomo. Prior to this, in 1185, two years before Eisai left for his second visit to China, the Taira (or Heike) warrior clan was decisively defeated by the Genji (or Minamoto) clan in a battle famous in Japanese history. The Taira afterward disappeared from the world of politics but they are said to have continued to financially support Eisai's activities in Kyushu. The warrior clans possibly saw in Eisai a truly reliable spiritual guide who could see beyond the contemporary political situation of Japan.

The imperial mandate issued in 1194 to ban the propagation of Zen reads as follows:

> [Emperor] Gotoba, fifth year of Kenkyū (1194), July 5, *kinoe-ne:*
>
> Buddhist monks of the Tendai school reported to the Throne that they had heard that elder monks like Eisai, who had been to China, and Nōnin, who abided in the capital, had established the Daruma school, and that they should be made to stop its propagation. The Emperor proclaimed that thereafter they should stop their activities.

This is found in fascicle ten of the *Hyakurenshō* (*Finest Style Excerpts,* seventeen fascicles, *Kokushi taikei* new ed., vol. XI, 1929). This record, made up of reliable annual records dating from the reign of Emperor Reizei, which began in 967, through that of Emperor Gofukakusa, which ended in 1257, gives the reason for the ban as nothing other than the introduction of a new school. For most Tendai priests, as well as priests of other traditional schools, the existence of any new school was perceived as a threat and could not be permitted.

In the continuation of Gate III in Fascicle Two of the *Treatise* (p. 118), Eisai himself refers to those who called themselves the Daruma school and criticizes this naming of the Zen school. He introduces the view of this school, refers to its followers as "those who have no wrongs that they would never commit," and mentions "this kind of person," who is a "holder of a fixed view on emptiness" that "no one can sit and talk with." Eisai goes no further and does not mention the name of "this . . . person." However, Kokan Shiren (1278–1346), a Rinzai Zen monk and author of the *Genkōshakusho* (*A Book on Buddhists Compiled in the Genkō Era,* 1322), identifies the person alluded to by Eisai as Nōnin, cited above in the *Hyakurenshō*.

According to Shiren, in the year of *tsuchinoto-tori* (1189) a person named Dainichibō Nōnin heard that in the land of Song the Zen school was flourishing, and sent his disciples by sea to ask Chan Master Fozhao Deguang (Busshō Tokukō, 1121–1203), who lived on Mount Yuwang (Ikuō), his view on ultimate reality. Master Fozhao pitied the foreign monks, with their burgeoning seeds of confidence in the true self, and comforted and encouraged them heartily. He entrusted them with a Dharma robe and a painting of Bodhidharma with words of praise written above it. Emboldened by Fozhao's entrustment, Nōnin then disrespectully began advocating the Zen school in Japan. Since he lacked a proper teacher inheritance and certificate (*inka*), people in the capital despised him. Until the time when Eisai began propagating the school of the Buddha's mind, the officials, gentry, and common people tended to regard Nōnin and Eisai as being of the same ilk and denounced them both. Aside from this, a Tendai monk named Ryōben of Hakozaki, Chikuzen Province, Kyushu, jealous of Eisai's Zen practice, persuaded the Tendai students in Mount Hiei to bring suit to the throne to exile the two.

As previously mentioned, it was due to Eisai's efforts that propagation of the Zen school was eventually officially sanctioned. According to the Japanese Buddhist historian Shiren, Eisai blamed Nōnin for his neglect of morality and practice. However, Nōnin is said to have had printed a Chan text on morality for students, which his disciples had brought along with other gifts from Fozhao. This was the

Weishan Jingce (*Isan Keisaiku; Weishan's Staff of Vigilance*). According to Professor Seizan Yanagida and Tsuji Zennosuke (*Nihonbukkyōshi* [*History of Japanese Buddhism*], Vol. III, *Chūseihen* no. 2, Tokyo: Iwanami-shoten, 1957), this was the first Zen text to be printed in Japan. Both Shiren and Eisai failed to appreciate the significant role that Nōnin might have played, as a man of Zen among the common people, in the history of Japanese Zen. It is said that Nōnin was accidentally killed by his nephew Taira Kagekiyo.

In 1198, the year Eisai wrote this *Treatise,* the Pure Land Buddhist teacher Hōnenbō Genkū (1133–1212) also wrote his main work, *Senchaku Hongan Nembutsu Shū* (*A Collection of Passages on the Nembutsu Chosen in the Original Vow,* English translation by Morris J. Augustine and Tesshō Kondō, Numata Center, 1997). In 1207 Hōnen was exiled to a remote region far from Kyoto, the capital at the time. The reason given for his exile was that the Pure Land teaching had caused serious moral problems in society. In both instances of new schools being advocated, in this case Zen and Pure Land, repression came from the traditional schools of Buddhism, in the form of imperial sanctions. The old forces regarded themselves as guardians of the state and wielded great influence on the nobles represented by the emperor. For priests of the traditional schools, the safety of the nobles meant the safety and security of their respective schools; anyone who might threaten their respective order was an enemy. Advocates of Zen and Pure Land practices, who were regarded as being concerned with their own religious life instead of contributing to the stability of the society, and thus outside the influence of the nobles and priests, were seen as such enemies.

Eisai was a Tendai priest of the highest rank (*daihosshi*). On returning from his second trip to China, in 1191, he began advocating that Zen should exist as an independent school, rather than merely remaining one among other traditional Tendai teachings, but soon met with an imperial ban on his activities. Hōnen had also been a Tendai priest, who practiced the *nembutsu.* When he began advocating Pure Land practice among those outside the Tendai school he met with grave punishment. Zen and Pure Land teachings, however, had already begun attracting popular attention. Political repression made the Pure Land teaching first advocated by Hōnen decisively influential among the common people. Although the definitive establishment of an independent Zen school in Japan had to wait for some time, the significance of this event was publicly acknowledged through Eisai's efforts, and he was later considered the founder of Japanese Zen.

In 1217, two years after Eisai's death, a young way-seeker then eighteen years old, Eihei Dōgen (1200–53), who later founded the Sōtō branch of the Zen school, came to Kenninji to practice Rinzai Zen under the guidance of Myōzen, one of Eisai's disciples. In 1223 Myōzen and Dōgen went to Song China to practice with Chan practitioners there. Myōzen died of disease in 1225 in China. The same year, Dōgen finished his Caodong (Sōtō) Chan practice under Tiantong Rujing (Tendō Nyojō, 1163–1228). In 1227 Dōgen returned to Japan with Myōzen's relics. He entered Kenninji in 1228 but left in 1230. The next year, at Fukakusa in Kyoto, he wrote the *Bendōwa* (*Lecture on the Wholehearted Practice of the Way*, 1231); he was already beginning his Sōtō Zen activities.

Both Myōzen and Dōgen wanted Zen practice to be independent of Tendai and Shingon practices. This was the same direction Eisai had discerned that Zen practitioners in Japan should go as well. What Eisai insists on in his *Treatise* is nothing less than the independence of Zen as its own school, instead of existing only as parallel practices of the other schools, though he remained a lifelong Tendai mantra practitioner as well. Eisai believed that knowledge of emptiness (*prajñā; hannya* or *e*) which has become one with the practice of morality (*śīla; kai*) and self-concentration (*samādhi; sanmai* or *jō*)—not prayers attended by *goma* (*homa*) ceremonies (i.e., burnt offerings) or anything else—would protect the land and people under the emperor's rule. Knowledge of emptiness, together with the practice of morality and self-concentration, would ultimately open oneself to the truth of reality, and this opening was the way of bodhisattvas, who worked out of compassion for other beings.

As a Buddhist monk who practiced self-restraint and who knew the degenerate condition of the contemporary Buddhist schools in

Japan, Eisai insisted on the necessity among Buddhist priests of keeping both individual and social morality (*śīla* and *vinaya,* or *ritsu*). For Eisai, the prevailing view in Japan of the history of the degeneration of the Buddha's teachings in the latter-day world (*mappō*) worked in the opposite direction. The awakened nature of all humans was already there before this world came into being, and will never decay when this world suffers destruction. The *Mahāparinirvāṇa Sutra* describes this awakened nature as nirvana that is the eternal bliss of the formless self, free of all defilement. Eisai follows the view of Chinese Tiantai scholars after Zhiyi, in their interpretation of the above scripture, that nirvana, the cessation of suffering, offers the true ground for morality. (According to Zhiyi's *Profound Meaning of the Lotus Sutra,* Fasc. 4, Vol. 2, T. 33: 726b, nirvana stands as a support not only for *śīla,* or keeping precepts, but also for *samādhi* and *prajñā.*)

It seems to have been Eisai's belief that monks and nuns in the latter-day world are urged by ultimate reality to open themselves to ultimate reality itself, and that is why they should uphold both *śīla* and *vinaya*. What urges one to maintain morality is, ultimately, not any external authority but one's own awakened nature, nirvana. Following Zhanran's phrase, "the teaching on the permanence that supports *vinaya*" (see the passage from his *Elucidatory Comments* on Zhiyi's *Profound Meaning of the Lotus Sutra,* quoted in Gate III, pp. 84–5), Eisai calls nirvana the "Zen truth that supports morality." Because of this nirvana-support, Eisai believed, one could and should do one's best at once to keep precepts and to be in composure. From Eisai's viewpoint, making little of precepts while emphasizing the importance of attaining awakening constituted a serious offense against Buddhist practices.

It was on the basis of this understanding that Eisai advocated Zen practice in Japan. With this understanding, Eisai rejected Nōnin's popular Daruma Zen practice as evil. The Zen practice Eisai observed and experienced in Song China was that of the Chan school as a state-supported and state-supporting religion. He could never have dreamed of a time when Chan would have nothing to do with any sovereign support. Eisai felt it inevitable to remain a reliable Tendai priest, strange as it sounds, in order to obtain imperial support for his advocacy of an independent Zen school in Japan. He believed he had to wait for proper Zen practitioners to appear for such support to be granted. For Eisai, Tendai and Zen should be no different in being religious schools that both protect the state and are protected by the state. He believed that a person in whom the three basic Buddhist practices of morality (*śīla*), meditation (*samādhi*), and wisdom (*prajñā*) were one could be a protector of the state and thus enjoy state support. From Eisai's viewpoint, Nōnin was far from the type of Zen practitioner he looked for.

About twenty years after Eisai's death, Dōgen, in his vigorous activities leading followers of the Sōtō Zen school, emphasized the importance of keeping the precepts (*śīla*) and practicing meditation (*dhyāna*). Through his remarks, recorded by his faithful disciple and successor Koun Ejō, we know that Dōgen deeply respected Eisai for his religious and moral personality. Furthermore, according to Tsuji Zennosuke in the *Nihonbukkyōshi,* Dōgen read a work by Ejō's former master Kakuan, one of Nōnin's disciples, which Ejō had brought to him together with a gift from Nōnin to Kakuan. On his deathbed, Kakuan had recommended Ejō to go to Dōgen for guidance. Dōgen knew Kakuan was a person of discernment, and at the same time admired Nōnin, calling the latter Oshō (*heshang,* "respected master").

In his brief Note on the Future (*Miraiki,* 1197), Eisai predicted that half a century after his death the Zen school would greatly flourish in Japan. Kokan Shiren, the Buddhist historian, took up Eisai in his *Genkōshakusho,* Vol. 2, with choice quotations from the *Treatise on Letting Zen Flourish to Protect the State.* Toward the end of his introduction, Shiren refers to the prediction of the Zen school's future efflorescence by Eisai and states that it came to be realized in the following manner. First, Enni Bennen (1202–80) of the Tōfukuji in Kyoto, and then Lanxi Daolong (Rankei Dōryū, 1213–78, from China) of the Kenchōji in Kamakura, presided over Kenninji, in 1258 and 1259 respectively. Shiren writes that this successive appointment by the court, though brief in time and formal in nature, of these two Rinzai Zen priests as presiding priests of the temple dedicated to Eisai, revealed his contemporaries' high estimation of him.

The present text by Eisai has not attracted much attention, written as it was for the special purpose of defending the standpoint of Zen against groundless rebuke. Composed in Chinese, full of passages quoted often and repeatedly from one hundred Buddhist sources (mostly Indian and Chinese), it is not easy to read. Nevertheless, we have in the *Treatise on Letting Zen Flourish to Protect the State* a very passionate and sincere exposition of the Zen truth, based on the author's own deep experience. In this work we meet a very competent, committed person who devoted himself to exhorting people of the early Kamakura era to practice Zen, and to pray for the nation's protection from decadence both internal and external, for this was precisely what he meant by "protecting the state."

On reading this treatise, the first question one has to ask is why a *daihosshi,* the highest rank of priest in the Japanese Tendai school, would come to be in the position of defending the propagation of the Zen school against imperial prohibition and predicting its future in Japan. This question naturally finds its answer as one reads the work. The Zen school predicted by Eisai to flourish half a century after his lifetime was a form that Eisai believed his contemporary Tendai school would have to accept. That was the form the Tendai school had to develop from within itself, which in his time it had not yet done, as he mentions in this *Treatise*. It seems that he considered himself one of those few Tendai priests who could understand the close relationship between Tendai and Zen. Eisai observed in China that Tiantai had already been replaced by Chan as a state-supported religion. He quite possibly returned home with the firm belief that this ought to be the direction of Japanese Buddhism as well. Eisai was one of those rare Japanese priests who seriously considered the future of their contemporary religion.

The *Treatise on Letting Zen Flourish to Protect the State* is an excellent introduction to Zen principles and the Chan/Zen school, made for the first time in the history of Japanese religious thought.

Eisai introduced Zen to the people of Japan as a religion that would protect the state and which therefore was worthy of being protected by the state. Eisai believed that the Zen school, among the four forms of transmission inherited by the Tendai school, could realize this ideal in the near future. Indeed, Eisai's notion of the ideal form of religion—at once state-supporting and state-supported—had always been held by all the eight Buddhist schools (Hossō, Jōjitsu, Kegon, Kusha, Ritsu, Sanron, Shingon, and Tendai). But it does not seem that any of the leaders of these Buddhist schools, or Eisai himself, ever concerned themselves with how a political system in which the state protected particular religions had contributed to the degeneration of the nation's religious institutions. No doubt, however, Eisai considered Buddhism in Japan to have long since been nearly dead; the Buddhist religion had to be revived by taking the form of Zen in which the Tathāgata's *dhyāna* (*chan; zen;* meditation), a leading term from the *Laṅkāvatāra-sūtra,* contained the entire three teachings of Buddhism—*śīla, samādhi,* and *prajñā*—as the proper activities of bodhisattvas for benefiting other beings. This is why Eisai, while still a high-ranking Tendai priest, felt compelled to announce the future efflorescence of his ideal form of Buddhism in Japan with such passion.

After reading the *Treatise on Letting Zen Flourish to Protect the State,* few could deny that it is a superb extant record, composed in the Song-Kamakura periods by a Japanese Tendai priest, of the introduction of the Chinese Chan school as a model for the future Japanese Zen school, with the purpose of radically improving the religious situation of the country. The revised edition of the *Treatise on Letting Zen Flourish to Protect the State* published by Kōhō Tōshun (1714?–1779?) of the Ryōsokuin, Kenninji, Kyoto, in the seventh year of An'ei (1778) includes a Foreword by an anonymous writer, Tōshun's own Note on the Foreword, and his Postscript after the complete text of the *Treatise* and Eisai's Note on the Future. The Foreword was apparently written by a presiding priest of the Kenninji some time after 1225, when the *Notes on the Memorial Temple for Dharma Master Senkō from the Country of Japan* (*Ribenguo Qianguangfashi Citangji*, referenced in Eisai's Foreword, p. 64) was written, and before the last year of Hōtoku (1451) in the Muromachi period, when Nansō Ryōsaku, the seventh-generation presiding priest after Eisai of the Kenninji, went to Ming China. The unattributed Foreword was discovered in Nansō Ryōsaku's notebook, and he is presumed to be its author. The Foreword gives brief sketches of Eisai's activities in Japan and China and also mentions that after Eisai presented the *Treatise* to the court, and through it succeeded in gaining imperial sanction for propagating Zen, the text did not circulate outside the Zen school. A century after Eisai passed away, Kokan Shiren quoted many important passages from the *Treatise* in his *Genkōshakusho,* published in 1322. This seems to be the earliest extant record referring to Eisai's *Treatise.* Tōshun's Note on the Foreword and Postscript help us to understand how the present text has been handed down to us.

A Note on the Translation

The text of the *Treatise* in the Taishō Tripiṭaka, vol. 80, no. 2543, pp. 2–17, contains some wrong characters—at thirty-three places in the text itself, and one in the Note on the Future—which seem to be scribal or typographical errors. In addition, one word is marked as missing in the Note on the Future. The original Taishō Tripiṭaka text was the 1778 revised edition by Kōhō Tōshun. Eisai's text was first printed in 1666, in the sixth year of Kanmon, by Yatsuo Rokubei in Kyoto. All the wrong characters referred to above, except two in the Taishō Tripiṭaka text (T. 80: 4a24, note 59; 14a4, note 162), were corrected in a text using the Japanese reading (*kundoku*) by Professor Seizan Yanagida, published in a coauthored work entitled *Chūsei-zenke-no-shisō* (*Thoughts Expressed by Men of Zen in Medieval Japan*), *Nihon-shisō-taikei* No. 16, Tokyo: Iwanami-shoten, 1972. This volume includes Myōan Yōsai's *Kōzengokokuron* (*kundoku* text with headnotes), pp. 8–97, the Kanmon version in Chinese characters, pp. 99–122, supplementary notes, pp. 389–401, and an article entitled "Yōsai and his problems developed in the *Kōzengokoku-ron,*" pp. 439–86. I have relied on this work by Professor Yanagida (who prefers "Yōsai" rather than the more common "Eisai" for rendering the author's name) in tracing the sources of the passages quoted in the present text. Eisai quotes from one hundred parts of scriptures, and some passages include quotations from other texts. For these text citations, the English title is used and the source and page reference is given. The Appendix gives a complete list of all texts cited or mentioned in the *Treatise,* listed in order of their appearance, numbering 1–101, with the English title used in this translation, as well as providing more complete English titles and Sanskrit, romanized Chinese, and romanized Japanese titles, where applicable. Sources for the texts are also given.

In this translation, where terms have Sanskrit, Chinese, and Japanese equivalents, their romanization appears in that order. Most certainly the dates Eisai gives in the text are those of the lunar calendar. Dates and original terms appear in parentheses. Interpolatory words or phrases supplied by the translator appear in square brackets. The endnotes provide explanatory remarks and indicate the places where corrected words and phrases adopted from Professor Yanagida's work for the scribal errors mentioned previously have been incorporated.

An English translation of Eisai's Foreword and a brief introduction to his thought have been published in Chapter XII, "Zen Buddhism," in *Sources of Japanese Tradition,* compiled by Ryūsaku Tsunoda, William Theodore de Bary, and Donald Keene (New York: Columbia University Press, 1958). In the same volume see also "Zen Pioneers in Japan," pp. 235–6; "Eisai: Preface to *Kōzen gokoku ron* (*Propagation of Zen for the Protection of the Country*)," pp. 241–3; and the material on Eisai's "*Kissayōjōki*" ("Drink Tea and Prolong Life"), pp. 243–6.

The present translation represents an extensive revision of a previous English translation completed in November 1985, on which I received help from Mr. Jeffrey Shore, MA, University of Hawaii. At the time of preparing this revised translation, more than seventeen years later, I had completed a study of the four-fascicle Chinese version by Guṇabhadra of the *Laṅkāvatāra-sūtra,* which was of benefit in revising this translation of the *Treatise on Letting Zen Flourish to Protect the State.*

For this translation I owe much to Professor Seizan Yanagida's Japanese reading of the Chinese text and his annotations, and also to the group readings of Tang and Song dynasty Chan texts, guided by the late Professor Yoshitaka Iriya, as well as Professor Yanagida, which continued for many years on the Hanazono University campus. These readings gave me much greater familiarity with Eisai's quotations from these sources. I am deeply grateful for the critical contributions to Chan textual research by these two notable scholars.

A TREATISE ON LETTING ZEN FLOURISH TO PROTECT THE STATE

by

Myōan Eisai

Foreword

1a

After its completion this treatise has been circulating only in the gate of our Zen school. The master is the first patriarch in this country of the *busshin-shū*, the "school of the Buddha's mind."[1] Hence the appellation, "Founding Master" Senkō. His father, from the Kaya clan of Bitchū Province,[2] was descended from Emperor Kōrei.[3] His mother, from the Ta clan, prayed before an altar to the deity of music, the family's ancestral temple inside the Kibitsu Shrine, and, on dreaming of the morning star, felt herself pregnant. She gave birth to the master when the morning star appeared.

At the age of eight the master took leave of his parents and went to learn the meaning of the Buddhist treatises, the *Abhidharmakośa* and the [*Mahā*]*vaibhāṣā-śāstra,* in their Chinese versions, as transmitted in Mii Temple of the Tendai school. In the autumn of the third year of Ninhei, *mizunoto-tori* (1153), when he was thirteen years old, the master ascended Mount Hiei and was ordained a Tendai priest with the name Eisai. He learned the meaning of the "perfect principle" of Tendai, and his fame among those assembling for study already surpassed all others. However, on contemplating the world to be a floating illusion, his pessimism strengthened daily. When he was twenty-three years old, he descended from Mount Hiei and went to live on Mount Nichiō of Bizen Province.[4] He spent several years there, abstaining from [eating] grain while engaged in the esoteric practice of a rite called *samaya* ("pledge"). He dedicated himself to keeping his body and mind free of defilement, and was versed especially in a particular observance called *saṃvara* ("restraint").

The master had long intended to journey to Song China. However, for the past two hundred years in this country no Buddhist monks had visited China. When he happened to mention [his wish to go to China], he was ridiculed by others. Despite this, however, his determination never waivered. He said to himself:

> Careful reading of the holy teachings tells me that making sincere and concentrated prayers at places where former sages manifested miracles or where ancient Buddhas did their practices will leave no old desire unaccomplished.

Thus, every time he visited a sacred area, the master prayed without fail for the realization of his wish, and he would receive a response from the deity. When he was twenty-seven years old, the master stayed in the mountains of Daisen, Hōki Province,[5] to devote himself to intensive zazen practice for a summer retreat. There he happened to have a copy of the *Lotus Sutra* that had been brought from China; he regarded it as an auspicious omen of his crossing the sea. Thereupon, the master reported this to his parents, and went to Chiku Province.[6] He met an interpretor for the country of Song, named Li Dezhao, at Hakata Harbor. Hearing from him how the Chan school was flourishing over there, the master admired it as a rarity.

When he was twenty-eight years old, in the third year of Nin'an, *tsuchinoe-ne* (1168), on the eighteenth [day] of the fourth month, the master boarded a trading ship and went to sea. On the twenty-fifth [day] he reached Mingzhou of Song, on the nineteeth [day] of the fifth month he went up Mount Tiantai, on the twenty-fourth [day] he arrived at Wannian Temple, and on the twenty-fifth [day] he made the offering of tea to the [five hundred] arhats[7] [believed to have come from India to abide on the mountain]. In the bowl of tea offered to them, the master saw reflected the entire body of an arhat, and when he dared to walk across the [natural] stone bridge [that spanned a terrifying fall] he suddenly saw two blue dragons; thereupon, he came to feel something move him. He knew himself to have been an Indian monk in the former life who had come to abide on the mountain of Wannian.

On the twenty-seventh [day] the master returned to Mingzhou; on the tenth [day] of the sixth month of the year he reached Mount Yuwang, where he revered and bowed to the Buddha's relics, feel-
1b ing himself penetrated by the glory that issued from them. In this

way, during his pilgrimage for contemplation, there were more than a few occasions when the master experienced a spiritual response. In the ninth month of the year the master returned home, with the impression that his half-year stay in Song was far from sufficient.

During the next eighteen years the master came to call himself the leader of the two allied gates of Buddhism, the mantra-esoteric and the exoteric. In the Tendai school, in which he had originally been ordained, the master wore the seal of the One Mind with contemplation of the threefold truth, and in the mantra part of the school he obtained the official confirmation of having entered the *maṇḍala* seat and received consecration with water sprinkled upon the head. Because in this manner he had come to the root and depth of the school [in both gates], the emperor as well as the subjects regarded the master as their honored guide. His guidance accorded especially with Emperor Gotoba.

The master one day received an imperial order to offer prayers for rain in a park named Shinsen-en [in Kyoto]. The ten fingers of his hands emitted great rays of light and illuminated all the grasses and trees there. A great amount of rain fell from the heavens. Each drop of water on the surface of leaves of the park's trees had the master's reflection in it. The emperor celebrated the occasion by giving him the special title Yōjō ("On the Leaves").

The master once more wanted to go abroad, this time to visit India and make a pilgrimage to the eight stupas that hold the relics of the Tathāgata [Śākyamuni]. In the third year of Bunji, *hinoto-hitsuji* (1187) he entered the country of Song again. This was in the fourteenth year of Chunzi, under the reign of Emperor Xiaozong.

In Song the master presented a memorial to the emperor in a petition for traveling to India. No permission was granted since the three routes from China to India, which ran through foreign lands, all belonged to the Mongols in those days and were not open [to travelers from China]. Thus he was obliged to stop at Wannian Temple on Mount Tiantai. During the five years of his stay in Song, the master read the Tripiṭaka scriptures three times.

Further, the master dressed for burial the corpse of the Venerable [Tripiṭaka Master] Śrī Bhadra [from Nālandā, India], the first presiding priest of the Tiantai Wannian Temple, and repaired the surface of the pagoda which had been built in memory of the priest. The master did this because he believed the venerable monk was his own previous incarnation. Once the master composed a verse:

> Here where a monastery overseas has specially been built,
> Green hills welcome me with beaming smiles.
> The bones of the blooming plums remain undecayed for three lives.
> I ponder on a rock, sweeping away green moss.

This appears to have been composed around that time.

When the master saw that the pagoda built in memory of Dhyāna Master Zhizhe[8] had become broken down and ruined, he gave up [his own] daily expenses in order to manage building operations. Subsequently the master had the porches built on both sides of the gate of Wannian Temple, which had been missing. For rebuilding a pavilion named the "One Thousand Buddhas' Towering Pavilion" on Mount Tianton, there was so great a contribution from the master that people admired it and a record of it was engraved in stone. For details, see the *Notes on the One Thousand-Buddha Pavilion of the Celebrated Mountain Taibai* (*Taibaimingshan Qianfogeji*) by Louyao (d. 1213), a Song scholar, as well as the *Notes on the Memorial Temple for Dharma Master Senkō from the Country of Japan* (*Ribenguo Qianguangfashi Citangji*)[9] by Yuchu, General Taxation Officer. Both *Notes* are kept at the Celebrated Mountain Taibai.

The nation of Song was suffering from an epidemic disease, which worried both the emperor and his subjects. The emperor ordered several high-ranking priests to pray against its prevalence, with no effect. The emperor then ordered the master to do the same. A day after the master received the imperial edict, the epidemic had already ceased. Two days after, those who had died came back to life. The emperor praised him for this and said:

> You have the title Yeshang (Yōjō, "On the Leaves"). Does it not mean that on the leaves one thousand Śākyamunis made their appearance?

The emperor specially granted the master the title of honor Great Master Qianguang (Senkō, "One Thousand Rays of Light"). Those contemporary great masters who had practiced under their own masters all over the country praised the master, calling him an Incarnate.

The master himself practiced under Chan Master Xuan [Huaichang] at both Mount Tiantai and Mount Tianlong for several years; he was permitted to enter Master Xuan's room and received the transmission of the seal of the awakened mind. Between the two, there was giving and accepting everything concerning the Chan gate, and the master's appellation Ming'an (Myōan) was established. When the master took leave to return
east Chan Master [Xuan] wrote words in verse on tens of sheets 1c
of paper, and granted them to him, thereby certifying his final attainment. That was how the school of the Buddha's mind came to be transmitted and circulate to the east of the sea.

The master returned to his home country in the second year of Kenkyū, *mizunoto-i* (1191), and stayed in the provinces of Tsukushi[10] for a few years. Then the master entered the capital of Kyoto, and in the second year of Kennin, *mizunoe-inu* (1202), he had a Zen temple built on the bank of the Kamo River near the fifth-street bridge, and was granted the name of the year, Kennin, for the temple. Once the master advocated the school of the Buddha's mind, students gathered like clouds to learn Zen and practice *dhyāna* under him. The master widely circulated the great bodhisattva *śīla* (precepts);[11] at the same time he had [his students practice] the esoteric rites of the Tendai school as well. Then the master caused Buddhist practice to flourish and made religious influence prevail in the country. On every *upoṣadha* (sangha ceremony of reciting the Vinaya) occasion of the dark half and light half of the lunar month, the master gave a sermon on precepts with no deficiency in the teaching. As time passed, the hearts of [those in] the capital turned to the master's teaching.

When [a priest of the Kegon school named] Chōgen, who had been begging alms all over the country with the purpose of rebuilding the Tōdaiji[12] died, the imperial court ordered the master to be in charge of this work. It was soon accomplished. [In 1208] the nine-storied tower of the Hosshōji [in Kyoto] burned down in a big fire. And [when things did not go well for rebuilding,] the master, who could not but receive the imperial order to be supervisor of the rebuilding work, had three years' tax revenue collected from Suwō Province[13] in order to prepare for the work. He succeeded in this as well. Besides, in other provinces some monasteries were first opened by the master, other celebrated temples were restored by him, and still others were supervised by him; the number of such temples is too many to list [all] their names here.

The master had already been propagating the school of the "utmost vehicle," which is the "special transmission outside the scriptures," far and wide. Meanwhile, various lecturers of Buddhist scriptures in the southern capital of Nara and the northern ridges of Mount Hiei, who were extremely prejudiced, denounced the master and brought suit against him. Thereupon, the master wrote three fascicles of a treatise in which he quoted from Buddhist sutras and *śāstras* to prove his point and refute their rebuke. He entitled this the *Treatise on Letting Zen Flourish to Protect the State* (*Kōzen-gokokuron*). The master presented it to the emperor and obtained imperial sanction. It is because of this that our school has prevailed under heaven.

Those who personally entered the master's gate and attained the truth were Eichō (d. 1247), Gyōyū, Gen'yū, and Myōzen (d. 1225). Those who came from other gates were Kōben (Myōe, 1173–1232, of the Kōzanji) and Shunjō (1166–1227, of the Sennyū-ji). Those who came from the exoteric and esoteric gates of the Tendai school were too many to count.

Now I strongly expect that in coming ages, when masters of this school succeed one after another and cause it to flourish in all corners of the country—alas! this treatise might be found quite useless.

I have sketched the above outline to let our descendants know [how the treatise was made as well as what the master's life activities were].

[Note on the Foreword] 1c21

The above Foreword, whose authorship remains to be verified, and which I happened to find between the pages of a notebook written by Nansō [Ryō]saku, was not given in the old edition of the *Treatise on Letting Zen Flourish to Protect the State.*[14] I presume that it was composed in [Ryō]saku's days. Then the date was only two hundred years after the founding master's days, and there is no wonder that the phrases of the Foreword were still detailed enough to stand as proof of their credibility. About the few expressions in the Foreword that are different from what have traditionally been known, I think more information should be collected to verify them. It is my regret that for the present edition [printed in 1778] I have failed to obtain any original version of the entire text that may have included this Foreword, with which to collate the present one. Now I add it to the head of the whole text to be printed together.

By [Ryō]saku I mean a disciple of Zuigan Ryōsei, the seventh generation from our founding master. In the era of Hōtoku (1449–51) [Ryō]saku entered the country of Ming together with Kyūen [Ryō]chin (d. 1498), and nothing is known about his end.

Noted by [Kōhō] Tōshun, [presiding priest of Ryōsokuin, Kenninji]

Preface

2a

By Eisai, An *Ajari* of Japan, Who Studied Abroad in Mount Tiantai of the Great Song, in the Rank of *Daihosshi* (Great Dharma Master) for Transmission of the Lamp

How great is the Mind![15] The height of the heavens is such that it is impossible to reach its end; the Mind rises above the heavens. The thickness of the earth is such that it is impossible to measure its extent; the Mind comes out from beneath the earth. The rays of the sun and moon travel so far that it is impossible to exceed them; the Mind extends beyond the reach of their rays. The great thousands of worlds, comparable to [the number of] grains of sand in the Ganges River, are boundless; the Mind encompasses these worlds. You might speak of the great void and the primal energy that fills it, and the Mind envelops the great void and is pregnant with the primal energy. Heaven and earth wait for Me and then cover and uphold one another. Sun and moon wait for Me and then circulate. The four seasons wait for Me and then change. A myriad of things wait for Me and then are procreated. Great indeed is the Mind.[16]

I have no other way than to forcibly name this Mind. This has been named the best vehicle (*śreṣṭhayāna*), ultimate reality (*paramārtha*), the true characteristics of reality (*dharmatā*) revealed through the knowledge of emptiness (*prajñā*), the one true mode of being (*dharmadhātu*), the unsurpassed awakening (*anuttarā samyaksaṃbodhi*),[17] the calm self in heroic advance (*śūraṃgama samādhi*), the eye and treasury of the True Dharma (*saddharmacakṣukośa*), as well as the sublime mind (*hṛdaya*) of nirvana.[18] This being the case, it is in this Mind that all the expositions classified as the three wheels, the eight treasuries, the four trees, and the five vehicles find their source.[19]

The Great Hero Śākyamuni transmitted this truth of mind (*cittadharma*)[20] to the golden ascetic Mahākāśyapa,[21] calling it the special transmission independent of scriptural teachings.[22] When Vulture Peak[23] turned its head and was met by the smiling face of Cockfoot Ridge,[24] the flower picked up [by Śākyamuni] budded on a thousand branches, and the profound source poured into myriad streams. Inheritors of this truth in India and students succeeding it in China could be known in great number.

Indeed, teachings on the awakened truth having been widely propagated by those who have already become Buddhas, their Dharma robes have also been transmitted of their own accord. And the norms by which former sages (*muni*s) practiced have solidly been established. The characteristics of the teachings on the awakened truth have made the weaving by teacher and disciple complete, and the norms for practice have been free from the mixture of right and wrong. Thereupon, Bodhidharma, the great master from the west, struck oars on the southern sea, and ever after he carried his staff to the eastern river [and to Luoyang (Rakuyō)], the teaching of Fayan (Hōgen) reached Korea, and the teaching of [Mount] Niutou (Gozu) came to Japan. As people have studied this, various vehicles have prevailed. As they have practiced this, they have had the ultimate knowing open up in one life. That which externally has the support of the teaching of nirvana for monastic discipline,[25] and which internally has the awakening of the wisdom of emptiness (*prajñā*), is none other than the Chan (Zen) school.

Our court, bright with the glory of the Imperial Sun, carries virtuous winds so far and free that people from the land where roosters are worshiped (Korea) or from the land where elephants are honored (India) reach the ground with their heads at its red stone steps; people from the land of Jinlin (Sumatra) or the Yu Ridge (in the western regions) present their allegiance at its green stone steps. In this country lay officials put into practice Confucian classics on administration; Buddhist priests propagate the path for going beyond worldliness. Even the teachings of the four Vedas have their use. As for Zen of the five branches, how could it be abandoned?

This fact nothwithstanding, there are some who slander Zen as a religion of dark testimony. Others are suspicious of Zen and speak of it as an evil attachment to emptiness. Some say Zen is not 2b
a religion suited to the latter-day world. Others say it does not meet the demands of our country. Some despise my capacity, and insist that I have had no scriptural verification. Others make little of my natural capacity, and consider it hard to stir up what is on the wane. This means nothing other than that the very upholders of the teachings on the awakened truth extinguish the Dharma treasure. Could anybody other than me know my mind? They not only block the principal gate of the Zen barrier (i.e., the Zen school) but also might possibly be ruining our patriarchal path of Mount Hiei (i.e., the Tendai school) as well. How sad and grievous! Is this right or wrong?

This being the case, I have brought together general principles from the three collections of the Buddhist teachings to show them to contemporary people of wisdom. I have noted the pivotal points of the Zen school itself so as to leave them behind for posterity. I have arranged them into three fascicles, with the division of ten separate gates. I name the whole text the *Treatise on Letting Zen Flourish to Protect the State* (*Kōzengokokuron*), so as to accord with the original intent of the Lord of the Awakened Truth and the Lord of the World.[26]

It is only on the presumption that my talks, wild as they are, would not contradict the true characteristics of reality that I have completely forgotten myself in playing with theory, for which both priests and laypeople are to be blamed. It is because of my recollection of the benefit from Linji, which the latter-day world will certainly receive, that I have become free from the shame of errors of my pen. May the proclamation of transmission of the Lamp of Truth not be annulled but illuminate each dawn of the three Dharma meetings under the future Buddha Maitreya![27] May the bubbling spring of ultimate reality be inexhaustible and keep flowing into the world throughout the country for eons under a thousand Buddhas![28] A list of titles of the [ten] gates will be given hereafter, as you see.

Fascicle One

2b13

First Gate: Having the Buddha's Teachings Abide Long
Second Gate: Protecting the State
Third Gate: Eliminating People's Doubts
Fourth Gate: Scriptural Verification by Ancient People of Virtue
Fifth Gate: The Sects of the Zen School's Lineage
Sixth Gate: Scriptural Evidence for Promoting People's Confidence in the Zen School
Seventh Gate: Citing a General Principle and Exhorting People to Practice Zen
Eighth Gate: Establishing a List of the Essential Patterns of Activity in the Zen School
Ninth Gate: Information from the Large Countries
Tenth Gate: Merit Transference and Making Vows

Gate I

By the first gate, "Having the Buddha's Teachings Abide Long," I mean what follows.

The *Sixfold Prajñāpāramitā Sutra* (T. 8: 868c) says:

> The Buddha [Śākyamuni] said, "So as to have the teachings abide long, I expound a collection of precepts for monastic discipline (Vinaya-*piṭaka*)."

The *Mahāprajñāpāramitā Treatise* (T. 25: 130b) says:

> The Buddha's disciples are grouped into seven: monks (*bhikṣu*s), nuns (*bhikṣuṇī*s), young monks to be ordained (*śrāmaṇera*s), young nuns to be ordained (*śrāmaṇerī*s), female novices (*śikṣamāṇā*s), laymen (*upāsaka*s), and laywomen (*upāsikā*s). The former five are mendicants, while the rest are householders.

Insofar as these seven groups of disciples are free from transgressions, the Buddha's teachings will abide long in the world. Hence the statement in the *Chan School Monastic Rules* (*Zokuzōkyō* 2–16, 439a):

> Indeed, it is by establishing precepts for monastic discipline and getting the practitioners free from transgressions that the school can have models for all the threefold world. Therefore, practicing *dhyāna* (*chan; zen*) and investigating into the Way[29] presuppose moral conduct that follows precepts. Unless one gets free from transgressions and keeps oneself away from wrongs, how could one attain awakening and become a patriarch? Accordingly you should obtain benefit by reciting items from the *Vinaya in Four Divisions:* the four grave
> 2c offenses that result in excommunication (*pārājikā*), the thirteen transgressions short of excommunication (*saṃghāvaśeṣa*), the two faults of indefinite character, the thirty faults concerning priests' possessions (*naiḥsargikāḥ pāyattikā*), the ninety moral transgressions (*pātayantikā*), the four [kinds of conduct] that must be confessed concerning receiving meals from others (*pratideśanīyāni*), a hundred rules to be observed concerning personal behavior (*śaikṣadharmaḥ*), and the sevenfold decorum for appeasing quarrels (*adhikaraṇaśamathā*).[30] Also items from the *Brahmā Net Sutra on the Bodhisattva Śīla* (T. 24: 1004–9)—that is to say, the threefold collection of purifying precepts, especially the ten weighty and the forty-eight less weighty precepts.[31]
>
> By doing all this you should be well versed in both keeping and transgressing precepts, besides in [knowing] what is prohibited and what is not. You should take recourse only to the noble words that come from the Buddha's golden mouth. You should not indulge in obeying people of mediocre capability.

The *Mahāparinirvāṇa Sutra* (T. 12: 472b) says:

> Should this scriptural treasury be extinguished, the Buddha's teachings would be extinguished on the spot.

Indeed, this scripture advocates religious observances for the days of deterioration.

The *Mahāsāṃghika Vinaya* (T. 22: 227b) says:

> The Buddha said, "If Buddhas don't prescribe rules for moral conduct, their authentic teachings will not abide long."

The *Buddha Treasury Sutra* (T. 15: 787bc) says:

> The Buddha said, "This person, dear Śāriputra, has forsaken the unsurpassed treasury of truth and deteriorated into embracing evil views. He is among those way-seekers who are likened to outcastes.... This will relegate my teachings, dear Śāriputra, which are free from defilement, to gradual extinction. The teachings of mine on the awakened truth (*bodhidharma*), which I have attained after the long period of birth and death I suffered from, will be ruined in those days by people of such evil views.... From such people I would not allow myself to accept a drink of water."

The *Brahmā Net Sutra on the Bodhisattva Śīla* (T. 24: 1009a) says:

> Those who violate the moral conduct they have vowed to keep on their way to attaining awakening are unable to receive any offerings from lay devotees, unable to walk the ground in the monarch's land, and unable to drink the monarch's water. Should they dare to walk, some five thousand hungry ghosts (*preta*s) will always stand in their way. Ghosts will call them "big thieves." Should they enter a monk's residence, a town, or a house, ghosts will sweep their traces away from the ground.... Those who violate the moral conduct of their own vow are no different from beasts.

The *Sutra of the Benevolent King* (T. 8: 833bc) says:

> In the ages, Lord of the World, when my teachings on the awakened truth are almost [completely] neglected, there may be monks who see the four kinds of sangha members (i.e., monks, nuns, laymen, and laywomen) often being treated by the king and his ministers in a manner that goes against the teachings. The latter will make willful transgressions against the Buddha, Dharma, and Sangha (the community of mendicants who seek awakening). The offenses committed by them are against the Buddha's teachings and against the moral precepts. They will bind monks with cords as in criminal law. When things go like this, the extinction of the teachings of the Buddha's truth will not take long.

The *Mahāprajñāpāramitā Sutra* (T. 6: 539ab) says in effect:

> Dear Śāriputra, after my death, in the last time, on the last occasion, in the last five hundred-year period[32] when my teachings are lost, a scripture that accords with the profound knowledge of emptiness (*prajñā*) will play a great part in helping people attain awakening in the direction of the northeast [as well]. This is because all the Tathāgatas[33] will make much of that kind of scripture, and pray for its preservation in that direction [as well] forever, without extinction.

This statement clarifies how the awakened truth of Zen that supports people in keeping precepts[34] will cause the Buddha's teachings on the truth to abide long. The *Great Dharma Torch Dhāraṇī Sutra* (T. 21: 677a) says:

> By protecting the Buddha's teachings I mean that at the time when the Buddha's teachings are exposed to extinction, bodhisattvas, realizing this, will resort to various means[35] to protect and preserve them, whereby they can have the teachings abide long. It is for this reason that those bodhisattvas will also come to have the protuberance (*uṣṇīṣa*)[36] on their heads as Buddhas have.

Herewith I have established the [first] gate "Having[37] the Buddha's Teachings Abide Long."

Gate II

By the second gate, "Protecting the State," I mean what follows.

The *Sutra of the Benevolent King* (T. 8: 832b) says:

> The Buddha entrusts realization of the knowledge of emptiness to monarchs and ministers of various countries, large and small, in present and future ages, and wishes to have them realize that this knowledge is the secret treasure for protecting the state.

By the knowledge of emptiness is meant the principle of Zen;[38] 3a
the above statement comes to mean that insofar as there are people within the land who keep precepts for moral conduct, deities will protect the state. The *Supreme Deity King's Prajñāpāramitā Sutra* (T. 8: 689a) says:

> Suppose a bodhisattva who practices to know emptiness for all beings as well as for himself happens to become a monarch, and some people who suffer from extreme poverty and humiliation come to curse and slander and disgrace him. On that occasion the monarch will refrain from intimidating them with punishment by saying, "I am ruler of this country; the law will subject you to capital punishment." Instead, he will immediately think this way: "For many lives gone by I have vowed in the presence of the World-honored Ones that I would rescue all living beings from their suffering by causing them to attain unsurpassed awakening. Should I arouse wrath now, it will go against the original vow of mine."

The *Sutra of Forty-two Sections* (*Zokuzōkyō* 1–59, 36a) says:

> Feeding a hundred evil people won't be as good as feeding a single good person. Feeding a thousand good people won't

compare with feeding a single keeper of the five precepts (*pañcaśīlāni*). Feeding ten thousand keepers of *pañcaśīla* won't exceed feeding a single new enterer into the stream of nirvana (*srota-āpanna*). Feeding a hundred thousand *srota-āpanna*s won't be equal to feeding a single attainer of the stream of nirvana who has one more birth and death left before final attainment (*sakṛdāgāmin*). Feeding a million *sakṛdāgāmī*s won't be like feeding a single attainer of the stream of nirvana who has no more birth and death left before final attainment (*anāgāmin*). Feeding ten million *anāgāmī*s won't surpass feeding a single attainer of the stream of nirvana who is worthy of respect because he has nothing more to attain (arhat). Feeding a hundred million arhats won't go beyond feeding a single solitary enlightened one (*pratyeka-buddha*). Feeding a billion *pratyekabuddha*s won't supplant feeding one among the Buddhas who appear in the three times of past, present, and future. Feeding ten billion Buddhas who appear in the three divisions of time won't be on a par with feeding a single person who thinks of nothing, abides nowhere, makes no-practice, and has nothing to attain.

"Thinks of nothing" and so on stand for none other than the principle of this Zen school. The *Sutra of Śūraṃgama Practices* (T. 19: 133 *ff*)says:

Dear Ānanda, you should keep these four kinds of restraint[39] with you, become as clear and bright as ice and frost, and be singleminded in reciting my mantra verse named "white umbrella" (*sitātapatra-dhāraṇī*).[40] You should select the most pure of the keepers of ethical precepts for your teacher, wear a new and clean robe, burn incense, abide quietly, and recite this divine series of mantras uttered by my heart-Buddha (*xinfo; shinbutsu*),[41] one hundred and eight times. Then fix a place to make it a depository for rules of morality (*sīmā-bandha*) and there build a seat of awakening (*bodhimaṇḍa*), seek for a quick presence of the fulfillment (*siddhi*) of the

> mantras, give rise to a bodhisattva vow in the *bodhimaṇḍa,* bathe and cleanse yourself every time you leave and enter the place, and six times a day circumambulate the Buddha statue. You should practice in this way without sleep for three rounds of seven days consecutively. Before such a person I shall manifest myself, stroke his head with my hand and comfort him, and cause him to open up awakening....
>
> If people constantly recite this series of mantras, no fire can burn them, nor can water drown them. They will attain perfect self-concentration (*samādhi*), so that no curse or any evil star could impose evils on them. Dear Ānanda, you should know that this series of mantras always has a bodhisattva named Vajradhara ("Thunderbolt Bearer") and his whole family, as many as eighty-four thousand and *nayuta*s, as protectors of the mantras. Every member of Bodhisattva Vajradhara's family has followers as many as that family, and all of them will attend the mantra reciter day and night. Even if either mentally or verbally they keep this series of mantras in their distracted mind, Vajradhara will always attend them. How much more so with those who are firm in their aspiration to attain awakening (*bodhicitta*)!...
>
> Dear Ānanda, in this suffering world are eighty-four thousand disastrous stars that evoke evil fates and twenty-eight stars of great evil, and when they appear in the world they can arouse various portents. On the ground where this series of mantras is alive, however, all those portents disappear.
> You may establish an area of twelve *yojana*s[42] to make it a 3b
> depository of rules of morality. No evils or disasters will ever enter there. That is why the Tathāgata propounds this series of mantras, so that in a future world all those mendicants who newly begin their practice may be protected from evils.

The recitation of this "white-umbrella" series of mantras is constantly practiced in Chan temples. This will suffice to prove that the significance of the Zen school lies in protecting the state.

In the *Official Document Presented to the Emperor,* Great Master Chishō[43] of the Tendai school says:

> Great Master Jikaku,[44] in the days when he was in China during the Tang dynasty, made this vow: "I am here after having crossed the four-stretching waves of the blue sea to seek for the stainless truth (*śukladharma*). Supposing I could return to my native land under the rule of our emperor, by all means I will build a Zen temple." By this the master meant specially that the state must be protected and that ordinary beings be helped toward their attainment of awakening through Zen practice.

As one of those who want to propagate the principle of Zen, I just follow these noble forerunners. Herewith I have set up the [second] gate, "Protecting the State."

Gate III

The third gate, "Eliminating People's Doubts," discusses two doubts to be eliminated. One is the doubt caused by ignorance through confusion and suspicion. The other is the doubt that scholars tend to embrace through bigotry.

Question: Someone asks, "People in the last five hundred-year period when the Buddha's teachings are lost are dull-witted and not very wise. Who can practice the principle of this school?"

Answer: The Great Sage Śākyamuni took time into consideration when he handed down the teachings to posterity. Why should we trust our worldly feelings to conclude that?

It is said (in the *Mahāprajñāpāramitā Treatise,* T. 25: 125c) that in the past the Buddha lived in Jetavana[45] for twenty-five years. [During that period,] among the nine hundred thousand families in the city, one-third saw the Buddha with their eyes, another one-third heard him speak with their ears but failed to see him, and the last third neither heard nor saw him.

On the part of the Buddha, to people of one capacity he manifested eight forms of being;[46] for others he left his relics, for others he left remains of his teachings; for still others he enabled them to listen to his teachings in the land beyond after this life. He even provided some people with adverse circumstances. The *Sutra on the Abiding of the Dharma* (T. 12: 1112c) says:

> The Buddha said, "Dear Ānanda, soon I shall assume the form of death. I have already finished everything a Buddha has to do. I have finished helping those who were to cross the sea of suffering to do so. For those who have not, I have provided them with the conditions in which they all can cross it. I have already made non-Buddhists, the army of demons, and others submit to the way of awakening. I have fulfilled my previous vows. For the future world I shall be the unsurpassed Awakened Eye."

Do you not see that the Buddha has already provided us with the present-life benefit? The same is true with the principle of the Zen school. If a person happens to have the conditions for it, he will practice it. Otherwise, no one would seek it. Even if he does not practice it, occasions of seeing, hearing, encountering, or knowing about it will lead one to attain ultimate liberation. You see in India that not all people have practiced Zen. In China there are some who have never practiced it. In Japan the same will be true. If there is one out of ten thousand people who practices it, how could it be impossible? If on the grounds that no one can do it you won't exhort anyone to practice it, then people will lack both the proper and adverse occasions for it. Moreover, the *Mahāprajñāpāramitā Sutra* (T. 6: 539ab, quoted above, p. 78) has this:

> Dear Śāriputra, after my death, in the last time, on the last occasion, in the last five hundred-year period when my teachings are lost, a scripture like this that accords with the profound knowledge of emptiness will play a great part in helping people attain awakening in the direction of the northeast

> as well.... Innumerable men and women of noble mind will gain unimaginable benefit.

Further, the *Middle Treatise* (T. 30: 1b) says in effect:

> *Question:* Why do you compose this treatise?
>
> *Answer:*[47] During the last five hundred-year period after the
> 3c Buddha assumed the form of *parinirvāṇa,* people are dull-witted and deeply attached to various forms of his teachings, and seek something final in them. Instead of realizing what the Buddha meant by them, they merely cling to their verbal expressions. While they hear about ultimate emptiness in the Mahayana teachings, they don't know for what reason things are empty of self-nature. Therefore, they give rise to fixed views and doubts about emptiness. Why do various faults arise in the midst of ultimate emptiness? In order to [clarify] this, the author composed this *Middle Treatise.*

The Tiantai school's *Elucidatory Comments* (T. 33: 858b) says:[48]

> Here is a doubt: The *Lotus Sutra* has already revealed the ultimate truth through provisional teachings. Why does the *Mahāparinirvāṇa Sutra* further propagate what is provisional? Master Zhiyi in the treatise explains that the latter teaches about the life-redeeming valuable treasure. The *Mahāparinirvāṇa Sutra,* fascicle 14, says:[49]
>
>> Seven varieties of gems, which their owner does not take out for use, are called treasures. The reason this person keeps them hidden is that he thinks of their future use. When the cost of grain is high, when enemies invade the country, or when the nation happens to have an evil king, the possessor can use the treasures so as to redeem his life. When it is hard to get some property, he can take them out for use.
>>
>> The same is true with the Buddhas' hidden treasure. It may happen that in the latter-day world evil members

> of the sangha will hoard prohibited properties, or that all the four groups of sangha members will insist that the Tathāgata (Śākyamuni) finally entered into complete extinction, and will read and recite non-Buddhist scriptures without respecting[50] Buddhist sutras. At the time when such evils appear in the world, those evils must be destroyed. That is why the Tathāgata expounded this sutra. Should this sutra disappear, the Buddha's teachings will disappear on the spot.

What the author of the treatise means by pointing to the *Mahāparinirvāṇa Sutra* as the valuable treasure is this: passages of the sutra that appear before and after the above quote all propound the eternity of nirvana, the extinction of suffering, the very teaching that truly supports morality. In this latter-day world evil sangha members who break the moral precepts (*śīla*), or who make no efforts [to learn] the Mahayana teachings as well as [to uphold] moral conduct, will lose the life of eternal abiding. But let this sutra be trusted; it propounds the eternity of nirvana, the very teaching that is the true support for morality. It is fully equipped with both *yāna* (vehicle) and *śīla* (precepts).

The Tiantai school's *Solutions for Propagation* (T. 46: 345b) says:[51]

> Then again the *Mahāparinirvāṇa Sutra* is specially meant for the latter-day world because it carries the exposition of expediency.

In addition, [Zhanran's] *Calming and Contemplation: Their Meaning and Examples* (T. 46: 447b) says:

> We need the *Mahāparinirvāṇa Sutra* because, although everyone in the various vehicles, relying on the *Lotus Sutra,* returns to the one real truth, people of the latter days, who are dull-witted, will see their own practice fall flat should

they lack support. Only their own practice and support from the ground of their being together can cause them to proceed further. The Buddha in transformation himself looked upon his death as the end of his lifetime activities. Much more so with our latter-day world, where practice will not advance without support. Therefore, the sutra expounded the eternity of nirvana as the true support for morality, and revealed the reality.

The *Lotus Sutra* (T. 9: 37c) says:

> In a latter-day evil world...a bodhisattva may sit in a secluded place and practice calming himself, contemplating that everything that has form is empty of self-nature, and that [all phenomena] are in their forms as they should be. . . . He may always be willing to contemplate on such forms as they are in their original way, and abide unmoved and stable like Mount Sumeru.

Great Master Tiantai,[52] in his commentary on the chapter "Abiding in Bliss" [in the *Words and Phrases in the Lotus Sutra*] (T. 34: 120b), says:

> By "contemplating," the scripture means the wisdom of contemplating the Middle Way. By "everything that has form," it means everything in all ten directions. . . . Contemplation goes with nineteen phrases. The first [phrase][53] expresses what is general; the other eighteen phrases correspond to the eighteenfold emptiness (*śūnya*) expounded in the *Mahāprajñāpāramitā Sutra*.

Further, the [*Lotus Sutra*] (T. 9: 37c–38a) says:

> In a latter-day world after the Tathāgata manifested *parinirvāṇa,* a bodhisattva who wants to preach on this Dharma Lotus truth should abide in bliss. No matter whether it is when he is explaining the truth to others or when reading the scripture, he may not speak of the faults of any other person or

> scripture. He may not despise other preachers. He may not talk about his like or dislike of others or of their merits or flaws.

It further says (T. 9: 38c):

> In the latter-day world where the Tathāgata's teachings are about to be extinguished, those who want to hold the truth 4a
> of this *Lotus Sutra* as their guide should be friendly and amiable to everyone, both laypeople and mendicants. They should be compassionate to those who have not been seeking awakening, making this vow: "When I attain awakening, no matter where I may find myself then, I will exercise to the full my possible supernatural power and wisdom to enable them to abide in this awakened truth."

These passages on four blissful ways of being from the *Lotus Sutra* all refer to a latter-day world. Then we know that all three sutras—the *Mahāprajñāpāramitā,* the *Lotus,* and the *Mahāparinirvāṇa*—expound the essentials of self-concentration (*samādhi*) in seated posture (i.e., zazen) and the contemplation based on it that were intended for the latter-day world. If the generations of [people of] the latter-day world lacked the capabilities and occasions for attaining awakening, the Buddha would not have expounded them. Since, however, this is not the case, the practice flourishes in the great land of Song. Only out of their ignorance do some people in the contemporary world believe that Buddhism, a religion based on the Buddha's teachings, has been extinguished. But they are wrong, as you will see from the details noted in the ninth gate.

Above I quoted a passage from the *Mahāprajñāpāramitā Sutra,* "[people attain awakening] in the direction of the northeast [as well]." This indicates China, Korea, and Japan. The Buddha's teachings have already been transmitted into China. Korea has had the transmission of the Fayan sect of the Chan school. When Deshao, the State Master of Tang, had some missing fascicles of Tiantai school texts sought in Korea and Japan, he knew that the Chan school was flourishing in Korea.[54]

It has been nearly three hundred years since State Master Deshao of China passed away. Before this, in Japan in the Tenpyō era, a master from Tang China, Daoxuan (Dōsen),[55] who stayed at Dai'anji in Nara, transmitted the teaching of the Chan school to Reverend Gyōhyō.[56] Great Master Dengyō (Saichō)[57] says in his *Genealogy* (*Zenshū* 1):

> According to the permit for my joining the sangha as a monk, the guiding master was Gyōhyō, Dharma Master for Transmission of the Lamp, who lived at Dai'anji, in the left quarters of the capital.
>
> My forefather in the Dharma, Reverend Daoxuan, had brought with him from the Great Tang a copy of Great Master Bodhidharma's treatise on Chan, which has been stored in the treasury of Mount Hiei. Toward the end of the Enryaku era (782–805) I visited the Great Tang to ask for further guidance about Great Master Bodhidharma's transmission. On October thirteenth, the twentieth year of Zhenyuan (Jōgen, 804), from Xiaoran (Shōzen or Yūnen, dates unknown), a monk of the Chanlinsi (Zenrinji, present-day Dacisi; Daijiji) on Mount Tiantai, I received transmission of the lineage of the Dharma through the two countries, India and China, as well as Bodhidharma's Dharma transmission, a Dharma treatise fom Mount Niutou, and so on. I brought home these texts with high esteem to be preserved on Mount Hiei.

Four hundred years have passed. I, Eisai, who regret the severance of this school, have recourse to the Buddha's sincere expositions meant for the last five hundred-year period, and eagerly wish to let flourish what has been abandoned and to carry out what has been cut off. As for direction and time, they accord with the Buddha's words. How dare you say we have neither the capability nor occasion for attaining awakening?

Besides, since the [time when the] Tathāgata manifested his *parinirvāṇa,* which corresponds to China's Zhou (Shū) dynasty, the fifty-second[58] year of King Mu (Boku), the year of *renshen* (*mizu-*

noe-saru, 949 B.C.E.), counted through to the present ninth year of Kenkyū in Japan, the year of (*wuwu*) *tsuchinoe-uma* (1198 C.E.), it has been two thousand one hundred and forty-seven years. This means that we are now within two hundred years in the last five hundred-year period after Śākyamuni. Great Master Tiantai says [in his *Words and Phrases* [*in the Lotus Sutra*] (T. 34: 2c)]:

> The last five hundred-year period receives the benefits of the living truth of awakening that originated in the distant past.

Great Master Miaole (Myōraku, i.e., Zhanran; Tannen) comments on the above statement [in his *Notes to the Words and Phrases*] (T. 34: 157b):

> At the beginning of the latter-day world the great teachings flourish. Hence, "five hundred."

Now you have said [that contemporary people have] "neither capability nor occasion" [to attain awakening]. This goes against our Original Teacher's (i.e., the Buddha) edict. It also finds fault with the knowledge of emptiness; it disparages Buddhas and bodhi- 4b
sattvas[59] as well.

The *Mahāprajñāpāramitā Sutra* (T. 7: 189b) says:

> Among the mendicants who practice my teachings on the awakened truth and monastic precepts, there will be ones so foolish and stupid that although still calling me Great Master, they will slander and destroy my expositions of the profound knowledge of emptiness. Dear Subhūti, you should know that slandering the knowledge of emptiness is slandering Buddhas and bodhisattvas.[60] Slandering awakening is slandering the Buddhas' knowledge of all forms.

The same scripture, in the passage preceding the one quoted above (T. 7: 189a), says:

> If I explain in detail what forms and measures of evil rewards a transgressor of my teachings on the awakened truth will

> come to have, on hearing me he will be horrified, vomit hot blood, and immediately his life will end as if [he were] shot by a poisoned arrow.

All this means that for those who have become mendicants in the Buddha-Dharma to give rise to the view of self even for one moment will amount to slandering the knowledge of emptiness.

The *Buddha Treasury Sutra* (T. 15: 786a) says:

> Dear Śāriputra, in my teachings on the awakened truth one has the base of all fixed views rooted out; one has all the verbal ways cut off, like hands in the empty sky that have nothing to touch and be obstructed by. The right way of being for way-seekers (*śramaṇa*s) should always be like this.

The *Sutra of Pleasure and Garlands* (T. 14: 931abc) says:

> Being free from the mind and from discrimination is the way-seeker's right mode of being; to protect one's sense faculties in their functioning is the way-seeker's right mode of being.

This being the case, even if some may try propagating the ancient texts of the Vedas in this country, people of wisdom will not stand in their way. You may take good care of your sense faculties in working them, and never obstruct the Buddha's teachings from flourishing.

The *Lotus Sutra* (T. 9: 50a) says:

> All the various productive activities in the world to help sustenance accord with the true mode of reality and don't contradict it.

The school of Zhenyan (Shingon, i.e., the Mantra school) [in the *Commentary on the Mahāvairocana Sutra*] (*Zokuzōkyō* 1–36, 459b) says:

> Insofar as you find yourself in the Tathāgata's teachings for helping people attain awakening, you may make a vow

and practice in that direction. Don't belittle the scriptural teachings of any of the three vehicles. If you do, you will be slandering the Buddha, Dharma, and Sangha; you will be slandering people's great aspiration for awakening (*bodhicitta*).

Since every means in the treasury of esoteric teachings is the Buddha's expedient, to find fault with any of them is to find fault with all his teachings. Various things of the world, efforts of livelihood, industries, the arts, and so on, have their right reasons. They accord with what the Buddha has preached. You cannot slander them. Much less so with the teachings of the three vehicles.

In addition, the *Mañjuśrī Inquiry Sutra* (T. 14: 501a) says:

> In the future there will be twenty divisions among my disciples. They will enable my teachings to abide long. They will all acquire the four grades of attainment culminating in arhatship. In their inheritance of my teachings in the three collections (Tripiṭaka) they are equal, without relative superiority or inferiority or even without medium. Like seawater, whose taste has no difference in being salty, and like the same person having twenty children, as the true expositions of the Tathāgata, dear Mañjuśrī, the original two divisions come from the Great Vehicle; they come from perfection of the knowledge of empiness (*prajñāpāramitā*).

According to *The All-pleasing: A Commentary on the Rules of Discipline* (T. 24: 796c) as well as other sources, we have this expression:

> For what reason did the Buddha [at first] not permit women to be ordained as sangha members? He could not do so before he established regulations for female members to respect male ones. If he had permitted women to be ordained without the regulations, his teaching would have diminished five hundred years from its original duration, which was one thousand

> years. Establishing the eight rules of respect for nuns toward male mendicants reestablished the longevity of the teachings to the full one thousand years.
>
> After the period of the authentic teachings comes that of another thousand years when what has the appearance of authentic teachings prevails. Then comes the period of ten thousand years when the teachings come to an end. During this latter-day period, for the first five thousand years people practice to attain the three kinds of wisdom and the four grades of attainment. After six thousand years, there will be no attainment of arhatship. After ten thousand years, there
> 4c will be no practice of the Buddha's teachings; scriptural expressions will be lost of their own accord.

What you say is contrary to the significance of these passages, by falsely making arguments and hindering their circulation. This already violates reason.

The *Mahā[prajñāpāramitā] Treatise* (T. 25: 416a) says:

> All arguments have faults of transgression. Only the Buddha's profound wisdom extinguishes all discursive thought and speech.

The *Lotus [Sutra]* (T. 9: 10a) says:

> The Tathāgata appears for the purpose of
> Proclaiming the Buddha's wisdom.

Also this (T. 9: 15a):

> What you now have to attain is
> None but the Buddha's wisdom.

Generally speaking, the Tathāgata's original intent to appear in the world is to cause living beings to destroy evil views and abide in the broad mind of no-dispute, which is the knowledge of emptiness.

The Tiantai school's *Great Calming and Contemplation* (T. 46: 63b) says:

> The Tathāgata's teachings show people the truth of no-dispute. Digested, [the teachings] will make sweet dew; otherwise, they will turn into poison.

The *Solutions for Propagation* (T. 46: 317c–318a) comments on the above passage:

> The expression following "the Tathāgata" means that the original intent of the Buddha's teachings is to show people no-dispute. Disputation is a human fault. How could one relate it to the Dharma and find fault with the Dharma? Now the Buddha wants to show people the truth of no-dispute. Therefore, he expounds the *Mahāprajñāpāramitā* [*Sutra*]....
>
> All this means that the Buddha's teachings, either great or small, originally show people the truth of no-dispute. Heavenly sweet drops of dew originally grant longevity to the taker; foolish people take them undigested [and as a result] they shorten their natural lifespan. The same is true with the Buddha's teachings. Originally they make one directly realize the extinction of suffering (nirvana) as one's eternal abode. As one gives rise to disputes, he enters into one of the three evil modes of existence.

The *Sutra* [*of the Brahmā Called*] *Excellent Thinker* (T. 15: 36c) says:

> Buddhas don't appear in the world to cause living beings to quit the suffering of birth and death and enter nirvana. They appear in order to cause beings to become free of the two fixed views of birth and death and nirvana.

Because what you say is contrary to these passages, you slander *prajñā,* the knowledge of emptiness.

Question: Someone says, "The principle of the Zen school does not set up words out of which to make any dogma, so it lacks verbal evidence. Without any scriptural verification, however, the lord of the state will have difficulty in trusting and accepting it.

Besides, you are such a worthless character. How dare you abruptly surprise the lord's hearing!"

Answer: The *Sutra of the Benevolent King* (T. 8: 833a) says:

> The Buddha said, "As I clearly see the kings in the three divisions of time now with my fivefold eyes, it is because of their attendance with five hundred Buddhas in their past lives that they have become sovereigns. That is why all the sages and arhats come to see them in their lands and bring about great benefits. If the sovereign exhausts his good fortune, sages will abandon him and quit the land. The land, abandoned by sages, will necessarily suffer seven disasters.
>
> "Lord, if in a future world kings uphold the Three Treasures [of Buddha, Dharma, and Sangha], I shall have the five powerful bodhisattvas visit and protect their lands.... Those five great beings, assisted by five thousand great deity-kings, will bring about great benefits in your lands.
>
> "Lord, you and you all may uphold *prajñāpāramitā*."

Therefore, all the kings, on hearing the Buddha's teachings, will naturally have confidence in them and accept them. Insofar as monarchs esteem the Buddha's teachings, who should first have to gain evidence for the teachings and then allow them to prevail?

The violent king of Qin (Shin) ordered the burning of books (213 B.C.E.). During the Huichang (Kaishō) era (842–5 C.E.) Buddhist monks and nuns were injured. The Daoist minister Lingsu (Reiso) suppressed the Buddhist religion (1117 C.E.), and his emperor Huizong (Kisō, r. 1101–25 C.E.) disfigured Buddha statues. None of these rulers were those who enjoyed their sovereign status as a reward of their attendance with Buddhas in past lives. They belong to those whose existence was formed by their evil desires. You should not say that the Buddha's teachings are too subtle for monarchs to trust in.

5a

Thus, a monarch who succeeded to the throne through abdication of the previous monarch had already attended five hundred

Buddhas, hadn't he? The same is true with mendicants who transmit the lamp of truth. They have planted excellent roots of virtue, not merely with two, three, four, or five Tathāgatas. With Buddhas as numerous as the grains of sand in the Ganges River they have deeply planted the seeds of vast *prajñā*, and now they realize the living truth of one phrase.

The *Diamond Sutra* (T. 8: 749ab) says:

> The Buddha said, "You should know that these people planted roots of virtue not just with one, two, three, four, or five Buddhas. They have already planted roots of virtue with an innumerable thousand, ten thousand Buddhas, and on hearing these phrases they will have even one moment of calm pleasure."

It will be the monarchs who will be the most pleased [with the phrases of the sutra], won't it? So what fault could there be in surprising the emperor's ears with my wish to let Zen flourish in this land?

Generally speaking, destitute people's grief is likely to reach the emperor's notice. Much more so must it be with the appeal from a monk who has been granted a royal certificate of ordination! How could it be otherwise with me, Eisai, who has risen to the present priestly rank? Xuanzang's *Great Tang Dynasty Record of the Western Regions* (T. 51: 907c) says in effect:

> In ancient times in Central India in a country named Yudhapati there were three Buddhist mendicants coming from the northern direction, on their way to make a pilgrimage to the Buddha's holy traces. Meanwhile, temple priests in India despised these three mendicants, calling them "men from out of the way" (i.e., non-Buddhists), and would not let them stay overnight in their temples. The [mendicants] were always turned away with the reason that in all the five parts of India mendicants had their ears pierced with hanging rings but these monks did not. Exposed to the rain and mist, they were skinny, wan, and sallow.

> It happened that the king came out to take a walk in the street and, on seeing the three mendicants, said to them, "From which direction have you come, revered mendicants, to find yourselves [in such a condition]?" They answered, "We are from the northern country of Tukhara. Once a few of us promised one another, 'The living principle of the Buddha's teachings is so subtle and deep, words or talks cannot penetrate it. Fortunately the Holy One's traces still exist. Paying a respectful visit to them may extinguish our human transgressions. Let us share the same wish and be pilgrims together.' Having made this promise among ourselves, we traveled this far. But the way-seekers of India don't dare show compassion toward us. On the contrary, they have always rejected us, shutting us out of their monasteries, and so on. That is why we have become like this."
>
> Hearing the mendicants talk, the king's sympathy increased. He chose a beautiful place, had a monastery built, and on a white piece of cotton wrote an inscription: "Our Royal Self, most honored among the people, enjoys this status through the graceful protection of the Three Treasures. Being lord of the people, I have already been entrusted by the Buddha to help his teachings be propagated throughout the land. Those who wear the dyed robes of monks will be in my gracious service. I have had this monastery built to invite traveling way-seekers here. From now on those mendicants who have ears pierced with hanging rings will not be allowed to stay overnight in this monastery I have built."

What an honest and sincere remark this is! The *Sutra of the Benevolent King* (T. 8: 833b) says:

> Therefore, I entrust kings with [the Three Treasures].

It also says (T. 8: 833a):

> Their attendance with five hundred Buddhas in the past lives enables them to become sovereigns.

It also says (T. 8: 833a):

> Great Lord, I now entrust you with the Three Treasures.

It also says (T. 8: 833c):

> Great Lord, after my death in the future world the four [kinds of sangha members] (monks, nuns, laymen, and laywomen), my disciples, and the lords and princes of all the small countries will be those who preserve and protect the Three Treasures.

The monarch of Japan is not a descendant of this king of India but the most honored of the imperial palace is always a child who takes shelter in the Buddha. The great lord of Yuezhi (India), on hearing of the three mendicants' trials, had a monastery built for them. Why would the noble lord of Japan not respond to an appeal from a poor monk and grant an edict on paper? Your hindrance 5b
and reproach against me is something that will cause the destruction of the Buddha's teachings; it will ruin the land itself. You should not be so insistent [on denouncing me]. The *Sutra of the Benevolent King* (T. 8: 833c) says:

> [The Buddha said,] "In the future world monarchs of small countries as well as the four [kinds of sangha] disciples will all commit this transgression. It will cause the destruction of the country, a result they must suffer themselves. They run counter to the Buddha, Dharma, and Sangha.
>
> "Great Lord, in the future world let people have the truth of this scripture circulate among them, for this is the vessel of the truth awakened to by the past seven Buddhas; this is the path that all the Buddhas in the ten directions unfailingly tread.
>
> "Evil mendicants mostly look for fame and profit. In the king's presence they will preach what will directly or indirectly cause the destruction of the teachings of the Buddha-Dharma. The king, not discerning, will trust [them] and listen to their

words, and willfully establish laws without having any recourse to the Buddha's moral precepts (*śīla*). I take this for the direct and indirect cause of the destruction of both the teachings of the Buddha-Dharma and their land. It will be precisely at this time that the authentic teachings of the Buddha-Dharma will be lost."

Hearing this exposition by the Buddha, the kings of the sixteen larger countries wept with grief. They cried their hearts out and their tears moved the three thousand great worlds. The sun and moon, the five planets, and the twenty-eight stars lost their brightness and became invisible. Then, each of the kings in his sincerest heart accepted and upheld the Buddha's words, "We should not restrain people from becoming mendicants to practice the Way as one of the four [kinds of] sangha members; we should do as the Buddha teaches us to."

The *Mahāparinirvāṇa Sutra* (T. 12: 381a) says:

Now with the propagation of the Buddha's unsurpassed authentic teachings does the Tathāgata entrust kings and ministers as well as the four [kinds of] sangha members. These sovereigns and four [kinds of] sangha members should admonish way-seekers to make their [practice of] morality (*śīla*), self-concentration (*samādhi*) and knowledge of emptiness (*prajñā*) become[61] powerful. If there are those who would not learn to practice these[62] three kinds of vessels of the truth, who are lazy, who violate precepts, and who slander the Buddha's teachings, then the kings, ministers, and four [kinds of] sangha members should try hard to cure them of such wrong ways of being. Dear Kāśyapa, the kings who do this are free from transgressions.

As you see, the Buddha has already entrusted kings with *prajñā,* the unsurpassed, authentic teachings of his truth. Monarchs should give directions for themselves. Why should wicked minds be left uncontrolled to create obstacles? I want to let the declining Zen [school] flourish in this country, whereas you forcibly find fault with it. I am a poor mendicant, unworthy of the name, but how does that mean that the Zen truth can be faulted? This kind of inference betrays the Buddha's children, who then find fault in the Buddha's teachings. The *Mahāparinirvāṇa Sutra* (T. 12: 380c–381a) says:

> For those who slander the Buddha's teachings, the sangha should decide either to expel them from the sangha or to chastise them within the sangha. . . . Dear Kāśyapa, the reason the Tathāgata demands a decision for taming those who find fault with the Buddha's teachings is that he wants to show that evildoers will have their own retribution.
>
> After my death, in every direction there will be mendicants who keep the moral precepts, who live in full dignity in their conduct, and who wish to preserve and protect the authentic teachings. When they see those who destroy the teachings, they respond actively, curing them through punishment, such as expelling or chastising them. These mendicants will surely acquire immeasurable and incalculable merit.

Monarchs, therefore, should think well of the Buddha's entrustment and have no objection to it.

Question: Someone says, "Zen is a principle commonly applied in the various schools. Why do you dare to set up an independent school for it?"

Answer: For naming an independent school with a common principle or for making a single truth represent two fields, we can
cite more than one example. The so-called religious observance of 5c
restraint (*saṃvara-śīla*) is a common concept among the schools. Nevertheless, it establishes the Vinaya school. Mendicants' morality cannot be different but all the five parts of India have five divisions of the Vinaya (monastic rules). The three collections of Buddhist [teachings] (Tripiṭaka, i.e., sutras, Vinaya, and *śāstras*) is the truth of the one same path but the eighteen [plus two basic]

branches in India had their own Tripiṭakas. The *Middle Treatise* directly discusses the one real truth, and it has become the basic text of the two schools, Sanlun (Sanron) and Tiantai (Tendai). The Zhenyan (Shingon) school is an esoteric vehicle, and it has the two temples, Tōji[63] and Tendai.[64] Still more so with the Chan (Zen) school, which represents the ultimate principle of all the schools and the capital of the land called Buddha-Dharma. In setting up one independent Zen school, there should be no hindrance at all.

Because of this, Great Master Dengyō's *Genealogy (Zenshū* 1, 199–248) says:

> It has been a long time since the genealogy came into being. The Buddha's teachings had their source in Central India. They came through the Great Tang and flowed into Japan. In India, transmission of the teachings already included sutras and their commentaries. In China also, transmission from one to another formed a lineage. Transmission of the Buddha's teachings down to me (Saichō) in Mount Hiei has had no genealogy from master to master as yet.
>
> Therefore, I respectfully compile the transmission of the Buddha's teachings through the three countries, and want to show them to those of our school who will come in later ages. They are:
>
> A lineage genealogy, in Great Master Bodhidharma's entrustment, of master-to-master transmission;
>
> A lineage genealogy, in the Tiantai Lotus school, of master-to-master transmission;
>
> A lineage genealogy, in the Tiantai perfect teaching (*yuanjiao; enkyō*) of the bodhisattva *śīla,* of master-to-master transmission; and
>
> A lineage genealogy, in the two fields of activities of the esoteric deities (*maṇḍala*), matrix (*garbha*) and thunderbolt (*vajra*), of master-to-master transmission.

Great Master Chishō's *Similarities and Dissimilarities of the Teaching Forms* (T. 74: 312c) says:

Question: Traditionally it has been said that the Buddha's disciples are of three sorts: Dhyāna masters (*zenji*), Vinaya masters (*risshi*), and Dharma masters (*hōshi, hosshi*). Of the contemporary schools, which school has which master?

Answer: The three schools of Zen, Tendai, and Shingon have Dhyāna masters. All the other schools [except the Vinaya school] have Dharma masters. These three sorts of masters are found in Dharma Master Shenfang's (Shinbō) *Brief Commentary on the Ten Wheels Sutra.*

Question: As for the Zen school, what kind of school is it?

Answer: This school is not included among the eight schools.[65]

Question: What is the characteristic of this school?

Answer: The Zen school has the *Diamond Sutra* and the *Vimalakīrti Sutra* as its main references. Its principle is that the mind is nothing other than the Buddha. A mind freed from clinging to anything constitutes its religious act. Its purpose is [to cause people to realize] that everything that has its own characteristics is empty of self-nature. Since the Buddha handed down the robe and bowl to Kāśyapa, transmission from master to disciple has not changed. Details are known from the records.

Question: Who has introduced this school to Japan?

Answer: Great masters one after another left Mount Hiei, entered the Great Tang to seek the truth, personally received this transmission, and returned home.

Venerable Annen's *Treatise on Teaching Time Polemics* (T. 75: 355b and 362a) says:

> In the three countries, various schools have had times of rise and fall but the nine schools have been practiced side by side. . . . According to the degree of depth of their doctrines,

> from deep to shallow, the nine schools are as follows. First, the Shingon school, with its doctrine, the one perfect principle, which is the mystery of all the Buddhas, expounded at all times and places by the Tathāgata Vairocana ("Great Sun"), who is eternal and free from change, naturally stands first. Then the Zen school, with its traps and nets amply employed by Śākyamuni all his life, and ultimately with emphasis on the transmission of mind to mind without
> 6a reliance on scriptural authority, constitutes the heart of all the Buddhas' [teachings] (*sarvabuddhapravacana-hṛdaya*). For this reason it counts as the second in order. . . . The Kusha (*Abhidharmakośa*) school stands as the ninth.

The *Song Dynasty Biographies of Eminent Monks* by Zanning (Sannei) (T. 50: 724b) says in effect:

> Buddhism in China has had three teachings: exoteric, esoteric, and [the teaching] of the Mind. The exoteric teaching has [Kāśyapa-]Mātaṅga[66] as its first patriarch. The esoteric teaching has Vajrabodhi[67] as its first patriarch. The teaching of the Mind has Bodhidharma as its first patriarch.

We have seen how in China and Japan the Chan (Zen) school has been interpreted; in the three countries the nine schools have been practiced together. This school arose in the Liang dynasty, flourished in the Song dynasty, and in the Chen and Sui [dynasties] brilliant scholars did not argue whether Chan was a general principle or a particular school. Wise emperors of the Tang and Song let it be practiced along with other schools. Gyōhyō and Dengyō transmitted it to Japan. Chishō and Annen both practiced it. As soon as young people heard the name "Zen," they began arguing about it. Whose shame is this?

Question: Someone says, "Establishing a new school is a rare[68] matter. You are far from the right person. Why do you want to accomplish such an important matter?"

Answer: Two thousand years ago when Śākyamuni passed away, he entered into perfect calmness (*parinirvṛta*) together with his teachings as many as the grains of sand in the Ganges River. Śānavāsin was the third [after Kāśyapa and Ānanda] who was entrusted with transmission of the teachings of the Buddha-Dharma. He entered into extinction and simultaneously carried away eighty thousand teachings from each of the threefold collection (Tripiṭaka). Since then, as time passed, the number of teachings gradually decreased, and the practice of morality (*śīla*) became more leaky and faulty, depending on the decline of practitioners. However, in India Aśvaghoṣa (second c. C.E.) and Nāgārjuna (second–third c. C.E.) realized the truth of one reality. In China Nanyue Huisi (Nangaku Eshi, 515–75) and Tiantai (Tendai; Zhiyi; Chigi, 538–97) attained *samādhi*. The Dharma light illuminated the four distant quarters; the practice of morality reached the [latter-day world in its second] five hundred years. If by identifying ourselves with mere commonality and vulgarity we did not practice following these holy footsteps, how would the teachings of the Buddha-Dharma continue? How could you not feel sorry about the extermination of the Zen truth but instead scrutinize the faults of humans and the truth?

The *Lotus Sutra* (T. 9: 38b) says:

> You should not belittle and rebuke those who learn to practice the Buddha's Way so as to uncover their merits and demerits.

Venerable Annen[69] says [in his *Treatise on Teaching Time Polemics*] (T. 75: 355a):

> Publicizing oneself while belittling others cannot be called propagating the Way.

The *Mahāprajñāpāramitā Treatise* (T. 25: 63c) says:

> If one slanders and rebukes others' religion because of strong attachment to one's own, even a practitioner of morality won't be exempt from the torture of hell.

The Mantra school's [*Commentary on*] *the Mahāvairocana Sutra* (*Zokuzōkyō* 1–36, 276c) says in effect:

> What is the demonic (*rākṣasa*) mind? It is that which gives rise to evils in the midst of goodness. Let me explain this. Someone may believe in the Buddha's words and build places of worship. Finding blame in this, the demonic mind will say, "You are injuring innumerable worms and giving much trouble to the benefactors. What could be the benefit of this? You deserve only the retribution of pain." This kind of evil mind is what I mean by the demonic mind. Simply observing the merit and benefit of that person's faithful act, without looking for his faults, counters the demonic mind.

The *Sutra of Śūraṃgama Practices* (T. 19: 107a) says:

> It is because the Tathāgatas in the ten directions are of one and the same path. What makes one free from the suffering of birth and death is always the genuine mode of his being (*āśayamaṇḍa; jikishin*). It is because his mode of being and words are genuine and not artificial.

This being the case, when both one's mode of being and words are not genuine but artificial, and when he looks to find fault in both humans and the truth, how could that person know the path? The *Mahāprajñāpāramitā Treatise* (T.25: 129b) says:

> One hundred years after the Buddha passed away, a man named Upagupta attained arhatship and became a great guiding master for the world. In those days there was an old nun, aged one hundred and twenty. As a child, she had seen the Buddha. Upagupta came to hear from her how the Buddha had looked and comported himself. The nun wanted to exam-
> 6b ine the master's behavior so she attached a bowl filled with oil to the back of the door. Upagupta approached and slowly opened the door. A little of the oil was spilled. After he entered and sat, he asked how the Buddha had emitted light from

> himself. He also asked how the sangha members had comported themselves. The nun answered: "In the days when the Buddha was alive, there was a group of six sangha members who were very evil mendicants, yet their behavior accorded with the regulations and excelled yours. In walking, standing, sitting, and lying down they never missed established rules. When the group of six entered this door, they never caused any oil to be spilled. You are an arhat who possesses the six supernatural powers. Nevertheless, you cannot equal them." Hearing this, Upagupta felt deeply ashamed.

However, in the days when the Buddha was alive, of the group of six mendicants two fell into the *nāga*'s (serpent demon) mode of existence and two rose to the realm of the *deva*s (heavenly gods). On the other hand, Upagupta was a man who had gained all the four attainments.[70] Does this not tell us that in the latter-day world not even a single precept should be made little of? Still less so with our intention to benefit other beings. Since our intention can never go against the Buddha's, how could ours be distinguished from the Buddha's intention?

The *Mahāparinirvāṇa Sutra* (T. 12: 590a) says:

> As for the aspiration to attain awakening (*bodhicitta*) and attaining ultimate awakening (*anuttarā samyaksaṃbodhi*), these two cannot be separated. Of these two the first is very hard; it is the aspiration to have others attain awakening before oneself does so. Therefore, I respectfully salute people of original aspiration.

Although this is a rare thing in the history of this country, and although I am an unworthy person to promote it, my daring to follow in the footprints of preceding sages with the practice and vow of great compassion won't meet any obstruction, will it? Besides, although the latter-day world would not have any appropriate vessel, examples of an important position to be officially established in founding a new school have not been lacking. If we want a

Taigong[71] for the ministry, we shall wait in vain for a thousand years. If we need a Kumārajīva as a model for teachers, ten thousand generations will pass without a Kumārajīva. However, even "half a verse" on the awakened truth was not belittled.[72] Why should the citer be strongly despised? As for me, I have already ascended to the official position for Transmission of the Lamp. Concerning the matter of reviving what has been abolished, why should we not expect imperial sanction? I sincerely hope there will be thorough investigation into this matter.

Question: Someone says, "Ancient patriarchs were all those Tathāgatas who had manifested themselves as bodhisattvas. You have no special virtue. How could imperial sanction be afforded to you for reviving what has been abolished?"

Answer: Do you abandon the gems that lie buried within ore, saying that the ore does not yet emit bright luster? No one would give up [a bag of] gold [for the reason] that the leather bag stinks. For the valuable brocade from Shu (Shoku; Sichuan Province) no one asks who the owner is. Betel palm is sought only for its taste. The Zen school alone expounds that the Dharma causes living beings to cross the sea of birth and death. Besides, the teachings of the Buddha-Dharma for the latter-day world mostly work with hidden benefit. Not necessarily do they seek supernatural transformation. The recent rebuke against Eisai is far from a digrace to Eisai alone, isn't it?

The *Vinaya in Four Divisions* (T. 22: 568c) says:

> It is said that the following once happened. The World-honored One accepted an invitation from a man of priestly caste (brahman) at Veranjā. Misled by the destroyers (*māras*), the priest forgot his dedication to the World-honored One whom he had invited, and made no meal offerings. The World-honored One had arrived at Veranjā with five hundred mendicants. It was already the summer rainy season [when the sangha dwelled together in one place] (i.e., summer retreat).

> Unable to return to Rājagṛha, they stayed in the woods of a nearby hamlet. There they met with famine, and it was extremely hard to obtain any food from almsrounds.
>
> At that time a horse trader from Parikhā came around with five hundred horses. He happened to see that the Buddha and his disciples were starving, and immediately donated half of his horse barley to the five hundred mendicants. To the Buddha he donated a peck of [the barley].
>
> Then Maudgalyāyana said to the Buddha, "I shall fly to Uttarakuru in the north and obtain rice there." The Buddha 6c
> said to Maudgalyāyana, "You have the supernatural power to do so. As for ordinary mendicants, how could they do the same thing?" Maudgalyāyana said, "I can take them with me, using my supernatural power." The Buddha said, "Give it up. You possess supernatural power but in the future how could ordinary mendicants accomplish this?"

It also says in effect (T. 22: 946c):

> Venerable Piṇḍola (Bhāradvāja; Binzuru) displayed his supernatural power for a benefactor. The Buddha scolded Piṇḍola, saying, "How dare you display supernatural power to a benefactor for one meal! It's like a prostitute who for the profit of half a coin will show her body to others. I am punishing you. You may not enter final extinction but will abide in the world to be a field of merit for the latter-day world."

The above shows how the Tathāgata made this regulation against displaying supernatural power for the latter-day mendicants. In ancient days[73] the king of Pengcheng (Hōjō) blamed Chan Master Farong (Hōyū, 594–657) of Mount Niutou,[74] patriarch of Great Master Dengyō. Later the king saw a true friend in the master and put his confidence in him. As for the hidden fragrance of divine responsiveness, who could know its omen?

Question: Someone says, "The Zen school insists that it does not set up words out of which to make any dogma. This will make lazy people more disinclined to study the holy teachings and will lead to the extinction of the Buddha-Dharma."

Answer: The *Buddha-contemplation Samādhi Sutra* (T. 15: 648a) says:

> My disciples in the future world, if they want to contemplate the Tathāgata, should practice three things. The first is to recite the profound scriptures expounded by the Buddha. The second is to keep the moral precepts and the four basic postures (sitting, standing, walking, and lying down) without transgression. The third is to concentrate [their] thoughts on the essential features of the Tathāgata and not scatter them.

Therefore, this school studies all the eight treasuries,[75] and practices all the six perfections (*pāramitās*). If anyone says that the Zen school advocates the mind as nothing other than the Buddha, and won't examine the traces of the Buddha's teachings, how would this be different from a person who, [while traveling] in the night just before dawn when it is not yet bright enough, discards their lamp and thus falls down a rocky precipice?

Question: Someone says, "Great Master Dengyō, in his *Notes to the Latter-day World Dharma Lamp* (*Zenshū* 1, 418) says:

> The latter-day world has no one who will keep the moral precepts. If anyone should say to the contrary, it will be a strange matter. It would be like a tiger roaming in a marketplace.

[How would you defend your position against this view?"]

Answer: The *Mahāprajñāpāramitā Sutra* (T. 7: 939a) says:

> A lion would bite a man, while a mad dog would chase a clod of dirt thrown by a man.

This may be applied to your case. Let me ask you: Why do you chase one clod of letters and words after another, whereas you have long forgotten that we have people who keep the moral precepts and practice good? When we see the skillful means of the holy teachings comprehensively, we come to know that the Buddha examined living beings' acts of good far into the future. As we saw above, the *Mahāprajñāpāramitā Sutra* (T. 6: 539a) mentions "in the last five hundred-year period when my teachings are lost," the *Mahāparinirvāṇa Sutra* (T. 12: 472b, Northern version) says "in the latter-day world" and "to redeem his life," and the *Lotus Sutra* says "in a later, latter-day world." The *Mahāprajñāpāramitā Treatise,* the *Middle Treatise,* and the *Great Calming and Contemplation* also have similar expressions. The *Diamond Sutra* (T. 8: 749ab) says:

> In the last five hundred-year period there will be those who keep morality, practice for the sake of merit, and have delight and confidence in these phrases. You should know that these people planted roots of virtue not just with one, two, three, four, or five Buddhas. They have already planted roots of virtue with an innumerable thousand, ten thousand Buddhas, and on hearing these phrases they will have at least one moment of calm pleasure.

All these exhort [those in] the latter-day world to practice morality. It seems that every time the Tathāgata opened his mouth,
the phrase "latter-day world" came first. Patriarchs moved their 7a
tongues both for the present and the future. Great Master Dengyō's interpretation, quoted above (p. 108), may be taken in this sense. Otherwise he may have meant the Small Vehicle (Hinayana) precepts of restraint, and not the Great Vehicle bodhisattva precepts of morality.

Queston: Someone says in rebuke, "Why does the Zen school newly call itself [a school] that will cause the Buddha's teachings to abide long?"

Answer: Moral precepts (*śīla*) and monastic precepts (*vinaya*) are what causes the Buddha's teachings to abide long. Now, the Zen school regards *śīla* and *vinaya* as its principles. Therefore it has the meaning of causing the Buddha's teachings to abide long. The Tiantai school's *Great Calming and Contemplation* (T. 46: 4b) says:

> Ordinary beings' indulgence in things for pleasure is what people of wisdom and sages chastise and for which they find fault with them. Breaking evils is achieved by pure wisdom (*prajñā*). Pure wisdom comes from pure concentration of the total being (*samādhi*). Pure concentration derives from pure morality (*śīla*).

Question: Someone says in rebuke: "How can the Zen school alone be the religion that keeps the state protected?"

Answer: The *Sutra of Forty-two Sections* (*Zokuzōkyō* 1–59, 26a) says in effect:

> At that time the World-honored One, having already attained awakening, had this thought, "Getting free from desire, keeping calm and composed—this is the supreme way of being. Abiding in this great concentration of the total being, I have defeated all the evil modes of existence. I will begin turning the wheel of the Dharma to expound my teachings and cause living beings to cross the sea of the suffering of birth and death."

The *Bequeathed Teaching Sutra* (T. 12: 1111a) says:

> Dependence on this morality will give rise to various sorts of concentration and the wisdom that extinguishes suffering.

Therefore, we know that without the concentrating force of the total being it will be very hard to break every evil. That is why we consider promoting the Zen school to be the most essential of all means for protecting the state.

Question: Why does the Zen school vigorously exhort people to practice morality?

Answer: It expresses what the *Mahāparinirvāṇa Sutra* meant by the teaching that the eternity of nirvana offers ultimate support to monastic discipline (*vinaya*). The *Bequeathed Teaching Sutra* (T. 12: 1111a) says in effect, "Dependence on morality gives rise to concentration; it also gives rise to wisdom."

The Tiantai school's *Great Calming and Contemplation* (T. 46: 4b) says:

> Breaking evils is achieved by pure wisdom. Pure wisdom comes from pure concentration of the total being. Pure concentration derives from pure morality.

Question: If that is the case, can those who have transgressed morality achieve self-concentration after they repent?

Answer: The *Mahāparinirvāṇa Sutra* (T. 12: 477c) says: "Repentance is called the second purification."

The *Essentials for Chan Practice* (*Zokuzōkyō* 2–15, 419b) says:

> If in the Great Vehicle one can cease the mind, one will be in true repentance. Because of this, hindrances will vanish and morality will naturally come. Because of this, concentration of the total being will be achieved.

The Tiantai school's *Great Calming and Contemplation* (T. 46: 39c) says:

> The *Sutra on Contemplation of Samantabhadra* (T. 9: 393b–394a) says in effect: "Taking the [seated meditation] posture and focusing one's thought on the true mode of reality . . . this is called the first repentance."
>
> The *Sutra on the Most Wondrous Supreme Dhyāna* says: "Transgressors of the four grave offenses and the five grave transgressions[76] will, except for deepening their thought (*dhyāna*), have no way to be saved."
>
> The *Vaipulya Sutra* (T. 21: 645c) says in effect: "As for the three refuges, the five moral precepts, and the two hundred and fifty precepts, there can be no reason for their not taking place with those who repent in this way."

Therefore, the Zen school has morality as its starting practice and concentration of the total being as its ultimate practice. If a transgressor of morality can make his repenting heart cease evils, then he may be called a person of Zen. Much more so with those who abide in the compassionate heart. In that case all sorts of morality and wisdom will not fail to be developed. Therefore, with the Zen school, which is understood to have great compassion as its original basis, I wonder what kind of transgression would be left unextinguished? The *Bodhisattva Garland Sutra* (T. 16: 87a) says:

> Men and women of good heart, from the beginning of their aspiration, should practice the bodhisattvas' heart, and in deepening their thought should fully develop the practice of all six perfections (*pāramitā*s).

The *Sutra of Supra-sunlight Samādhi* (T. 15: 53bc) says in effect:

> The Buddha said, "The destroyers (*māra*s) represent four things to disturb you. . . . When your ego-thought ceases, when your ego-thought is cut, the destroyers will surrender.
> 7b Those four destroyers all derive from yourselves; they never come from outside."

Therefore, the Great Vehicle has it that when our mind is brought to rest, morality presents itself and *dhyāna* is achieved.

Question: Why do you strongly expect an imperial sanction to be issued?

Answer: The Buddha's teachings must necessarily wait for the monarch to allow them to prevail. Therefore, the Buddha was solicitous to entrust monarchs with the propagation of his teachings. The benefit gained by kings who were entrusted with them was also unbounded. Concerning the reason why the Buddha's head emits light from its protuberance (*uṣṇīṣa*)—this is what a Buddha of the past, named Raśmipramokṣa ("Ray-Emitting"), himself said in the *Great Dharma Torch Dhāraṇī Sutra* (T. 21: 676c):

> There are three roots of virtue: 1) renouncing envy and rejoicing in what is taught and indicated; 2) when working for the sake of others, not seeking any reward; and 3) not abusing or injuring others so as to accomplish one's own good. Besides this, there are two things: 1) protecting the teachings of the Buddha-Dharma, and 2) expounding the teachings well.
>
> By protecting the teachings I mean this: When the teachings of the Buddha-Dharma are about to be lost, bodhisattvas realize this well, protect them so that they may be propagated through various means, and cause them to abide long. Because of this, one also gains the unique feature of a protuberance on the head (*uṣṇīṣa*) that emits light.
>
> By expounding the teachings well, I mean that when a bodhisattva expounds the teachings to the four [kinds of] sangha members, if there is anyone who misses the teachings even for a moment, the bodhisattva takes care of that person and repeats the teachings for him.

The *Mahāparinirvāṇa Sutra* (T. 12: 383b) says:

> Because I have protected the teachings of the Buddha-Dharma, I have gained this indestructible body.

The story of a mendicant named Buddhadatta and King Bhavadatta [who saved the life of the mendicant] is also related in the same section of this scripture.[77]

End of Fascicle One

Fascicle Two

Gate III (*continued*)

Question: Someone says, "This school already insists on not setting up any words.[78] This makes it almost the same as those [who are] ill-attached to emptiness and those of obscure evidence. If that is the case, the Tiantai school has already denounced it. The *Great Calming and Contemplation* (T. 46: 52b) explains the contemplation of what goes beyond thought, and says:

> This is far from what is known to a Dhyāna master of obscure evidence or a Dharma master who recites passages.

The *Profound Meaning* [*of the Lotus Sutra*] (T. 33: 686a) says:

> If a person contemplating himself should say that he, as he is, is approved of since he is equal to the Buddha, never looks into scriptures such as sutras and *śāstra*s (commentaries on sutras and independent treatises), and thus falls into a kind of self-conceit that he has attained awakening, then this is [like] embracing a torch to burn oneself.

The *Elucidatory Comments* (T. 33: 829c) says:

> The one who grasps a torch named obscure evidence burns his hand called excellent *dhyāna*.

As for the motto of the Zen school, "not setting up any words," how could it be exempt from the above reprobation?

Answer: This Zen school hates masters of obscure evidence, and rejects those who become ill-attached to emptiness. It is like the bottom of a great ocean that dislikes corpses to lie there. Just abiding in the "perfect rank" (*yuanwei; en'i*),[79] practicing the "perfect and immediate" awakening (*yuandun; endon*),[80] and externally practicing the precepts of restraint to prevent wrongs while internally

benefiting others out of compassion—this is called the principle of the Zen school; it is called the Buddha-Dharma. This significance
7c is lacking in those who advocate Zen without discernment, those who are ill-attached to emptiness. They are thieves, as it were, in the midst of the Buddha-Dharma. The *Collection of Records from the Ancestral Mirrors* (T. 48: 496bc) says:

> Internal reason (*li; ri*) really responds to external conditions (*yuan; en*); no reason obstructs phenomena (*shi; ji*). Phenemena stand depending on reason; there are no phenomena that have lost their reason. Nowadays all those who won't have "confidence in the perfect awakening" (*yuanxin; enshin*) belittle themselves as having nothing to do with awakening. They suppose the Buddhas to be the remotest beings. Such people have not only lost sight of phenomena; reason is also completely lacking in them. Only when one realizes the principal aim (*zong; shū*), which is the One Mind that is free from hindrance and is self-abidingly free, reason and phenomena, according to their own nature, will be seen mutually permeated, and the unworldly and the worldly will be known to interpenetrate. If one were attached to phenomena and becomes lost in reason, that person will perish for long *kalpa*s of time. If one realizes reason but neglects phenomena, this is far from the "perfect attainment" (*yuanzheng; enshō*). The reason is this: neither reason nor phenomena go beyond the Mind that is self (*zixin; jishin*). How can [reason and phenomena or, in Buddhist terms,] original nature (*xing; shō*) and forms (*xiang; sō*) go against the meaning of oneness?
>
> If you attain the ancestral mirrors and immediately realize the true mind, then there will not be even the description: "neither reason nor phenomena." How could there be clinging to "either reason or phenomena"? However, when one attains one's original ground (*ben; moto*), one will never cease to be engaged in the "perfect practice" (*yuanxin; enshū*). . . .
>
> As for those who advocate Zen without discernment, those of obscure evidence, how could they know living beings'

"sixfold immediacy" of awakening (*luji; rokusoku*)?[81] As for those who are mad with intellect and who just follow words, how could they know the One Mind? Now people first need to establish confidence in the perfect awakening, have no doubt in it, and abide in the rank of "contemplating practice" (*guanxing; kangyō*) through which one immediately attains awakening. An ancient one[82] says: "One should discern what is real and true all through one's life." How could it be false?

The *Ancestral Mirrors* (T. 48: 866bc) further says:

The Tiantai teaching clarifies two kinds of cessation and contemplation: relative and non-relative. The former is a clumsy crossing,[83] and the latter a clever crossing.[84] The relative kind has three cessations and contemplations, respectively. The three relative cessations are putting something to rest, stopping oneself, and getting free from cessation. The three relative contemplations are penetrating what is contemplated, the contemplator himself being penetrated in contemplation, and getting free from contemplation. The non-relative kind also has three cessations and contemplations respectively. The three non-relative cessations are self-nature[85] being true cessation; taking the form of something external as skillful means for cessation; and cessation as putting to rest dualistic discrimination. The three non-relative contemplations are starting from the falsity of appearances and ending in attaining emptiness, starting from emptiness and ending in attaining provisionality, and abiding in the middle as the ultimate principle.

Now this *Ancestral Mirrors* only discusses the significance of the perfection and immediacy of the One Mind. As for the cessation and contemplation that are perfect and immediate, they have the following characteristics. When through cessation reality (*di; tai*) is realized, reality is at once one and three.[86] When through reality cessation is realized, cessation is at once one and three. . . . When contemplation has something on which to contemplate, the object is at once one and

> three. When something external arouses contemplation on itself, contemplation is at once one and three. Like the three eyes on the face of the god Maheśvara, they are three but on one face.... Oneness immediately makes three. All three make one. They don't make one line either vertical or horizontal. Neither are they juxtaposed or separated.... All these meanings lie in the One Mind. What are their characteristics?... Thus you may know that the principle of the Zen school is not obscure evidence or ill-attachment to emptiness. Much less is it a false religion, isn't it?

Question: Someone falsely calls the Zen school the Daruma school (Bodhidharma school), and insists as follows: "We make no practice or any cultivaton, for originally being free from self-afflicting passions, one is basically awakened. Therefore, there is no use for any particular precept or practice. There should only be use for lying down. Why should one take the trouble of making such practices as the *nembutsu,*[87] worshiping the Buddha's relics by making offerings, practicing a longtime observance of taking one meal a day before noon, being moderate in one's consumption of food,
8a and so forth? What do you think about this?"

Answer: That person is to be counted among those who have no wrongs that they would never commit. It is to this kind of person that the holy teachings refer to as a holder of fixed views on emptiness. No one can sit and talk with such a person. One should keep a hundred *yojana*s' distance away from them. The *Sutra of Treasure Clouds* (T. 16: 278c) says:

> You may keep arousing an ego-view, which, piled up, may rise as tall as Mount Sumeru; you should never, with a fixed view on emptiness, give rise to the self-conceit that you have attained awakening. The reason I say this is that we can become free from all fixed views only through our realization of emptiness, and that if we give rise to a fixed view on emptiness [itself], then we would have no way to be cured.

An ancient venerable master (unidentified) said,

> A Dhyāna master who embraces a perverted view on emptiness is like one who goes without the guiding function of the eyes and falls down into a fiery pit. A Dharma master who clings to letters is like a parrot that can speak human words but lacks human feelings.

This being the case, the Zen school, which learns from the treasury of the Buddha-Dharma and keeps the Buddha's purifying precepts, can be called "the Buddha's Zen" (*fochan; butsuzen*). Besides, the Tiantai school's *Great Calming and Contemplation* (T. 46: 18c) says:

> In the northern districts of the Huai and Huang Rivers ("River Huai" in Zhiyi's text) there are Mahayana practitioners of emptiness. They are snake catchers without cages. Let me explain this in detail. Their late teacher practiced contemplations on the quality of good. After a fairly long time without success in penetrating the good, he turned, feeling free from anxiety, toward contemplating the quality of evil, [and then] gained some composure and a slight realization of emptiness. He was not versed in living beings' capacities and occasions for attaining awakening, nor did he reach the Buddha's true intention. He simply taught this quality of evil to others as empty. Long after[88] he began teaching others, he came upon one or two who benefited from his teaching. When the result was something like a worm eating wood and leaving traces that happened to form certain letters, he approved of this as their attainment of awakening. He said this was a real matter and rejected the rest as false words. He laughed at those who kept precepts to cultivate good, saying that it was not the path. He simply allowed people everywhere to do wrong. Those who had no discerning eyes and did not discriminate right from wrong, whose mental strength was dull, and whose self-afflicting passions were heavy, heard this

> exposition by the teacher, knew it accorded with their natural inclinations, and accepted it in faith. They followed him in obedience, gave up observing restraints and, leaving no wrong uncommitted, their transgressions acculmulated into a high mountain. This finally led the common people to regard sins as something as trifling as weeds, and the monarch and ministers to destroy the Buddha's teachings. Poison deeply infiltrated people's minds, and there has been no improvement. . . .
>
> This is a monster destroying the Buddha's teachings, a monster of the contemporary age. How could it have anything to do with my so-called spontaneous practice of self-concentration? I say this because such stupid persons, lacking the understanding based on wisdom, believe in their original teacher, admire their predecessors, and say decidedly that this is the path. They consider what agrees with their feelings to be easy to follow. They run after pleasure without restraint, and won't improve their delusional way of life.

As we see, to the north of the Huai and Huang Rivers long ago there was a madman. As soon as he heard the truth of Chan, [he knew it] to be remarkably excellent. But not knowing how to practice, he practiced only *dhyāna* in sitting posture (zazen) as he liked. He abolished activities both practical and theoretical. He was a man trapped in the net of false views. This person is to be called a master ill-attached to emptiness. This is a corpse in the midst of the Buddha's teachings. The *Ancestral Mirrors* (T. 48: 689ab), defeating a hundred and twenty fixed views, says:

> Some, in their attempt to imitate the one who has attained freedom from hindrance, relinquish practice; others, following their self-binding passions, presume emptiness to be the original nature of the passions. Both of them are deluded [as to] the principle and miss its significance. They are contrary to what is profound and true. . . . They break ice so as to get fire, climb a tree in order to seek fish.

This is a remark made out of disgust for those who do no practice, not to speak of those who give up *samādhi* and *śīla*, or those 8b
who blame true wisdom. Vinaya Master Daoxuan [in his *Instructions and Admonitions on Observing Restraints*] (T. 45: 869b) says:

> Those who don't practice *dhyāna*[89] or *samādhi*[90] long deviate from the mind of true wisdom. Those who don't practice various virtuous restraints (*saṃvara-śīla*) will hardly accomplish excellent activities. That is why persons of great virtue throughout history have really been good fields of merit for the world.

In addition, the Tiantai school's *Solutions for Propagation* (T. 46: 262a) says:

> If there is no keeping of a particular precept, there will be no practicing of a worldly *dhyāna*. Much less will there be realization of the three modes of reality.

Therefore, the Zen school considers keeping precepts to be what precedes everything else. The *Chan School Monastic Rules* (*Zokuzōkyō* 2–16) says:

> Practicing *dhyāna* and investigating the Way presuppose moral conduct that follows precepts.

Question: Someone says, "Venerable Chōnen,[91] in the rank of *hokkyō* ("Dharma bridge"), entered China, and on returning home wanted to establish the Sangaku school.[92] Because of the accusations made against him by the contemporary Buddhist schools, his plan was abandoned. Is this school identical with or different from what you refer to?"

Answer: The names are already different; there can be no confusion between the two. I am not sure what Chōnen's intention was. The present Zen school advocates the nondiscriminating (*śubha; shōjō*) *dhyāna* of the Tathāgatas (*nyoraizen*).[93] It has never assumed the name "Sangaku." Since the Liang dynasty it has only been called the Chan (Zen) school. There has been no other name or idea for it.

Question: Someone says, "The [practice of the] *nembutsu samādhi* (*nenbutsu-zanmai*) has prevailed all over this country without receiving any imperial sanction. Why does the Zen school expect one?"

Answer: Propagation of the Buddha's teachings has always been entrusted to monarchs. Therefore, [the Zen school] must wait for an imperial sanction before it can prevail in this country. Besides, concerning the Nembutsu school, it is said that the late emperor established it by imperial order in the Tennōji.[94] The prevailing *nembutsu* practice among people high and low displays its remaining fragrance. Why should the Zen school[95] not [also] be blessed with the issuance of an imperial sanction?

Question: Someone says, "The Buddhist schools prevailing in the world are eight in number. Why should there be nine?"

Answer: Venerable Annen's *Treatise on Teaching Time Polemics* (T. 75: 355b; quoted above, p. 101) says:

> In the three countries, various schools have had times of rise and fall but the nine schools have been practiced side by side.

Great Master Chishō says [in the *Similarities and Dissimilarities of the Teaching Forms*] (T. 74: 312c):

> [The Zen school] is not included among the eight schools.

As for the names of the nine Buddhist schools that have prevailed in the three countries of China, Korea, and Japan, you can find them out for yourselves.

Question: As for this Zen school in relation to *śīla, samādhi,* and *prajñā,* what would you say it is?

Answer: Its principle is the Tathāgata's *dhyāna,*[96] which does not set up words out of which to make any dogma. Positively expressed, it is common to all the Mahayana schools. Negatively stated, it is free from mind, ego consciousness, and perceptive consciousnesses; it is free from verbal expression.

Question: If it is common to all the Mahayana schools, why is it to be separately established?

Answer: The Buddha said (quote unidentified):

> My intention does not have any different aspects. It comes to have different appearances only because it follows living beings' various capacities.

We must respectfully look up to and delightedly accept the Tathāgata's skillful means as well as the patriarchs' kindly intentions. The foreword to the *Sutra of Perfect Awakening* says:[97]

> Directly expressed, the Way is without duality. Differences come into being in learning the Way. When the Buddha and Laozi talk about the Way, they are the same. When they discuss the means, they come to differ from one another.

Jizang, the Sanlun school master, in his *Commentary on the Middle Treatise* (T. 42: 3a), says:

> All the Mahayana sutras express the Way as being without differentiation. Since the Way is without duality, how could the teachings be different?

Although the Way has no differences, distinctions, or divisions, it comes to establish separate schools because of the different means. There is nothing in which to find fault here; much less in the Zen school, which arose in the Liang dynasty and has flourished up to the present Song dynasty in China. How could younger people argue over "common" or "separate" [in regard to this historically important school]?

Question: If that is the case, does this school have any sutras 8c
and *śāstras* as its scriptural sources?

Answer: Positively stated, all the great Tripiṭaka writings (sutras, Vinayas, and *śāstras*) are its scriptural sources. Negatively expressed, it has not a [single] word as its scriptural source.

Question: Someone says, "The Zen school has more than a thousand volumes of books. How can this be explained?"

Answer: They are records of Zen persons; they are like extracts in the secular world. Should one speak of any scriptural sources for the Zen school, it would be like [speaking of the] hair of a tortoise or the horns of a hare, which do not exist. However, this does not mean [these texts] have no profound, original purport. People of wisdom should deliberate on this.

Question: If that is the case, the very profound characteristics of reality will hardly be within the reach of ordinary, unawakened people's struggling efforts. By what means and practice can one attain them?

Answer: The *Bequeathed Teaching Sutra* (T. 12: 1111a) says:

> Dependence on this morality will give rise to various sorts of concentration and the wisdom that extinguishes suffering. Therefore, mendicants should keep their [practice of the] moral precepts clean, and never spoil or be lacking in [it]. Without precepts kept clean, no merit or virtue will come into being. Hence you should know that keeping precepts is the primary abode of tranquility and merit.

The *Foreword to the Brahmā Net Sutra* says:[98]

> Keeping precepts, like a stable area of ground, plus practicing *dhyāna,* like a house built on the ground, can produce the light of wisdom from within.

The *Lotus Sutra* (T. 9: 8a) says:

> I tell such people that they will [attain awakening in the midst of future birth and death] because they cultivate moral precepts and keep them clean.

The Tiantai school's *Great Calming and Contemplation* (T. 46: 4b) says:

Pure concentration derives from pure morality.

Referring to a passage in the *Mahāparinirvāṇa Sutra* (T. 12: 432a–c), the *Great Calming and Contemplation* (T. 46: 38a) says:

> If *śīla* (morality) is not pure, one falls into any of the three evil paths;[99] no *dhyāna-samādhi,* no *prajñā-jñāna* (wisdom-knowledge), will be developed.

The *Sutra of Śūraṃgama Practices* (T. 19: 131c) says:

> Practitioners of *dhyāna,* if they don't break off lust, will continue to transmigrate through the three evil modes of existence, unable to escape. It is like steaming grains of sand and gravel in the hope of cooking them into boiled rice; cooked for one hundred thousand *kalpa*s, they will still be [only] heated sand. Which path could ever be practiced for the Tathāgata's nirvana to be attained? My exposition like this is called the Buddha's exposition. What is not like this is the exposition of a devil.

The Buddha's teachings regard keeping precepts as preceding everything else. If anyone breaks moral precepts regulated by the Buddha, and calls himself a child of the Buddha, it can be compared to a subject who won't obey the monarch's orders but who [still] calls himself a subject of the monarch. [The *Afterword to*] *the Mahāparinirvāṇa Sutra* (T. 12: 901ab) says:

> Ānanda said to the Buddha, "After your passing away, who will be our master?" The Buddha said, "Moral precepts [in the perfection of *śīla*] will be the master for you."

How much more so it is with the three basic learnings and the five components of the Tathāgata's being![100] They have *śīla* as their first constituent. Therefore, this school has *śīla* as regulated by the Buddha as its master. By practicing *śīla,* one attains to it.

To summarize, the person who breaks all evil views, and who cures various evil acts as well, is called a Zen person. Concerning the evil acts, The *Sutra of [Bodhisattva] Samudrajñāna* (T. 17: 948a) says in effect:

> At that time the bodhisattva Samudrajñāna said to the Buddha: "Now I would like to talk about the twelve evil enticements. They are: 1) for a bodhisattva not to bestow on others what is dear to oneself; 2) for one who, on seeing those who break morality, hate and despise them; 3) for one who is patient in acts of body and speech not to be so in acts of mind but to remain arrogant; 4) for one who teaches living beings to lead them into either of the two paths of the Small Vehicle (i.e., *śrāvaka*s and *pratyekabuddha*s), and to be fond of professional female singers and dancers, etc.; 5) for one who rises from the four stages of *dhyāna* to return to the world of desire (*kāmadhātu*), to wish for a long life and not
> 9a see hundreds of thousands of Buddhas appearing in it; 6) for one whose knowledge of emptiness is still immature to find fault with the five perfections (*pāramitā*s), to praise the sixth perfection, and to sink into an evil path; 7) for one who favors dwelling in a forest (*āraṇyaka*) not to practice for benefiting others; 8) for one not to teach the Buddha's teachings to those who are capable of being taught; 9) for one to expound treatises not related to the Buddha's teachings and hinder the latter from being manifested; 10) for one to call evil friends truly good ones; 11) for one to remain conceited, not to humble oneself either to one's master or one's parents; and 12) for one to be indulged in being wealthy, remaining lazy and arrogant—these are the twelve evil enticements."

The *Sutra of Ratnakumāra* (T. 17: 952c–953c) says:

> The Buddha said, "Self-cultivating bodhisattvas have three kinds of agreement between what they say and what they are: 1) They don't deceive Buddha Tathāgatas; 2) they don't deceive any living beings; and 3) they don't deceive themselves. Because they are determined to attain awakening,

they don't long for lesser fruits. Even though they may suffer in various ways, they won't be alarmed or upset. This is how they don't deceive Buddhas, living beings, or themselves.

"Further, there are four modes of being in which bodhisattvas don't deceive Tathāgatas: 1) being firm and stable, 2) inspiring awe, 3) exerting themselves to the utmost, and 4) being strenuous in keeping precepts. The four modes of being in which they don't deceive living beings are: 1) being firmly determined to keep learning and cultivating themselves, 2) imparting delight to others out of friendliness, 3) sympathizing with suffering people out of compassion, and 4) accepting living beings without exception. The four modes of being in which they don't deceive themselves are: 1) being firm and stable, 2) being firm and stable without end, 3) not flattering, and 4) being free from deceit."

The *Foreword to the Brahmā Net Sutra*[101] says:

> When you keep moral precepts and don't feel guilty, your longings will also be fulfilled.

If we keep our *śīla* or moral precepts clean, then without fail our *samādhi* and *prajñā* will be fulfilled completely.

No other blame against or doubt about the Zen school, if there were any, need to be taken up for our consideration, and thus the [third] gate, "Eliminating People's Doubts," has been established.

Gate IV

By the fourth gate, "Scriptural Verification by Ancient People of Virtue," I mean the proofs that ancient people of virtue practiced the principle of this school. There are ten.

1. According to the *Biography of Prince Shōtoku* (*Dainihon Bukkyō Zensho,* vol. 112, 25) and Great Master Dengyō's *Single Mind Moral Precept* (T. 74: 645c), vol. II:

> Dhyāna Master Nanyue [Hui]si (Nangaku Eshi) of Chen (Chin) came across Great Master[102] Bodhidharma (Daruma) and received direct teachings from him.

Besides, the *Postscript to A Treatise on the Contemplation of Mind* of the Tiantai school[103] says:

> The Great Master of the Shaolin (Shōrin) Temple on Mount Song (Sūzan) handed down the truth of Chan to Dhyāna Master [Hui]si of Nanyue; [Huisi] handed down the Chan truth to Dhyāna Master Zhizhe (or Zhiyi; Chisha or Chigi) of Tiantai.

2. Dhyāna Master Zhizhe constantly practiced this *chan* (*dhyāna; zen*). When reciting the *Lotus Sutra* he came to the passage (T. 9: 53b), "This is the true exertion; this is named the true honoring of the Dharma (*dharma-pūjā*) of the Tathāgata (*tathāgata-pūjā*)," he suddenly attained great awakening. He saw for himself that the dignity of the very meeting on Vulture Peak in India, where the sutra had been expounded, remained without being dispersed.

3. From the Second Patriarch of Chan [Huike] down through the present Twenty-fifth Patriarch [Eisai], the Chan truth has prevailed in the world.

4. During the eighteen dynasties since the Later Han (Gokan) through the Tang there were more than two hundred Buddhist scholars, both priests and laymen, who engaged themselves in translating original scriptures into Chinese. Their translations included many scriptures on the essentials of *dhyāna*.

5. Daoxuan of the Tang came to Nara, Japan, and entrusted
9b Gyōhyō with this truth of Chan.

6. Japan's Great Master Dengyō, in Nara, first heard about this school and, finally crossing the ocean, reached Xiuchansi (Shūzenji) on Mount Tiantai and personally received transmission of [Mount] Niutou; great awakening suddenly dawned on him.

7. Great Master Jikaku (Ennin) always practiced this Chan. One day when he was staying in Tang China, he made a vow: "On

returning home to my native land under the rule of our emperor, I will have a Zen temple built."

8. Great Master Chishō (Enchin) selected[104] the principle and substance of this school.

9. Venerable Annen expounded the essentials of Zen.

10. Prevailing in the contemporary China of the Great Song is a scripture of ten fascicles, the *Chan School Monastic Rules* (*Zokuzōkyō* 2–16). The gist of it is as follows: All the scriptures, i.e., sutras, Vinayas, and *śāstra*s, which derive from Śākyamuni's lifetime teachings in their five periods, clarify the essentials of the Buddha's *dhyāna*. The Buddha's four basic postures come from *dhyāna*. A sutra (unidentified) says: "Abiding in the self-concentration of *dhyāna*, one is compassionate toward living beings."

These are none other than so many examples of scriptural verification for the Zen school.

Thus established is the [fourth] gate, "Scriptural Verification by Ancient People of Virtue."

Gate V

By the fifth gate, "The Sects of the Zen School's Lineage," I mean that this seal of the mind[105] was transmitted down through the past seven Buddhas, and that the close transmission that has been continuing, one lineage[106] after another, makes it uninterrupted. *Reasons for the Rise of the Chan School* (*Shōwahōbō Sōmokuroku*, General Index 2, 770a) says:

> And the Chan school is observed to have started in the times of the preceding Buddhas, as long ago as *kalpa*s as numerous as dust particles.

According to the *Longer Records of the Buddha's Words:*[107]

> During the past *kalpa* of supernal mainfestations (*vyūhakalpa; zhuangyanjie; shōgongō*), there appeared a thousand Buddhas in the world; the last three of them were counted as the first

> three of the seven Buddhas with whom the present [auspicious] *kalpa* began.

The seven Buddhas kept entrusting one after another with the seal of the mind. Their oral transmission exists apart from this. Their lineage relationship is as[108] follows: The Buddhas 1) Vipaśyin, 2) Śikhin, 3) Viśvabhu, 4) Krakucchanda, 5) Konakamuni, 6) Kāśyapa, and 7) Śākyamuni.

Śākyamuni, forty-nine years after attaining awakening, was with a large assembly at a shrine named Bahuputraka ("Having Plenty of Children")[109] on Vulture Peak.[110] He praised Mahākāśyapa, offered him half his seat, and said:

> I am entrusting you with the eye of the Dharma that is pure and clean, the sublime mind of nirvana, the reality that is without form, the authentic truth that is subtle. You should protect and uphold this.

He also ordered Ānanda to help Kāśyapa preserve the eye of the Dharma and not let it be interrupted. He also composed a verse.[111]

The *Sutra on Handing Over a Lotus Flower* (T. 16: 127b–128c) says:

> The Buddha, looking at Kāśyapa far in the distance, said to him, "Welcome, Kāśyapa. It's a long time since we met. You should take this half of the Buddha's seat." When the Buddha moved aside, the three thousand worlds quaked. Kāśyapa said to the Buddha, "I don't dare sit at the seat of the Buddha's robe and bowl. The Buddha is a great master, while I am a disciple. In the past, from the Buddha I received a *saṃghāṭī* robe.[112] Holding it high with esteem, I didn't dare wear it. . . . Since that time I have had no lust. I received the Buddha's robe when I was in the process of self-cultivation. When I raised it in my hands above my head, I attained the ultimate fruit of no-cultivation. I followed the Buddha's suggestion and received the Tathāgata's robe. Although it is in
> 9c my possession, I dare not think it has lessened in value. I

> only hold it in my hands but dare not place it beneath me. If [my hands are] not washed and cleaned, I also dare not hold it. How could I make little of it by placing it below my head? . . . The Lord of the Dharma had no master to follow but in a self-effected manner has attained awakening. That is not common to any *śrāvaka* or *pratyekabuddha.*"[113]
>
> The Buddha said, "Well said, well said. It is as you have said." . . . The Buddha then said to Kāśyapa, "Now take this seat, and ask me anything you are wondering about. I shall expound my view for you."
>
> Kāśyapa then rose from his seat, bowed his head at the Buddha's feet, and, as he was told to, sat.

The *Sutra on the Great Drum of the Truth* (T. 9: 291c) says:

> Kāśyapa said to the Buddha, "The Tathāgata is great enough to treat me respectfully. By 'respectfully' I mean the Tathāgata once told me, 'Come and sit with me.' It is for this reason that I naturally feel deeply obliged to the Tathāgata."
>
> The Buddha said, "Well said. That is why I treat you respectfully."

[What follows is the Dharma transmission in the Zen school:][114] The first, Mahākāśyapa; the second, Ānanda; the third, Śānavāsin; the fourth, Upagupta; the fifth, Dhītika; the sixth, Miśraka; the seventh, Vasumitra; the eighth, Buddhanandi; the ninth, Buddhamitra; the tenth, Pārśva; the eleventh, Puṇyayaśas; the twelfth, Aśvaghoṣa; the thirteenth, Kapimala; the fourteenth, Nāgārjuna; the fifteenth, Kāṇadeva; the sixteenth, Rāhulātta; the seventeeth, Saṃghanandi; the eighteenth, Gayāśaṭa; the nineteenth, Kumāralāta; the twentieth, Jayanta; the twenty-first, Vasubandhu; the twenty-second, Manorhita; the twenty-third, Kroñcaratna; the twenty-fourth, Siṃha; the twenty-fifth, Vaśiṣṭha; the twenty-sixth, Puṇyamitra; the twenty-seventh, Prajñottara; and the twenty-eighth, Bodhidharma.

Great Master [Bodhidharma] crossed the South Asian Sea and reached Guangfu (Kōfu) in Putong (Futsū) the eighth year of Liang

have heard that in the land of Japan the Buddha's teachings have prevailed. Fortunately I have met you, my respected master. I must present you my view in written words.

"Yes, human beings have the difference of Chinese and non-Chinese. But the Buddha's teachings have the single truth of the mind. The moment one realizes oneness of the mind,[118] one knows that the truth is a single gate. It is what the *Diamond Sutra* (T. 8: 749c) says, 'You should give rise to the mind that abides nowhere.'

"When you want to know its original streams, please pay a visit to me. I shall speak with you about each of them. Extensively knowing the way of the patriarchs exceeds inference made from the viewpoint of the Small Vehicle."

10b This was in Qiandao (Kendō) the fourth year of Song, the year of *wuzi* (1168). In the autumn I returned to Japan. Then, reading Annen's *Treatise on Teaching Time Polemics,* I knew the names of the nine Buddhist schools. Besides, carefully reading Chishō's *Similarities and Dissimilarities of the Teaching Forms,* I knew the details of Dharma transmission in the Japanese Tendai school on Mount Hiei. Next, I saw Great Master Dengyō's *Genealogy* and knew that our Mount Hiei had received the transmission of the Dharma. Since then I kept nourishing this thought, and twenty years passed. I intended to pay a visit to the eight holy stupas that had been built in memory of Śākyamuni in India. In March, the third year of Bunji in Japan, the year of *teimi* (*dingwei,* 1187), I left my native land. I took with me a list of the lineages of the various schools as well as a book on the geography of the western districts. On reaching the land of the Song I first went to the capital, Lin'anfu, visited the Undersecretary of Pacification, and reported my wish to travel through India. I presented to him a paper which conveyed my wishes as follows:[119]

> Dragging this half-shadow of mine on planks laid across a precipice,
> I shall terminate the whole body on the equable diamond seat of awakening.

However, he did not give me a certificate; he just told me that my case was on record, and kept me from leaving for the west. I could not but weary myself thinking about India: "Is the time not yet come? Does my attainment not accord with oneness?"[120] It was in Chuxi (Junki), the fourteenth year of the Brilliant Song, the year *dingwei* (1187). Then I climbed Mount Tiantai, and took a rest in Wannian Temple. Seeking instruction from the head priest of the temple, Chan Master [Huai]chang (Eshō), I practiced Chan with him and asked the Way of him. Through him I gained a good understanding of the style of the Linji school. I recited the precepts of the *Vinaya in Four Divisions*. I finished reciting the precepts of the bodhisattva restraints. Finally, in July, the autumn of Shaoxi (Shōki) the second year of Song, the year of *xinhai* (*shingai; kanoto-i,* 1191)—the second year of Kenkyū in Japan—I returned home. When I parted with the Chan master, he brushed a calligraphy[121] for me which read:

> The Great Dharma Master of the Senkōin, Japan (by which he meant me, [Ei]sai), has had an ingenious disposition ever since his previous lives. He swiftly abandoned worldly life with its heavy entanglements of obligations and affections, followed the Buddha to receive the tonsure, wore a *saṃghāṭī* robe, magnaminously held this teaching, and, not minding the distance of ten thousand *li,* arrived by sea in our land of the Brilliant Song to search out the mysteries of the principle.
>
> In the year of Qiandao *wuzi* (1168) he sauntered on the mountain of Tiantai and, upon seeing the excellent beauty of the mountains, rivers, and land, as well as the special purity of the seat of awakening, he greatly rejoiced. Once he gave a faithful donation, making offerings to those bodhisattvas who had gathered from the ten directions to learn to practice *prajñā*. He also went to the stone bridge, where he offered incense, made tea, and saluted the living five hundred great arhats.
>
> Soon he returned to his native country. He remained in our dream for exactly twenty years. Although they did not hear

> from him, elder mendicants in this mountain were vividly reminded of those days. Now memories of his previous visit have been revived. Our old relationship seems to have been far from shallow. With his diligence and determination deepened, I could not but indicate the essence of the Dharma to him.
>
> In the past, when the aged Śākyamuni was about to manifest perfect cessation (*parinirvāṇa*), he entrusted the mind of nirvana, the eye and treasury of the Dharma, to Mahākāśyapa, which has been transmitted generation after generation up to me. Now I entrust this Dharma to you. Protect and uphold it and, bearing the patriarchs' seal on yourself, return home to help the latter-day world attain awakening. Reveal the Dharma to living beings, and keep the authentic truth continuously alive among them. I also give you a *kaṣāya* ("dyed yellowish-red") garment. Great Master [Bodhidharma], in the past, transmitted a robe to help people have trust in its bearer. It was an expression of the truth that originally
> 10c there was nothing to which to cling. When it was handed down to the Sixth Patriarch, its transmission ceased.
>
> Although the style is out of vogue now, I give you a *saṃghāṭī* robe only for the sake of its bearer gaining people's trust in a foreign country. I ordain you in the bodhisattva *śīla*. A staff, a bowl, and the other essentials of a monk—all of these are given to you without exception. Listen to my verse of Dharma transmission. . . .

This school, ever since the Sixth Patriarch, has gradually divided itself into sects, and has caused the Dharma to circulate over the four seas. Its generations [from Master Nanyue Huairang up to me] have grown to twenty; its lineage streams became five (i.e., the five leading Chan sects: Fayan [Hōgen], Linji [Rinzai], Weiyang [Igyō], Yunmen [Unmon], and Caodong [Sōtō]). The one that most widely flourishes now is the Linji sect. Since the seven [past] Buddhas down to Eisai, about sixty generations have succeeded in the lineage. Indeed, it is with good reason that the teachings of the

Buddha-Dharma have had public verification. In the above I gave a single branch of Dharma transmission alone. For the rest of the branches, you may see them in a diagram separately prepared. We have come to the end of the [fifth] gate, "The Sects of the Zen School's Lineage."

Gate VI

By the sixth gate, "Scriptural Evidence for Promoting People's Confidence in the Zen School" I mean what follows:

The principle of this Zen school does not set up any words out of which to make dogma. It has been specially transmitted outside of scriptural teachings. It does not cling to passages taught; it only transmits the seal of the mind. It is free from letters, being without words. Through directly pointing to the source of the mind,[122] it has one attain awakening. We see verification for this scattered in various sutras and *śāstras*. Let me show you a few of them to have them serve as proofs of the present school.

The *Flower Ornament Sutra* (T. 9, no. 278, 449c) says:

> At the time of original aspiration (*bodhicitta*) one attains authentic awakening.

It also says (T. 10, no. 279, 89a):

> Upon realizing that everything that has its own characteristics is immediately the self-nature of the mind, one fulfills the body of wisdom; no realization through others achieves this.

The *Heap of Jewels Sutra* (T. 11, vol. 52, 308c) says:

> The original nature of the mind is like the moon reflected in water.

It also says (T. 11, vol. 62, 361b):

> The self-nature of everything that has its own characteristics is unobtainable. As in a dream one tries to satisfy desires,

every attempt is made in vain. Things arise according to imagination and turn out to be unreal. This is also how the World-honored One knows things.

The *Vimalakīrti Sutra* (T. 14, I, 538c) says:

As the mind is free from discrimination, the Buddha's land becomes free from discrimination.

It also says (T. 14, IX, 551c) in effect:

Vimalakīrti remained silent.[123]

The *Laṅkā[vatāra]-sūtra* (T. 16, II, 492a) says:

The Tathāgatas' nondiscriminating *dhyāna*.[124]

The *Mahāprajñāpāramitā Sutra* (T. 7, fasc. 409, 49a) says:

What is seen as having form does not have its own being, and is unobtainable. Even all-knowing wisdom (*sarvajñajñāna*) has no being of its own and is unobtainable.

It also says:[125]

There being no words is called the Buddha-Dharma.

And this:

The ultimate way of reality has no words; all verbal expressions are so many secular explications.

The *Diamond Sutra* (T. 8, X, 749c) says:

You should give rise to the mind that abides nowhere.

It also says (T. 8, XXVI, 752a):

If anyone insists that the Tathāgata has any truth that is verbally expounded, he is blaming the Buddha without reason.

It also says (T. 8, XXVI, 752a):

If anyone sees me as form, his practice is deluded.

The *Lotus Sutra* (T. 9, II, 5c) says:

> Only the Buddha with other Buddhas can exhaustively investigate the real form of all that has its own characteristics.

It also says (T. 9, XVI, 42c):

> It is not like this; it is not different from this.

It also has this (T. 9, II, 10a):

> It is impossible to manifest reality in words.

The *Mahāparinirvāṇa Sutra* (T. 12: 406b) says:

> The Tathāgata eternally abides and does not suffer change. . . . Anyone who expounds the truth in this way is a true disciple of mine.

It also says:[126]

> Not a word have I expounded.

The *Mahāprajñāpāramitā Treatise* (T. 25: 190b) says:

> Perfection (*pāramitā*) of the knowledge of emptiness (*prajñā*) is the real truth, free from perversion, where memory, imagination, and contemplation are already removed, where ver- 11a
> bal truth is extinguished, and innumerable transgressions are done away with. It is free from discrimination; it is the mind that is constant and one. People of such honorable, deep wisdom can see the truth, knowing emptiness. It is like space, free from contamination, deceit, and words. If anyone contemplates in this way, he is regarded as seeing the Buddha. If contemplated as they truly are, the three—Buddha, knowledge of emptiness (*prajñā*), and nirvana—are of one characteristic; in truth, there is no difference among them.

The Mantra school's *Mahāvairocana Sutra* (T. 18: 9b) says:

> Being awakened that I am originally free from birth and from

> verbal modes of being, I have attained liberation from all faults. I have become free from causal conditioning. I know emptiness like space. Wisdom that knows reality as it truly is has arisen in me. Already free from all kinds of darkness, I am of the ultimate nature and without defilement.

The *Middle Treatise* (T. 30: 1b; quoted above, p. 84) says:

> *Question:* Why do you compose this treatise?
>
> *Answer:* During the last five hundred-year period . . . people are dull-witted and deeply attached to . . . verbal expressions, [and give rise to perverted views. That is why] the author composed this *Middle Treatise.*

The Tiantai school's *Great Calming and Contemplation* (T. 46: 1c and 3a) says:

> Tiantai (Master Zhiyi, the speaker,) transmits Nanyue's three kinds of cessation and contemplation. . . . In spite of the latter's three passages, one should not be attached to any of them. Otherwise, tumors will grow on oneself. The [*Mahāprajñāpāramitā*] *Treatise* (T. 25, XVIII, 190c) says: "Knowing emptiness and not knowing emptiness—all make bondage and all make liberation." The same is true with the three passages. The *Mahāparinirvāṇa Sutra* (T. 12: 520b) says: "If anyone knows the Tathāgata never expounds the awakened truth, that one will be called a person of much hearing. This indicates that not making exposition is at once exposition."

The *Scripture on the Explication of Underlying Meaning* (T. 16: 712c) says:

> The self-attained truth that is formless is free from verbal exposition and the four things. It is the awakened truth free from polemics, which is the characteristic common to everything, and which goes beyond being an object of discriminating consciousness.

By the "four things" the sutra means seeing, hearing, and other [sense] perceptions, as well as knowing by consciousness.

The *Sutra of* [*the Jain*] *Satyaka's* [*Instruction*] (T. 9: 326a) says:

> It is because the nature of everything in the world is free from discrimination.

The *Sutra of Moonlight Samādhi* (T. 15: 550b) says:

> The self-nature of everything that has its own characteristics is equal, free from deceit, and in self-concentration (*samādhi*).

The *Mañjuśrī Inquiry Sutra* (T. 14: 495c) says:

> That this goes beyond calculation, being free from mind, ego consciousness, and perceptive consciousnesses, and that every verbal expression is cut off with it—this is the practice of *prajñā*.

The *Sutra of Examining through Divination* (T. 17: 907a) says:

> Bodhisattva Kṣitigarbha ("Earth Womb") said, "By the one real realm I mean the self-nature of living beings. From the beginning it is free from generation and extinction, free from discrimination by its self-nature."

The *Sutra of the Diamond Samādhi* (T. 9: 373a) says:

> Anything that has its own characteristics is originally free from existence and nonexistence. It is free from self and other, too. It has no beginning and no end. With it, success and failure have no place.

The *Sutra of King Longevity* (T. 3: 387c) says:

> Being self-effected, liberation is not the gift of any teacher. For my practice I am under no teacher's care. Determined to proceed alone, I have no companion. . . . The ultimate path is free from journeying to and fro; it is deep and subtle, pure, wondrous, and true.

The *Sutra of the Bodhisattva Precepts for Practicing Good* (T. 30: 973b) says:

> Bodhisattvas, for the sake of awakening, practice *dhyāna,* enjoy delight in this life, and keep body and mind calm and composed—this is called benefiting oneself. Because of the tranquility of body and mind, they do not worry living beings. This is called benefiting others.

The *Demonstration of Consciousness Only* (T. 31, X, 54–59a) says in effect:

> Everything of the world that has its own characteristics is nothing but what makes itself known (*vijñaptimātra*), without any substance.

The *Treatise on Awakening Confidence* (T. 32: 576a, Liang version) says:

> Free from the characteristics of verbal expression.

We might have to exhaustively quote passages on the essentials of Zen, which Śākyamuni expounded in his lifetime. Here, however, I have shown only a few. I hope readers will know the same is true with other sources. In other words, all the expositions by the Tathāgata that appear in the sutras, some being provisional
11b and others unconditional, are meant for living beings to accept and hold the nondual truth of the Buddha as no-mind and sentient beings as mind. For this purpose he first made the skillful means of traps and nets. Venerable Annen says [in the *Treatise on Teaching Time Polemics*] (T. 75: 355b; quoted above, p. 102):

> [T]he Zen school, with its traps and nets amply employed by Śākyamuni all his life, and ultimately with emphasis on the transmission of mind to mind without reliance on scriptural authority, constitutes the heart of all the Buddhas' [teachings].

Great Master Chishō says [in the *Similarities and Dissimilarities of the Teaching Forms*] (T. 74: 312c; quoted above, p. 101):

> Its principle is that the mind is nothing other than the Buddha. A mind freed from clinging to anything constitutes its religious act.

I pray that seekers of the Way in the latter-day world may undertake the study of the eight treasuries and cultivate the myriad practices, that they may not be deceived by the partial mind, and that they may use the strength of this Zen principle to extinguish grave sins. The *Commentary on the Mahāvairocana Sutra* says in effect (T. 39: 582b): "Attaining *prajñā* without relying on *dhyāna* is quite impossible."[127]

If anyone can realize the aim of *prajñā,* his sins are certain to be extinguished. The reason is that for causing the extinction of sins nothing surpasses the real characteristics of *prajñā*. The Tiantai school's *Great Calming and Contemplation* (T. 46: 39c; quoted above, p. 111) says:

> If anyone commits grave sins of the nature of phenomena (*dharmas*), he will find the practice of four kinds of self-concentration to be the way of repentance. The *Sutra on Contemplation of Samantabhadra* says in effect: "Taking the [seated meditation] posture and focusing one's thought on the true mode of reality . . . this is called the first repentance."
>
> The *Sutra on the Most Wondrous Supreme Dhyāna* says: "Transgressors of the four grave offenses and the five grave transgressions will, except for deepening their thought (*dhyāna*), have no way to be saved."

All this provides scriptural evidence for the Zen school. Hence the [sixth] gate, "Scriptural Evidence for Promoting People's Confidence[128] in the Zen School," has been established.

Gate VII

The seventh gate, "Citing a General Principle and Exhorting People to Practice Zen," has three aspects. They are: 1) teaching, 2)

Zen, and 3) the general aspect. First, by teaching I mean various teachings. People of not very brilliant capacity will first examine the admirable ideas of various teachings and schools. When they learn the essentials of Zen, those teachings will serve as the means for cultivating themselves to enter Zen. The *Collection of Records from the Ancestral Mirrors* quotes sixty sutras and *śāstra*s, collects the excellent purports of the three schools,[129] and comments on the expressions of more than three hundred authorities. It does so in order to expound the essentials of the Chan school.

Second, by Zen I mean the Buddha's *dhyāna*. It is not adhering to words, not being bound by mind or thought. Therefore, one penetrates this by getting free from mind, ego consciousness, and perceptive consciousnesses. One learns this by transcending the paths of the unawakened and the awakened. In this way Zen concerns people of superb brilliance.

Third, by the general aspect I mean what follows. The so-called teachings and so-called Zen are nothing but names. To say "penetrating" and "learning" are also provisional matters. "I," "others," "living beings," "awakening" (*bodhi*), and "nirvana" are all names, too. They don't substantially exist. The teachings expounded by the Buddha are also names; there is nothing expounded. Therefore, the Zen principle is free from the characteristics of words, free from those objects of the mind. It is beyond thought and deliberation and ultimately unobtainable. Concerning the Buddha-Dharma (lit., "the Buddha's awakened truth"), what has no Dharma to be expounded is called the Buddha-Dharma. What I now call Zen is an expression of that characteristic.

Since the three aspects mentioned above are provisional names, if anyone insists that the Buddha's *dhyāna* has letters and words, he is blaming the Buddha, Dharma, and Sangha. Therefore, the patriarch [Bodhidharma] did not set up words out of which to make any dogma but, by directly pointing to the human mind, causes one to see one's self-nature [as no-mind] and attain awakening. This was the so-called Chan (Zen) gate.

He who takes hold of names and letters misses the Dharma. He who clings to characteristics and appearances is also perverted. 11c
Originally there being no moving and nothing to be obtained is called the Buddha-Dharma,[130] the Buddha's truth. The Buddha-Dharma lies just in walking, standing, sitting, and lying down. Adding even a bit to it is impossible, whereas taking away just a bit is also impossible. Realizing this, you will not waste even the slightest energy. As soon as you estimate it by deliberation to be something marvelous and mysterious, you already have nothing to do with it. Therefore, if you move, you will be arousing the base of birth and death. If you stay quiet, you will be getting drunk in the area that is dark and heavy. If you forget both movement and quietude, you will squander your Buddha-nature.[131] When nothing like this is available, what will you do?[132]

If you clarify the principle outside the scriptural teaching, you will never seek rules in words. Instead, immediately you will see, and pull up the garment and go. An arrow that has left the bow is not bound to return; none of the thousand sages would be able to grasp it.[133] If you have not reached this source of creativity, you should take care not to be so careless and arrogant as to try to cheat others. Otherwise, the final day of the year-end month[134] will see you incapable of making use of it.

Have you not heard this? [In the days of the Five Dynasties in China], a Chan monk laughed at Elder Monk Fu of Taiyuan (Taigen) [when he was expounding the *Mahāparinirvāṇa Sutra*]. Immediately then and there Fu realized Chan, with the result that his name came to be known throughout the nine divisions of the entire country. [As recorded in the *Blue Cliff Record*] (T. 48: 183ab, case 47, and 222bc, case 99), Fu said to the monk who laughed at him:[135]

> Since I began lecturing on Buddhist scriptures, I have been fidgeting with my nose on the body born of my parents. Hereafter I shall never dare behave like that.

If someone goes into the sea to collect treasures, he should seek[136] the "wish-fulfilling gem" (*cintāmaṇi*). If he cannot obtain one, nothing else will do. Among those who learn the Way, how can there not be one who knows a little but understands less? However, not attaining to this Great Matter is really to be grieved. A remark by an ancient man [of Chan] goes:[137] "Insofar as you have not clarified the Great Matter, behave like when you lost your parents."

Śākyamuni, the aged man, originally made his appearance in the world for the sake of this Great Matter. Now what is the Great Matter and how is it clarified? By this I mean that one should attain great awakening once and for all; that is, one needs to see it for oneself. That alone enables you to open your own mouth and give expression to your own thoughts. On the other hand, insofar as you don't attain, see, or reach awakening, however well you can expound the whole five thousand and forty-eight volumes of the Tripiṭaka, and with whatever skill during your exposition of them you can hold a bowl filled with water and not spill even a drop, this is only of the quantity level of the Dharma body. How remote it will be from the Great Matter!

Let me raise the case of the ancients who attained awakening. Try deliberating on this [passage from the *Eye and Treasury of the True Dharma*] (*Zokuzōkyō* 2–23, 63b):

> Venerable Luoshan[138] asked Venerable Shishuang[139] one day, "When arising and perishing don't cease, what shall I do?"
>
> Shishuang said, "You need immediately to make yourself like cold ashes or a withered tree. Make one moment ten thousand years. Have the container and the lid fit together."[140]
>
> Luoshan did not accord with [Shishuang]. [Luoshan] then went to Venerable Yantou[141] and presented the same question to him. Venerable Yantou, on hearing it, shouted, "Who is it that arises and perishes?"
>
> At these words, Luoshan suddenly became awakened.

Now tell me, to what was he awakened? The ancients kept thinking of this, abiding in this. During all the twelve divisions of the day they continued to struggle with this [question]. For Luoshan, attaining awakening was everything. Only because worldly anxieties confusingly arose and perished without stopping in his mind did he raise that single question so as to ultimately clarify this matter.

Venerable elder masters prescribed medicines according to the disease. Some will find one dose effective. Others will need a vari- 12a
ety of methods combined with the application of all kinds of acupuncture and moxibustion. Only with the disease gone and the medicine removed does the whole body become light and clean—that fact alone verifies the effect. Among later way-seekers, those who don't reach the original source are likely to distinguish between superior and inferior, and insist that Shishuang's words for Luoshan were dead, whereas Yantou's words for him were full of life. Discerning views like these are something held only after one buys sandals to travel on foot on a way-seeking journey.

One who fails to apprehend the aim of the steelyard hook wrongly clings to the measurement marks on the beam.[142] A lion bites a man while a mad dog chases a clod of dirt thrown by him. Generally speaking, venerable elder masters never make a remark in vain. Way-seekers should by all means be equipped with the eye of discernment critical enough to be able to throw a pepper seed onto the tip of a needle.[143] If one cannot discern what is right and what is not, it will be like poling a boat casually up the Shanxi (Senkei) Gorge.[144] How could one reach the other shore?

Venerable Tianhuang[145] said [in the *Jingde Records of Transmission of the Lamp*] (T. 51, XIV, 313b):[146]

> Roam through your own inclinations;
> Be free, carefree, following conditions.
> Exhaust the feeling of being unawakened,
> With no self-understanding of being awakened.

If instructions were needed, they would all, the master meant, be [like] painting legs for a snake.

[According to the *Eye and Treasury of the True Dharma*, fasc. 5] (*Zokuzōkyō* 2–23, 61b),Venerable Qinglin[147] said:

> What is inside the patriarchs' gate is as profoundly subtle as traces of birds [in the sky]. When [one's] efforts [have been] exhausted, all pass the crisis. Unless it is investigated, it can hardly be clarified. Reaching this point, you should penetrate it by getting free from mind, ego consciousness, and perceptive consciousnesses. Learn it by transcending the paths of the unawakened and the awakened. Only then can you hold it yourself. Otherwise, no one can be the child of the Chan school.

I wish I could give all such wonderful words of ancient masters, for they express the profound gist of their whole lives.

> Any way-seeker who wants to practice this Dharma[148] should be a bodhisattva who practices to know emptiness, to arouse great compassion, to make the comprehensive vow, to cultivate himself in self-concentration, to be equipped with a great bodhisattva's pure, wonderful precepts, and to exert all his efforts to cause living beings to attain awakening, seeking liberation not solely for himself.
>
> Thus[149] you may relinquish all connections with the world, put the myriad affairs to rest. Keep body and mind one, no matter whether moving or at rest. Drink and eat neither too much nor too little. Regulate your sleep, not making it too short nor too long. Sit cross-legged, keeping the eyes slightly open. In this posture, with the breath already regulated and worldly associations long forgotten, you will make yourself into one. If you realize the purport of this posture, spontaneously all the four elements of your physical being will become light and stable. You will enjoy the so-called truth of bliss and stability. For one who has already attained this, it will be like a dragon that has gotten [an ample supply of] water. To one who has not yet attained this, let me advise you to establish self-confidence and never withdraw in aversion.
>
> When you come out of *dhyāna,* move your body slowly at first, and be dignified and reserved in rising. All the time preserve the strength of *dhyāna* as if protecting an infant. Then

it will be easy for the power of *dhyāna* to grow. Just as divers prefer quiet waves for seeking pearls as in the moving water it is extremely difficult to find them, when the *dhyāna* water is clean and clear the pearl of the Mind spontaneously appears. The *Sutra of Perfect Awakening* (T. 17: 919a) says: "The unhindered nondiscriminating wisdom arises from *dhyāna*."

Herewith we know that transcending the unawakened way of being to enter into the Awakened Way requires quietude as its necessary condition. All our basic postures of walking, standing, sitting, and lying down should rest on the strength of *dhyāna*. This is something to be achieved most urgently.

If you want to attain *dhyāna,* you must depend on practicing morality. There is no reason for attaining *dhyāna* without the provision of moral precepts.

An Essential Understanding of Dhyāna Practice (T. 15: 292b) says:

> It is like a monkey tied to a post. All day long it runs about,
> and the chain always pulls it back. When it gets to the end 12b
> of the chain, it rests. The monkey's attention, like the chain, is directed to the post. Our mind is compared to this monkey. A practitioner's self-contemplation is also like this. Gradually the mind is controlled and made to abide in itself as the object of contemplation. If the mind abides here long, it accords with the practice of *dhyāna*.

Therefore, if you want to accomplish this *dhyāna,* keep yourself morally clean without a flaw; for controlling yourself with the help of moral restraints resembles that monkey. The *Sutra of Moral Conduct* says:

> Keep your mind tied to itself and prevent it from being negligent, just like a monkey that is attached to a chain.

I am an uncouth person born and brought up in Japan, living in a forest at the foot of a mountain. Following my predecessors' example, I undertook long journeys across rivers and seas. Wearing a soiled robe, I spent days sitting [in meditation], facing a wall in silence. I was content with my lot and refrained from stating my view to others, for I felt deeply ashamed at my way of life which was full of stupidities.

Recently, however, following the ancient masters' footsteps for awhile, I observed a Chinese master's style of awakening. He was often eagerly attentive but would also very often stop. However, as soon as I burned a stick of incense to salute the master (Xu'an Huaichang; Ki'an Eshō), the relationship of guest and host was established between us. Fortunately, raising the patriarch's instructions, I had an early opening of the eye of awakening. Repeatedly I cultivated the method of transcending birth and death and, entering the Way, I returned home. Since I have already achieved the unity of being, I would very much like to help the patriarch's Way greatly flourish in this country of Japan. That is the only reason I have taken upon myself the responsibility for its realization and at the same time pray heartily for that result.

Because of this I have made repeated cultivation of the method of transcendence, and when I look back[150] on it again and again, I see not one word to be transmitted and circulated. In the ancient days, to the repeated censure from a Jain, the Well-awakened One (Sugata) Śākyamuni retorted with the unity of silence. That precisely accords with the present case. Whether the school itself is shallow or deep is known by one who gains its purport. Please don't exhaust yourself by knocking at the gate or grasping at the sky. Great Sage Nāgārjuna means this when he says [in the *Mahāprajñāpāramitā Treatise*] (T. 25, XI, 139c):

> Existence is not anything; nonexistence is not anything; existence-nonexistence is not anything; neither existence nor nonexistence is not anything. This kind of exposition is also not anything.

He also says [in the same treatise] (T. 25, XVIII, 190b):

There is no verbal expansion; there are no words. If anybody can contemplate like this, he is regarded as seeing the Buddha.

We have seen the general principle of the Zen school. The *Laṅkā[vatāra]-sūtra* (T. 16: 492a) gives four kinds of *dhyāna:*

> 1) The kind of *dhyāna* that serves for ignorant people; 2) that which investigates the meaning of reality; 3) that which rests on the true mode of reality (*tathatā*) as its base (*ālambana*); and 4) that which, free from discrimination, is the Tathāgata's way of being (*tāthāgataṃ dhyānam*). The last is so called because when there is penetration into the mode of the Tathāgata stage, there is abiding in the personally attained noble wisdom.

These are the characteristics of Zen.

End of Fascicle Two

Fascicle Three

Gate VII (*continued*)

Now I would like to exhort youth of the latter-day world to make this Zen the right occasion for immediately attaining awakening. 12c
No matter whether you might think you have heard little and have slight understanding, or whether you consider yourself too dull to gain wisdom, if you wholeheartedly practice sitting *dhyāna*, you will inevitably attain awakening. The *Sutra of the Bodhisattva Precepts for Practicing Good* (T. 30: 973b; quoted above, p. 142) says:

> Bodhisattvas, for the sake of awakening, practice *dhyāna*, enjoy delight in this life, and keep body and mind calm and composed—this is called benefiting oneself. Because of the tranquility of body and mind, they do not worry living beings. This is called benefiting others.

The *Essentials for Chan Practice* (*Zokuzōkyō* 2–15, 419a) says:

> According to my ordination teachers both of *śīla* (*upādhyāya*) and of mantra (*ācārya*), what counts is to learn to practice *dhyāna* intently. It does not matter whether we have heard much or little.

For this reason a person of the latter-day world, no matter how dull-witted he may be, if he fastens his mind to the Buddha's *śīla*, tries making activity and rest no different from one another, remains concerned for all living beings, stops evil views, believes and accepts the Buddha's words, concentrates his mind on one object, and stops various associations and related obligations, then he is really a person of *dhyāna* cultivation. The *Bequeathed Teaching Sutra* (T. 12: 1111a; quoted above, pp. 110, 124) says:

> Dependence on this morality will give rise to various sorts of concentration and the wisdom that extinguishes suffering.

Generally speaking, attaining confidence in just one phrase of the Buddha is the immediate way among a myriad virtues for attaining awakening. We have examples of this: [According to the *Mahāprajñāpāramitā Treatise*] (T. 25, XIV, 164c), when Ānanda taught the essentials of the five supernatural powers, Devadatta acquired them through cultivation in just one summer retreat. [According to the *Sutra of Words of Truth on Great Acts*] (T. 4: 588c–589ab, story no. 16), Cūḍapanthaka, to whom the Buddha taught only one verse, attained the fruit of arhatship. A verse [in the *Song Dynasty Biographies of Eminent Monks*] (T. 50, XX, 837a) says:[151]

> If one quietly sits in *dhyāna* for but a brief moment, this will exceed the merit of building seven-jeweled stupas as numerous as the grains of sand in the Ganges River. Even a stupa of gems will ultimately turn into dust but a single moment of the composed mind will attain authentic awakening.

The *Sutra Treasury of Miscellaneous Jewels* (T. 4, 494ab, story no. 114) says:

> In olden days there was a monk who was aged and whose intellect was dark and hardened. When he saw young monks expound the truth of the four fruits of practice, he wished he could attain them. He told the young monks, "I pray that you will give me the four fruits of practice." The young monks laughed in derision and told him, "We have the four fruits of practice. You should prepare a good meal for us before we give them to you." Then the old monk rejoiced and managed to prepare a meal of rich food, and entertained them. The young monks, making a fool of the old monk, told him, "Sit in one corner of this shed. We are going to give you a fruit of practice." When the old monk heard this, he was glad and sat. The young monks then struck the old monk on the head with a leather ball, saying, "This is the fruit of the *srotaāpanna* ("entering the stream toward nirvana"). The old monk

> heard this, fastened his thoughts to it, not scattering them, and immediately acquired the first fruit.
>
> The young monks again made a fool of him, saying, "Although you have acquired the first fruit, still you cannot be free from seven births and deaths." Then they made him move to another corner and, as before, struck him with the ball. The old monk strengthened his concentration and immediately attained the second fruit. In like manner, the old monk, shifting to each corner [of the room], attained all four fruits of practice and greatly rejoiced. He provided them with various meals, incense, and flowers, and asked them to allow him to return their favors.
>
> He discussed with them the [thirty-seven] constituent factors of the Way to awakening. The young monks' lofty utterances soon stagnated and finally stopped. The old monk at that very moment told them, "I have already attained the fruit of arhatship." At this, all the young monks repented of belittling him.

Another story [from the *Sutra Treasury of Miscellaneous Jewels*] (T. 4: 494c, story no. 115) goes as follows:

> In the past there was a woman who had deep confidence[152] in the Three Treasures of Buddha, Dharma, and Sangha. She invited a monk to her house and made some offerings to him. After that the woman, with a sincere heart, closed her eyes, 13a
> sat calmly, and entreated him to expound a teaching. The monk failed to answer her request and stole away to his temple. However, she [continued to sit and] contemplate the reality of this conditioned life—impermanence, suffering, and emptiness—which keep living beings from gaining self-abiding in anything. She deepened her thought in that contemplation and acquired the fruit of the *srota-āpanna*. As she had been able to attain this fruit, she went to the temple to find the monk in order to express her gratitude to him. The monk, ashamed, hid himself to avoid meeting her. Hearing

> her entreaties, however, he came out, and she then thanked him for providing her with the occasion to attain the fruit of the Way. The monk was bitterly ashamed.

These two cases reveal the virtue of confidence in the Dharma. The *Mahāprajñāpāramitā Treatise* (T. 25: I, 63a) says:

> What leads people to the great sea of the teachings of the Buddha-Dharma is confidence in the truth.

The Mantra school quotes the above passage and comments on it [in the *Commentary on the Mahāvairocana Sutra*] (*Zokuzōkyō* 1–36, 264b):

> When the god Brahmā implored him to turn the wheel of the Dharma, the Buddha said in verse:
>
> > I now open the gate of the immortal dew.
> > Any people confident in it will have joy.
>
> This verse does not say that people who practice charity (*dāna*), morality (*śīla*), listening to many discourses, perseverance (*kṣānti*), great effort (*vīrya*), *dhyāna,* or the knowledge of emptiness (*prajñā*) will have joy. It refers only to those who have confidence. This is the Buddha's own suggestion. . . . For this reason, the power of confidence ranks first. It is not the knowledge of emptiness and virtues other than confidence that first lead one to the teachings of the Buddha-Dharma.

The *Diamond Sutra* (T. 8: 750b) says:

> Those in whom clear confidence arises that this is really true come to know the true characteristic of reality.

Ci'en's (Jion) *Commentary on the Diamond Sutra by the Dharmalakṣaṇa School* says:[153]

> I declare that a moment of confidence perfuming and staying with the mind can break the unbounded extensive cycle of birth and death.

Huizhao (Eshō) of Zizhou (Shishū) says in his *Commentary* [*on the Diamond Sutra*]:[154]

> Even if one cannot attain the formless *tathatā* (ultimate reality), the power of confidence also can remove evils.

Therefore, through first gaining confidence in a few words of one's master, one enters the *dhyāna* sea of the Buddha-Dharma. One can enter all the Buddha's teachings only through one's confidence in them. The *Treatise on Awakening Confidence* (T. 32: 590a, Tang version) says:

> *Question:* All the Buddhas, with boundless skillful means, can benefit living beings in the ten directions. Why do living beings not always see Buddhas, observe supernatural transformations, or hear them expound the Dharma?
>
> *Answer:* The Tathāgatas really have such skillful means. What is required is only that living beings be free from discrimination. Then the Tathāgatas will manifest themselves. In a mirror that has dirt on it no figures will appear. When the dirt is removed, [images then] appear there. It is the same with living beings. Insofar as they are not freed from dirt, their Dharma body never appears. When the dirt is gone, it appears.

The *Sutra on Attaining the Mudrā that Effects the Strength of Confidence* (T. 10, IV, 952b) says:

> The Buddha said to Mañjuśrī, "In this Jambu[dvīpa] world the sun and moon manifest their circles in the water of all vessels when the water is clean and not muddy, unless hindered. Meanwhile, the sun and moon have never moved from their original places. The Tathāgata is like this. Living beings who are to be transformed into their original way of being, can, with their own minds free from discrimination, all see the Tathāgata. Meanwhile, the Tathāgatas, as they originally are, do not move. In this way, the Tathāgata will be present in the living beings in the ten directions of the world in whom confidence arises."

Now, the monks of the Zen school who have chosen the way of being of body and mind that preserves both individual and sangha precepts (i.e., *śīla* and *vinaya*), with the water of their mind clean and clear will immediately see their own mind, and moment after moment they will accord with every perfection (*pāramitā*). However dull-witted and poor in wisdom they may be, because they keep morality pure and clean, the clouds of karma will vanish and the moon of the Mind will manifest itself brightly. The reason why
13b the *Mahāparinirvāṇa Sutra* advocates the eternity of nirvana as the true support for morality[155] is seen here.

Question: If that is the case, when we practice *dhyāna,* what precepts should we take?

Answer: The precepts given in the *Vinaya in Four Divisions* and the *Brahmā Net Sutra* [*on the Bodhisattva Śīla*] are considered to be appropriate. I say this because in practicing them externally we learn the basic postures of *śrāvaka*s and internally embrace the friendly social concern of bodhisattvas.

Question: The Vinaya regulations against the five definitive distinctions of offenses and the seven groups of transgressions[156] are Small [Vehicle] practices. Where is the need for our being equipped with the two vehicles? It is said that keeping the precepts for *śrāvaka*s is breaking the precepts for bodhisattvas. The *Bodhisattva Stages* (T. 30: 523a) extensively clarifies differences between the Great Vehicle and the Small Vehicle on keeping and breaking precepts, doesn't it?

Answer: The original intent of the Buddha's teachings lies only in avoiding evils and preventing wrongs. Concerning keeping or breaking precepts and permitting or restraining certain acts, if you grasp their purport and cultivate them, then it does not matter what vehicle you may choose. Vinaya Master Daoxuan says (in the preface to his *Instructions and Admonitions on Observing Restraints,* T. 45: 869b):

> There are some who insist: "I am a person of the Great Vehicle. I don't need the teachings of the Small Vehicle." Such people internally betray the bodhisattvas' heart and externally lack the *śrāvakas*' practice. Except for veterans in the Dharma, who could scrutinize it well?

How profound is this remark! It constitutes the central point of the Zen school. The Tiantai school's *Solutions for Propagation* (T. 46, IV–1, 254a) says:

> *Question:* "Why do we in the Great Vehicle apply precepts of the Small Vehicle and explain about the ten kinds of precept gainers?"
>
> *Answer:* The *Mahāparinirvāṇa Sutra* frequently expounds that the eternity of nirvana supports morality as its ultimate basis. We are thinking of the same principle here. The Small Vehicle works as skillful means. Then we know the mendicant bodhisattvas see no difference between themselves and *śrāvakas* in regard to the six kinds of friendly mutual respect and the ten benefits for regulating morality, but that they differ with respect to the six perfections and the four extensive vows, which are lacking in the practice of the Small Vehicle. For lay bodhisattvas the three refuges (Buddha, Dharma, and Sangha) and the five precepts will all lead them to the attainment of awakening. Still more so with the *Brahmā Net* [*Sutra on the Bodhisattva Śīla*]'s so-called eight myriad kinds of excellence appearing in one's every posture of those who have been ordained in the Great Vehicle. All seven groups of the Buddha's disciples actualize them. Beings of the five paths that suffer from their respective modes of existence will also commonly be equipped with such excellence. How could one tolerate the breaking of precepts and call it the "Buddha vehicle"? That is why a parallel elucidation is made with the use of four phrases concerning *yāna* (vehicle) and *śīla* (precepts) [with which one is either "relaxed" or "firm"].[157]

The same text says (T. 46: 255a):

> Both the *Mahā[parinirvāṇa] Sutra* (T. 12: 432bc) and the *Exposition of the Ten Stages,* referring to the [five] definitive distinctions of offenses and the [seven] groups of transgressions, say: "Bodhisattvas, great beings, hold those precepts of restraint." You should[158] know that precepts have no distinction of great or small. It depends on what the ordained expect of them. In other words, the Middle Way is not only a matter of emptiness and provisional forms; it also universally concerns respective precepts. Only then are we fully equipped with precepts.

The same text, in a preceding passage, says (T. 46: 254c):

> The five definitive distinctions of offenses and the seven groups of transgressions given in the *Mahāparinirvāṇa Sutra* (T. 12: 432bc) are the mendicant bodhisattvas' precepts of restraint.

These passages mean that precepts, both great and small, are skillful means, through the cultivation of which one enters the Tathāgatas' *dhyāna.*

Someone insists, "One who is relaxed with *śīla* (morality) while firm with *yāna* (vehicle or its principle) will encounter a Buddha's lifetime. Why then should it be indispensable to practice *śīla*?" But this kind of remark lacks reason. Who would wish to have *śīla* relaxed? By those who encounter a Buddha's lifetime while being relaxed with *śīla* are meant those in evil [modes of existence] like *nāga*s and other beasts. When they feel grateful for longevity, they come to live in a Buddha's lifetime due to the Buddha's vow-power. However, it is far better to meet a Buddha in a human life or above in heaven. Concerning this, the Tiantai school's *Great Calming and Contemplation* (T. 46: 39c) says:

> In this way between cause and effect there are differences with reduction in the degree of transgression and thus varieties of rise and fall as its rewards. How could one say, "Keeping *śīla*

> in reason leads to awakening; what is the use for keeping *śīla* in phenomena?" It is fortunate to attain awakening as a human or heavenly being. What meaning could there be in doing one's utmost to enter any of the three evil modes of existence (i.e., the realms of hell, hungry ghosts, and animals)?

In the present context, this passage sounds wonderful. We must, however, note the statement of the *Mahāparinirvāṇa Sutra* (T. 12: 400c):

> Being relaxed with *śīla* is not considered to be relaxed. It is with *yāna* (vehicle and its principle) that one is considered to be relaxed. 13c

This statement refers to those who are relaxed both with *yāna* and *śīla* [and emphasizes the importance of *yāna*]. It does not mean that one can favor being relaxed with *śīla*.

The *Great Calming and Contemplation* (T. 46: 20a) further says:

> A sutra mentions:[159]
>
> > One may rather be a Devadatta[160] than an Udraka Rāmaputra.[161]

This has the same meaning as the above statement [of the *Mahāparinirvāṇa Sutra*].

The *Solutions for Propagation* (T. 46: 254a, quoted above, p. 159) says: "How could one tolerate the breaking of precepts and call it the 'Buddha vehicle'?" This passage means that, however firm one may be with *yāna,* breaking *śīla* cannot be called the Buddha vehicle. How much less so with this Zen school? It does not seek for fulfillment in the distant future; it dares not expect some future benefit. It uses purifying precepts as skillful means. By drawing a poisoned arrow right before one's eyes, it expects the wonderful attainment of awakening immediately in this life. The *Sutra of the Bodhisattva Precepts for Practicing Good* (T. 30: 973b, quoted above, pp. 142, 153) says:

> Bodhisattvas, for the sake of awakening, practice *dhyāna,* enjoy delight in this life, and keep body and mind calm and composed—this is called benefiting oneself. Because of the tranquility of body and mind, they do not worry living beings. This is called benefiting others.

All that this passage means is a reward in a future life, which is the case with most of the schools of the Great Vehicle. In this respect, theirs is different from this school's intent. Their attainment cannot be considered very difficult. This Zen school, on the other hand, cuts through the devil's trap-net right before one's eyes. It seeks to be equal with the Tathāgata's practice. The *Sutra of the Bodhisattva Precepts for Practicing Good* (T. 30: 1005c) says:

> When the Buddha abides in *dhyāna,* no devils can find an opportune moment.

If someone has recourse to the remark, "One who is relaxed with *śīla* while firm with *yāna* will encounter a Buddha's lifetime," and favors breaking precepts, how is he any different from the one who carries a nugget of gold with him yet dies of hunger?

Besides, the passage from the *Great Calming and Contemplation,* "One who is relaxed with *śīla* will encounter a Buddha's lifetime," and the passage in the *Mahāparinirvāṇa Sutra,* "Being relaxed with *śīla* is not considered to be relaxed," are far from referring to those who break precepts and annul restraints. Those who commit grave sins are not said to be relaxed with *śīla;* they should be called breakers of *śīla.* So-called relaxation with *śīla* refers to the person who stops short of committing a minor offense. I say this because if one commits any of the four [grave offenses] or the five grave [transgressions], he will without fail fall into the hell of unremitting torture (Avīci). For him it will be impossible in any way to encounter a Buddha's lifetime. He who commits some minor sins will fall into the existence of a *nāga* or other beasts but in that existence he may feel so grateful for longevity that he will be able to encounter a Buddha's lifetime.

I sincerely hope you will abstain from using evil words, keep your body and mouth clean to follow the sincere truth of the noble teachings, keep your mind pure and clean to enter the wonderful gate of great compassion, and expect to attain Zen in this life. Does not the *Sutra of Śūraṃgama Practices* (T. 19: 131c; quoted above, p. 125) say:

> Practitioners of *dhyāna,* if they don't break off lust, will continue to transmigrate through the three evil modes of existence, unable to escape. It is like steaming grains of sand and gravel in the hope of cooking them into boiled rice; cooked for one hundred thousand *kalpa*s, they will still be [only] heated sand.

Someone says in rebuke: "The *Lotus Sutra* (T. 9, XI, 34b) says, 'If anyone holds this scriptural teaching, he will be called a precept holder. He will soon attain the Buddha's Way.' This passage means that he who is firm with *yāna* will attain awakening. [What is the use for further *śīla*?]"

This rebuke is wrong. We hear about being firm with *yāna,* whereas we have never heard of relaxation with *śīla*. What we understand by the above passage is only this: In the manner of perfect permeation, which leaves no room for artificiality, every being is originally endowed with *śīla*. It is on this basis that the holding of this scriptural teaching is mentioned. There cannot be any reason for acquiring the merit of *śīla* in reason while breaking *śīla* in phenomena. The Tiantai school's *Solutions for Propagation* (T. 46, IV–1, 254a, quoted above, pp. 159, 161) says, "How could one tolerate the breaking of precepts and call it the 'Buddha vehicle'?"

If anyone relies on the passage from the *Lotus Sutra,* "he is called a precept holder," and continues to violate *śīla* in phenomena, there cannot be any reason that reading the *Lotus Sutra* alone
will yield any expected result; it will be efficacious only for a dis- 14a
tant future. It is only through the practice of the contemplative gate of both phenomena and reason or, in other words, only with the application of both acupuncture and moxibustion, that the sick

are healed. The *Profound Meaning [of the Lotus Sutra]* (T. 33: II–1, 698b) says, "The eyes of wisdom and the legs of practice in unity will reach the pond clean and good."

The Tripiṭaka Dharma Master Yijing of Tang says [in his *Buddhist Monastic Traditions of Southern Asia*] (T. 54: 211c):

> People directly point to the gate of emptiness and regard it as the Buddha's real intent. However, they would rather know precepts also[162] to be the Buddha's intent. Their high valuation of one and low estimation of the other derive from mere assumption. While they never look into any text of *śīla* or related scriptures, they copy a couple of volumes of the gate of emptiness and insist that the reason [of emptiness] contains all three collections (Tripiṭaka) of Buddhist scriptures. They never think of the pain of thick, molten metal being poured down their throats. But that is the disaster they are inviting in this life at every step due to pretending to be monks, living clandestinely with other ordained monks.
>
> It is a bodhisattva's real determination not to let the floating bag of *śīla,* which helps one to cross the sea of birth and death, become deflated. One should not make little of a small transgression. Instead, one should join the Buddha's call made for our sake on his last day.[163] The truth of his call is that one should practice both the Great and Small [Vehicles], for this alone accords with the admonition of the Benevolent Honored One.
>
> Refraining from small transgressions while contemplating vast emptiness, accepting living beings while keeping oneself pure and clean—what fault could there be in doing this? All the eight myriad teachings of the [Great] Sage (i.e., the Buddha) will be summarized into one phrase or two: "Externally following secular ways while internally concentrating on true wisdom."
>
> The orthodox principle of Buddhism in the west regards keeping *śīla* as its basis. One should protect the floating bag

> from being punctured by even a small pinprick. One should be careful not to allow the great wrong of a needle hole. The very beginning of great wrong is blamable on improper ways of clothing and eating.
>
> To those who devote themselves to the Buddha's teachings, liberation is not a distant goal, whereas neglecting the Honored One's words will leave one long immersed in deep depravity.

It accords with the Buddha's immortal teachings on his deathbed for latter-day practitioners to trust in this practice. Those who follow it are really the Buddha's children.

The Tiantai school's *Solutions for Propagation* (T. 46, IV, 259a) says:

> In the world there are foolish people who insist that since the mind is free from birth everything that has its own characteristics is also free from generation, and who on that ground commit new sins. Committing crimes occurs necessarily through the three poisons [of greed, anger, and delusion]. A person who is really of no-birth will not make even a blessing, much less commit an offense. The reason is that both offenses and blessings follow the stream of birth and death.

Besides, the *Great Calming and Contemplation* (T. 46, IV–1, 41b) says:

> This is called penitence both in phenomena and reason. With the extinction of the offense that hinders awakening and with *śīla* kept clean and pure, self-concentration (*samādhi*) presents itself, opening up cessation and contemplation. Because the *śīla* in phenomena is kept clean, the root *samādhi* presents itself. Because the *śīla* that is none other than the Middle Way is kept clean, the king *samādhi* presents itself.

Commenting on this, the *Solutions for Propagation* (T. 46, IV–2, 262a) says:

> When "this is called" is mentioned, the author means this: If there were no *śīla* in phenomena, there cannot even be worldly *dhyāna*. How could there be the threefold truth [of emptiness, provisionality, and the Middle Way]? Wrong is the one who might insist, "In the Great Vehicle, why should one cling to *śīla*?"

Further, the same commentary says (T. 46, IV–1, 255b):

> You should know that no one can go without the Vinaya regulations against any of the [five] divisions of offenses or the [seven] groups of transgressions. As for those people of the world who despise phenomena and want only to value profound reason, they are certainly aloof, empty, and baseless in their practice of contemplation. Since they lack the objects of contemplation, contemplation will not follow.

The *Mahāparinirvāṇa Sutra* (T. 12, XVII, 467b) says:

> If anyone holds this scriptural teaching while violating precepts, he is kin to devils, far from being a disciple of mine. I won't allow him to hold and recite this scripture.

The *Lotus Sutra* (T. 9, II, 7c) says:

> Those whose practice of precepts has gaps and omissions cannot afford to hold this truth.

It also says in effect (T. 9, XIV, 37b):

> [Bodhisattvas] will not associate themselves with any of those who break precepts.

There should be no association with those who break precepts. How could any association be permissible with those who, while having recourse to the scriptural passage [in the *Lotus Sutra*] (T. 9, XI, 34b, quoted above, p. 163), "he will be called a precept holder," will violate precepts themselves? If anyone has recourse to the passage, "he is considered to be applying[164] himself toward the attainment of awakening," while wasting the four periods [of the day] or six periods [of the day and night] without practicing *dhyāna,* and if 14b anyone has recourse to the passage, "he is called a precept holder," while recklessly transgressing the fourfold or tenfold restraints, then such people will be transgressing the Great Vehicle, not to speak of going against the Small Vehicle, won't they?

The *Sutra of the Bodhisattva Precepts for Practicing Good* (T. 30, I, 962a) says:

> Then Mañjuśrī asked the Buddha, "The word *vinaya* means controlling and taming. Everything that has its own characteristics is ultimately under control in its self-nature. Why does the Buddha advocate *vinaya*?" The Buddha said, "If ordinary beings could realize that everything that has its own characteristics is ultimately under control, no Buddha would advocate *vinaya* at all. Because they don't realize that, Buddhas advocate *vinaya*."

The same scripture (T. 30, II, 969c) says:

> When igonorant people advocate the emptiness of all forms that have their own characteristics, they are committing grave transgressions. Even advocating something through explication for others' benefit through delusive[165] thoughts will also be a grave offense. Such will truly be disciples of a non-Buddhist path, such as Purāṇa [Kāśyapa]. Purāṇa insists that everything that has its own characteristics is nonexistent in its self-nature. But in the Buddha's teachings it is existent as well as nonexistent. If anyone advocates the emptiness of everything, you should know that he misses the mark. Abiding with such a person in the biweekly recitation of the Vinaya rules (*upoṣadha*) will cause grave sins. The reason is that he does not realize the meaning of emptiness. He is unable to benefit others, not to speak of benefiting himself.

When ordinary ignorant people like those described above delusively expound the meaning of emptiness while unable to hold precepts, they are non-Buddhists; they are people of the devil. The *Mahāparinirvāṇa Sutra* (T. 12: 467b, quoted above, p. 166) says: "He is kin to devils, far from being a disciple of mine."

That is why the Zen school strongly admonishes people to hold precepts; it expects them to attain the present-life benefit through a lifetime of effort. You should not, with shallow knowledge, speak of one as surpassing others and of another as falling short. Supposing that worldly talks and discussions lack real benefit, doctrinal arguments for or against either the Great or Small [Vehicle] will all be without benefit. Likewise, the perfect permeation free from artificiality, being orally expounded by one who does not realize it, is like a good taste and cool water that hungry and thirsty people talk about but which never enters their mouths and throats. It is also like the case of a rich man, who can recite a text on operating a boat but who cannot actually operate a boat, and who is drowned.

Herewith I have established the [seventh] gate, "Citing a General Principle and Exhorting People to Practice in the Zen School."

Gate VIII

By the eighth gate, "A List of the Essential Patterns of Activity in the Zen School," I mean the following ten, according to the *Chan School Monastic Rules* (*Zokuzōkyō* 2–16), as well as the prevalent "pattern of monastic activities" (*shi; shiki*) in the large countries.

1. Temples: Although they differ in size, all temples are modeled after the drawings of the Jetavana residence [of Śākyamuni and his disciples]; there are drawings of this residence separately.[166] A temple has corridors on four sides without any side gates. It has one gate alone. The single gate has door guardians, who close it at evening twilight and open it at daybreak. The door guardians check specifically nuns, laywomen, the destitute, and violent people and keep them from staying overnight in the temple. Destruction of the Buddha's teachings occurs solely through affairs with women and the like.

2. Ordination: Precepts, no matter whether of the Great or Small Vehicle, concern human passions. What matters here is only great compassion to benefit living beings. This Zen school has no preference in precepts as to whether of the Great or of the Small Vehicle. What it exclusively values is keeping morality with self-restraint (*brahmacaryā*).

3. Protecting morality: After ordination, if one does not protect morality but breaks it, then how could it be different from acquiring a gem but crushing it later? The *Chan School Monastic Rules* (*Zokuzōkyō* 2–16, I, 439a) says:

> After ordination one should constantly protect morality. You
> should prefer a moral death to an immoral life. Therefore, 14c
> mendicants should firmly hold their two hundred and fifty precepts, and lay way-seekers their threefold collection of purifying precepts, especially the ten weighty and the forty-eight less weighty precepts that constitute the first of the threefold collection (Tripiṭaka).

This being the case, [after ordination] one should follow the scriptural teaching on *śīla* and, on the occasion of *upoṣadha* assembly for recitation of the Vinaya rules every half-month, one should open oneself to the other practitioners. Violators of morality should be dismissed, like corpses in the great ocean, which does not allow them to remain on the bottom.

4. Scholarship: One whose learning covers all the eight treasuries and whose practice covers precepts of both vehicles; one who externally is possessed of the dignified demeanor of a sangha member (*bhikṣu*), which make him a field of merit (*puṇyakṣetra*) for humans and gods; one who internally keeps the bodhisattva's great compassion, which makes him a benevolent father for living beings—in such a person the emperor finds an important treasure and the country sees an excellent physician. Hence my wish for the flourishing [of the Zen school which produces such a person].

5. Regulations for conduct: In every kind of conduct, such as the longtime observance of one meal a day before noon, being

moderate in one's consumption of food, keeping temperance, and holding precepts with self-restraint, monks should obey the Buddha's words. What follows is the daily pattern of monastic activities:

The Time of Lighting at twilight, when monks gather at the Buddha hall to offer incense and worship;
The Time of Being in Calmness [9:00–11:00 P.M.], for *dhyāna* practice;
The Third Watch [11:00 P.M.–1:00 A.M.], for sleep;
The Fourth Watch [1:00–3:00 A.M.], for sleep;
The Fifth Watch [3:00–5:00 A.M.], for *dhyāna* practice;
The Time of the Hare [5:00–7:00 A.M.], same as twilight;
Daybreak, for taking gruel;
The Time of the Dragon [7:00–9:00 A.M.], for reading scriptures, studying, and listening to lectures by elder monks;
The Time of Yu (Gu) [9:00–11:00 A.M.], for *dhyāna* practice;
The Time of the Horse [12:00 P.M.], for taking a meal;
The Time of the Sheep [1:00–3:00 P.M.], for bathing and [attending to other personal matters];
The Time of the Monkey [3:00–5:00 P.M.], for *dhyāna* practice;
The Time of the Rooster [5:00–7:00 P.M.], for relaxation, released from work.

As you see, monks never slacken in their *dhyāna* practice, and moment after moment they repay their obligation to the state; in one period of practice after another they pray for the emperor's longevity. Indeed, they pray that the emperor's work for the people may long prosper and that the lamp of the Dharma may illuminate far and wide.

6. Impressive and dignified manner: Monks, both young and old, always wear the outer robe (*saṃghāṭī*) of either seven or nine strips of joined cloth. When they see one another, they first join their palms [in *gasshō*], lower their heads, and express their deep mutual amity and respect. While taking meals, walking in *dhyāna,* practicing [seated] *dhyāna,* studying, reading scriptures, and sleeping, they

never leave the community [of their fellow monks]. When a hundred or a thousand monks gather in a hall, all are careful of their deportment and their conduct toward others. If anyone's seat is empty, the steward monk will check [on the missing practitioner]. In this way, not even a minor transgression is allowed.

7. Clothing: For the upper and lower garments and the outer and inner ones, all monks should wear the Dharma robes used in the large countries. This is the bearing that best accords with "least desire and least material." Everything should be simplified.

8. The assembly of disciples: Those who are endowed with both morality and wisdom, and who possess the nonregressive mind at the beginning, should join the community. By all means they must be roundly endowed with the eyes [of wisdom] and the legs [of practice].

9. Benefiting and nourishing oneself: Monks don't engage in cultivating the land; *dhyāna* cultivation occupies them. They don't hoard property or treasures, for the Buddha's words are to be trusted. Except for a hot meal once a day, they cut off any other desire forever. The Dharma for mendicants is to have little desire and be content with one's lot.

10. The summer and winter retreats: On April 15 a summer retreat is formed, and it concludes on July 15. On October 15 a yearly [winter] retreat is undertaken, and it concludes on January 15. These two special retreats derive from the Buddha's original practice. They should be practiced with confidence. In our country this function has long been abolished, while in the Great Song monks have never dispensed with the two annual retreats. For one who has not come through special retreats, to count such a person's priestly age by the number of either of the two names, the "summer [retreat]" (*xia; ge*) or the "yearly [winter retreat]" (*la; rō*), is, in the Buddha's teaching, a laughable matter. 15a

The above descriptions of these ten items are [given in] outline only; details are given in "The Pattern of Monastic Activities" [current in the great state of Song].

Further, Zen temples have the following sixteen activities throughout the year:

1. The rite for the Emperor's Day: In the thirty days that precede the present emperor's birthday, sutras such as the *Mahāprajñāpāramitā Sutra, Benevolent King Sutra, Lotus Sutra,* and *Sutra of Golden Light* are recited every day, and prayers for the emperor's longevity are made.

2. Recitations: On the six days—the third, thirteenth, twenty-third, eighth, eighteenth, and twenty-eighth—of every month, there are rites for reciting the names of the ten Buddhas. This is to pray for the wind of the emperor's virtue to reach far, for the paths under the imperial reign to benefit long, for the Buddha-Dharma to unfold itself forever, and for living beings to have benefit far and wide. It is also to express gratitude to people for a donation even of a single piece of grass or leaf.

3. Rites for local gods: On the second and the sixteenth day of every month, the Dharma donation for local gods is conducted according to the places where the temples are located.

4. Requital for obligations: On the first day of every month, in respect for the present emperor, a lecture on the *Prajñāpāramitā Sutra* is given; and on the fifteenth, in respect for the previous emperor, a lecture on the *Mahāparinirvāṇa Sutra* is given. On both occasions prayers for protection of the gods are cited.

5. Monthly activities through the year: In January, an assembly for praising the arhats; in February, an assembly for making offerings to the Buddha's relics; in March, an assembly; in April, a celebration of the Buddha's birthday and of the beginning of the summer retreat; in May and June, lectures on the *Sutra of Golden Light;* in July, August, and September, lectures on the *Prajñāpāramitā Sutra;* in October, ordination; in November, the winter night activity; and in December, a great assembly for reciting the *Sutra of the Buddhas' Names.* Each activity has its [associated] rites.

6. Activities during retreat: Every day during the [summer and winter] retreats, along with other meetings, an assembly is held for reciting the *Sutra of Śūraṅgama Practices.*

7. Reciting Buddhist scriptures: Reciting one fascicle every day from the entire collection of the Buddhist scriptures, [which in the Song edition number as many as five thousand and forty-eight fascicles]. In a temple that has a hundred priests, the [entire collection of] Buddhist scriptures can be recited six times a year. Scriptures are recited when donors visit temples, for the donors' future merit, or for their prayers to be realized.

8. Activities in a mantra temple (i.e., a Shingon temple) [that is attached to a Zen temple]: Constant offerings are made to [the living beings of the] water and land—offerings for those in the unseen modes of existence. This is practiced so that donors may pray for bliss, for future merit, and for the deceased.

9. Activities in a calming and contemplation temple (i.e., a Tendai temple) [that is attached to a Zen temple]: Practices of self-concentration (*samādhi*) are performed, based on such sutras as the *Lotus Sutra,* the *Contemplation Sutra,* and the *Invitation of Bodhisattva Avalokiteśvara.*

10. Visiting the master's room: On the day when the master has leisure time, disciples visit him in succession in his room. For the Zen school this is a most important matter. The manner for doing this should be examined [in the *Chan School Monastic Rules*].

11. *Upoṣadha:* The biweekly recitation of the Vinaya rules continues as usual.

12. Inspection of the monks' official quarters: Once every five days each month, an elder monk gives admonition from the platform and then inspects the monks' official quarters. In the past the Tathāgata, for the sake of five matters, made an inspection of the monks' cells every five days. For "five matters," refer to the [relevant] Vinaya passages.[167]

13. Bathing: As an official duty or at a donor's expense, monks bathe every five days; in hot months, they bathe every day.

14. Meals served in memory of the deceased: For the sake of the previous emperor, the previous master, or deceased parents, [special] meals are served. There are rules for this.

15. Government-sponsored memorials: Ministers and nobili-
15b ties serve meals to monks. When government officals visit a temple, there are specific rites to follow.

16. Turning [the wheel of] the scriptural collection: An assembly of monks play festival music and turn a wheel with eight spokes, which holds the entire collection of Buddhist scriptures.

Question: Such regulations for conduct seem beyond the capacity of people of the latter-day world. They may instead cause practitioners to worry and regress. What do you think about this?

Answer: The teachings of the Buddha-Dharma are extremely easy to practice, easy to realize. The Buddha said, "This is the truth of bliss and stability."[168] The *Treatise on the Treasury of Analyzed Concepts of Buddhism* (T. 29, I, 2c) says in verse:

> Sangha members in harmony feel joy;
> All sharing austerities, they rejoice.

When men and women of the world see their parents' abilities, they think only of acquiring them. Sparing no effort, they succeed in inheriting their familial skills. Because of this, blacksmiths, tilers, weavers, magicians, farmers, and the like see their successors continue. Theirs, however, is painful and assiduous labor. Meanwhile, the skills inherited by the Buddha's heirs is "the truth of bliss and stability." It is unlike those worldly trades in which people [exert much effort], smashing their bones. Having a special liking for something, however, will in turn yield attachment to that particular matter. One who inhabits a big river and exercises vigorously there will, upon climbing up onto land, feel ill at ease. One that abides in the air and freely flies will be helpless on the ground. Likewise, one who has had comfort dwelling in the house of Buddhism will, on entering lay life, become troubled. Those who have been stained by and attached to evil acts will consider the teachings of the Buddha-Dharma to be extremely hard to practice.

The Great Master of Mount Kōya (Kūkai, Kōbō Daishi) says in his *Three Teachings Pointing to Where to Return* (*Kōbō-daishi Zenshū,* fasc. 9, 327):

> Going to where one likes is like a stone thrown into water.
> Going to where one dislikes is like oil poured on water.

Those living beings who are lost in ignorance regard suffering as something delightful. The Buddha said [in the *Lotus Sutra*] (T. 9, II, 9b):

> Deeply attached to the five desires,
> They behave like a yak that loves its tail.
> Deeply infatuated by evil views,
> They take suffering to discard suffering.
> For the sake of these living beings
> I give rise to great compassion.

This is not the case with the Buddha-Dharma. When one holds[169] precepts in clean practice, in body and mind one abides in bliss and stability. The *Bequeathed Teaching Sutra* says:[170]

> When your body is in comfort, the Way flourishes. For drinking and eating you should know the moderate measure.

One should deliberate on what this means. The Buddha's disciples, no longer inheriting the teachings of the Buddha-Dharma, can be likened to lion cubs that have grown into sheep or cats, can't they? They would also be like farmer's children who have gone mad, or weaver's children who have become prostitutes, wouldn't they? Worldly occupations with good successors will have richness and beauty that exceed the previous ones. The Buddha's teachings, having been exterminated, would leave idleness and indolence beyond sick children's endurance. The present-day offspring of the Buddha are compared to those farmers and the like who have failed to take up their family trade. When such people want to eat rice, they must instead eat sandy mud. When they want to put on a robe, they have to don a piece of bark.

[Herewith I have established the [eighth] gate, "A List of the Essential Patterns of Activity in the Zen School."]

Gate IX

By the ninth gate, "Information from the Large Countries," I mean that by mentioning the manner of practice now prevailing in India and China, I wish to have people of faith and practice enter the great sea of the Buddha's teachings. Concerning the Buddhist situation in India, I have heard the following four points:

1. At the harbor of Hakata,[171] Chikuzen Province, Chinzei (i.e., Kyushu), an interpreter for the two royal courts, Li Dezhao (Ri
15c Tokushō), then eighty years old, told me, "When I was over twenty years old, I saw a monk from India in Dongjing.[172] He wore a single undergarment and an upper *kaṣāya* robe. Even in the painful cold of winter he didn't wear any other clothes. The next spring before he returned to India he said to me, 'If I were to stay here, I would violate the Buddha's rules.'"

This was in Qiandao (Kendō) the fourth year of Song, the third year of Nin'an in Japan, *wuzi, tsuchinoe-ne* (1168).[173]

2. A monk from Chengdufu (Seitofu) told me, "In the first year of Chunxi (Junki), *jiawu, kinoe-uma* (1174) a monk from India, who was high-spirited and resourceful, came to Lizhou.[174] When he recited mysterious magical words his mouth emitted light, and those who heard [his words] were cured of disease. He wore a single undergarment and an unlined robe. In the winter months of extreme cold, he refused a cotton robe offered by the other monks, insisting that it was not permitted by the Buddha. Afraid of violating the monastic rules, he returned to India the following spring." I heard this in Shaoxi (Shōki) the first year of Song; the first year of Kenkyū in Japan, *gengchu, kanoe-inu* (1190).[175]

3. A monk from Guangfu told me, "Between China and more than fifty provinces of Kunlun (Konron) [on the South Asian Sea], there has been more and more oceangoing traffic year after year. At times Buddhist monks come from those places. They wear rings

pierced through the ears. They wear a single undergarment and an unlined robe, roughly the same as the monks from India. In the winter months they don't wear cotton clothes. When they see the observances of Chinese monks, they don't praise them."

4. The revered master Zuyong (Soei) of Xiuchansi on Mount Tiantai (present-day Dacisi; Daijiji) told me, "I hear that in Vaiśālī, India, there still stands Layman Vimalakīrti's room, the size of a square *zhang* (*hōjō*). Monks from the South Asian Sea continually make a pilgrimage to the place below the *bodhi* tree and worship the image of Bodhisattva Avalokiteśvara. In Nālandā Temple there are five thousand monks, most of whom recite the Tripiṭaka texts. There are also the Buddha's bowl and Śānavāsin's robe. Many people go on pilgrimage to where the eight memorable stupas stand."

All these belong to the contemporary age.

In the Song dynasty twenty miracles have been cited:

1. A monk from Weinan (Wainan) told me, "On Mount Qingliang (Shōryō, of Wutaishan; Godaisan) Mañjuśrī appeared riding a lion."

2. In Mount Tiantai at times live arhats appear, whose traces also emit light.

3. At the stone bridge (in Mount Tiantai) blue dragons appear, and when they do, it rains.

4. The holy traces such as those in Guoqing (Kokusei) Temple[176] still remain in dignity.

5. The Buddha's relics preserved in the temple in Mount Yuwang (Ikuō) emit light.

6. In Mount Yuwang eels appear, and as soon as they appear, it rains.

7. Monks maintain a dignified posture at all times.

8. Inside the temples it is calm and silent.

9. There are many who reduce themselves to ashes (i.e., die in *samādhi*). In the spring of Chunxi (Junki) the sixteenth year, *jiyou, tsuchinoto-tori* (1190) a monk of Xiangtian (Shōden) Temple reduced himself to ashes in *samādhi*. It is now the tenth year since then.

10. Among monks, many know when they are going to die.

11. Laypeople hold the precepts of the bodhisattva restraints.

12. Young novices hold the five precepts.

13. Both laity and clergy are selfless.

14. In Mount Dongye (Tōekizan), Bodhisattva Samantabhadra emits light.

15. The Buddha hall in each temple looks as if a living Buddha abides there.

16. The storehouses for Buddhist scriptures and monks' halls look as dignified as in the Pure Land.

17. Emperors are unfailingly ordained in the bodhisattva restraints.

18. No monks possess or cultivate rice fields.

19. Animals are often observed to have human sentiments.

20. Government laws are never perverted to wrong the people.

People in Japan, nevertheless, tend to refer to their favorite saying, "In India and China the Buddha's teachings have already been extinguished. They flourish only in Japan."

[According to the *Great Tang Dynasty Record of the Western Regions,*] after the passing away of the Tathāgata monarchs of
16a various countries were afraid that the "diamond seat"[177] would be buried, so they had the seat marked with boundaries and had two statues of Bodhisattva Avalokiteśvara built nearby. [According to the *Record of the Transmission of the Dharma Treasury*] (T. 50: 303c–304b), Śānavāsin, the Third Patriarch who transmitted the Buddha-Dharma to his successor, had a robe he had worn since being an embryo, and which had grown together with him after his birth. This natural robe has been preserved by mysterious power for the sake of people's faith in the Dharma. [According to the *Great Tang Dynasty Record of the Western Regions*] (T. 51, VIII, 915b), when Xuanzang visited the two sites, the Avalokiteśvara statues [near the diamond seat in Magadha] were buried half up to their chests; and (T. 51, I, 873b) a small part of Śānavāsin's robe [in Bāmiyān] had become tattered.

Xuanzang's pilgrimage to India was during the years of Zhenguan (Jōkan) (627–49) of the Tang;[178] it was sixteen hundred years after the Tathāgata passed away. The Tathāgata had been dead more than a thousand years when the statues had become half-buried and a small portion of the robe had become tattered. Now it is only four hundred and some years after Xuanzang's observation. How could they all be extinguished now? How laughable people here are in their lack of estimation!

The *Sutra of the Original Practice* says:[179]

> In the midland, under the *bodhi* tree, when a Buddha does not appear, a sage appears. When no sage appears, a god of great strength abides.

The *Mahāprajñāpāramitā Sutra* (T. 5, CIII, 570b) says:

> No matter whether man or beast enters the hut under the *bodhi* tree, no ghosts can find an opportunity to attack them.

A sutra says (unidentified):

> Tribes that lack virtue are not born in the midland.

The *Sutra of the Original Practice* says:

> Buddhas will not be born in borderlands; they will be born without fail in the midland.

The *Sutra on [the Prince Coming into Being with] Auspicious Responses* (T. 3, I, 473b) says:

> Kapilavastu is in the center of the three thousand worlds that have their own sun and moon, and of the twelve thousand heavens and earths. The reason is that the dignity of the Buddha made it impossible for him to be born in a borderland.

In the midland of India, the Tathāgata attained awakening (*bodhi*) under a tree. There remains the diamond seat at the very site. In such a holy land, how could the Buddha's teachings not be alive now? Indeed, what Eisai heard directly from people while staying in China must tally with the actual situation in India.

Question: According to what has been mentioned, the Buddha's teachings vigorously flourish in India and China. Now I wonder if there are people who have attained the fruit of practice.

Answer: As I have seen with my own eyes and heard with my own ears, there are those in China who reduce themselves to ashes in *samādhi,* just as those in India, mentioned above.

Question: If that is the case, will Japan also have such people?

Answer: Yes, there must be.

[*Question:*] Here is a criticism against this kind of answer: "India and China are supremely holy lands. There may appear those whose pure fruits of practice will mature to the attainment of awakening. Japan is just a borderland. Tribes that lack virtue reside here. Therefore, it is extremely difficult to have such attainers of awakening. Besides, people lack the practice of *śīla*. This makes things more difficult for them, doesn't it?"

Answer: The *Mahāprajñāpāramitā Sutra* (T. 6: 539ab, quoted above, pp. 78, 83) says:

> [A]fter my death, in the last time, on the last occasion, in the last five hundred-year period when my teachings are lost, a scripture [like this] will play a great part in helping people attain awakening in the direction of northeast [as well].

In the direction of the northeast is the land of Japan. There has been no dislike of this borderland, has there? As for *śīla* and *vinaya,* keeping the two hundred and fifty precepts of the Buddha's day ought to be equivalent to refraining from committing the four grave offenses in the latter-day world, far distant from the time of his *parinirvāṇa*. The *Record of the Transmission of the Dharma Treasury* (T. 50: 307ab) says:[180]

> A nun of one hunded and twenty years' age compared a group of six evil mendicants with Upagupta. Upagupta, then, felt much ashamed. The nun said, "Revered monk, you should not feel ashamed or regretful. The Buddha said, 'After my death, people of the first day will be better than [those] of the 16b
> second day, while people of the third day will be far meaner. This will continue until their beneficial virtue diminishes, their ignorance and dullness increase, and their good nature decreases.' Reverend monk, it has been one hundred years since the Buddha's *parinirvāṇa*. Even if people do things unworthy of the Buddha's disciples, this is only natural. How could it be strange?"

This being the case, the fruit of attaining awakening, the extinction of the self-afflicting passions (*āsravakṣaya*), won't necessarily depend on the dignity of one's demeanor; what is required is just the eagerly attentive, real cultivation.

In Central India monks go through the year in an unlined robe. In other places they don't. In China and Japan monks wear lay garments, yet their attainment of the truth is the same in nature. The efficacy with which their attainment works on others is also no different.

By "lay garments" I mean those other than the three robes for monks. The lay garments, which the Buddha prohibited monks from wearing, were two-shouldered robes, vests, and other [such clothing]. In cold districts, however, there was a robe permitted by the Buddha: the *repa,*[181] which is called the "waist robe" here. The cold of our land cannot be as terrible as that of Bāmiyān of the Himālayas, where snowflakes fly in June. And yet [monks in Bāmiyān] wear a waist robe alone! Both Xuanzang and Yijing saw this on their pilgrimages.

Meanwhile, in China, the great masters Nanyue (Huisi; Nangaku Eshi, 515–77) and Tiantai (Zhiyi; Tendai Chigi, 531–97) attained the fivefold [preliminary] stage [on the way to ultimate awakening], and the sixfold [second stage, namely] purification of the six sense perceptions, [on the way toward ultimate awakening], respectively. In Japan Kōkei (977–1049) and his disciple En'in (d. 1050) worked miracles, which surprised heavenly and earthly gods as well as humans, and they all wore lay garments. Although they did not show the dignity of uncovering the right shoulder [and kneeling on the right knee], they kept all the precepts in their practice. That is why they attained such excellent fruits.

Recently I heard about a monk named Kakuben, of Ōjōin Temple, Yamada-gun, Iga Province, Japan. Kakuben lectured on the *Mahāparinirvāṇa Sutra* from the platform. When he finished talking about Daosheng, a Chinese Buddhist who had endured death[182] [before he had a scriptural verification of his view that there should be no exception for attaining awakening], Kakuben entered into final calmness on the platform [just as Daosheng had done]. Since no one knows of this, it has not been recognized how miraculous it was. However, the *Essentials of the Single Vehicle* (T. 74, III, 351a) [praises Kakubenand] says:

> Throughout the whole country of Japan people's capacity for the perfect teaching has reached maturity; both officials and the public, those living near the capital and in remote areas, all have taken shelter in the One Vehicle.

Besides, this country, considering its physical features, is peerless, and the Three Treasures of Buddhism have vigorously flourished [here]. If people dedicate themselves to holding the Buddhist morality, have deep confidence in their true way of being, and cultivate the dignity of the Buddha, how could it be in vain? A layman of the Great Song named Wenbo (Bunhaku), who abides in Mount Emei (Gabisan), praised Japan, saying:

> Who would divide that land from this land? Separating them is a short distance. Shining with sixty-six provinces (*zhou; shū*), the land extends over three thousand *li*. Its mountains are mines of diamonds inexhaustible. Gems that are abundant adorn the earth. The Four [Noble] Truths pervade the

> people's attention. The triple Buddha image is set up deep and quiet. I look up casually, and see all this. Why do I wait for my legs to carry me there? Take good care of yourself.

This being the case, this land is a holy place, where the Buddha's teachings pervade. If you practice Zen assiduously and seriously, the Tathāgata will certainly be pleased; your attainment of the fruit will also be realized. I hope that you will stop arguing about whether the Buddha's teachings are flourishing or have declined in India and China, and will only cultivate the realization of selflessness, so that you will be able to let the Buddha's teachings flourish in this country.

Concerning the Buddha's teachings, the *Sutra on the [Excellence of] the Donation of a Lamp Fire* (T. 16: 803c) says:

> The Buddha has four kinds of excellent, living, good teachings: 1) *śīla,* 2) *dhyāna,* 3) *prajñā,* and 4) the Mind that is free of defilement.

Among these four, *dhyāna* comes first, because it comprehends 16c
all. The Tiantai school's *Great Calming and Contemplation* (T. 46: 39c; quoted above, pp. 111, 143) says:

> The *Sutra on the Most Wondrous Supreme Dhyāna* says: "Transgressors of the four grave offenses and the five grave transgressions will, except for [*dhyāna*], have no way to be saved."

To extinguish sins, *dhyāna* is essential. Giving rise to good is also [accomplished] through the power of *dhyāna.* The *Mahāprajñāpāramitā Treatise* says in effect:[183]

> Although the three vehicles have different spheres of activity, their attainment necessarily makes use of the power of *dhyāna* that is free from discrimination.

Since this is the case, the traditional eight schools of Buddhism, despite their differing spheres of activity, must always apply *dhyāna* to reach their respective attainments. The same is true with the practice of *chengming* (*shōmyō*) and *nianfo* (*nembutsu*),[184] for except for *dhyāna* nothing else would establish a practice for immediate fruition in the next life.

For this reason, when I think of the physical features of this land, considering the latter-day world, pitying the naivety of the people, and remembering the paths trodden by the patriarchs, I earnestly desire to make flourish what has been abandoned. Nevertheless, evil conditions of various kinds obstruct me from realizing this. Even some Buddhists, out of jealousy, want to suppress it. I wonder if I should give up this land now. The [*Great*] *Heap of Jewels Sutra* (T. 11, Vol. 92, 529a) says:

> Where there is talk just for the sake of talk, controversy just for the sake of controversy, there arise many self-afflicting passions. Wise people should keep away from such occasions; they should stay a hundred *yojana*s away from such places.

In the western seat of our government[185] is a person who reproaches me; in the eastern capital there are people who stand in my way. While I want to avoid them both, I have no place to go [that is] a hundred *yojana*s away from either of them. I want to examine myself critically but I am far from being a wise person. What should I do in this situation? I might have to cross the vast sea again to conceal my traces in the clouds of Mount Tiantai. But my only regret is that I shall give up benefiting my native land to share in the benefit of Dharma water in a foreign land. *An Approach to Truth through the Samādhi Called No Polemics*[186] (T. 46: 630a) says:

> If somone should praise themselves as a person of great wisdom and despise all the practitioners of *dhyāna,* it is comparable to killing humans of the three thousand great worlds, though the gravity of this offense even surpasses the latter.

Evil[187] persons who may stand in my way will naturally commit this transgression; they will be useless to the imperial court and the state. My wrongly being accused of being the root source of this is a most lamentable matter.

Herewith I have established the [ninth] gate, "Information from the Large Countries."

Gate X

By the tenth gate, "Merit Transference and Making Vows," I mean what follows.

The *Mahāprajñāpāramitā Sutra* (T. 7, fasc. 543, 794c) says:

> Subhūti answered Maitreya, saying, "Speaking of those men and women of noble mind who abide in the bodhisattva vehicle, who practice the profound perfection of the knowledge of emptiness (*prajñāpāramitā*), I would say this: If they want not to reproach the Buddha but to transfer merit to other beings, they should think in this way: 'Tathāgatas are really worthy of offerings; they have attained ultimate awakening. Just as the Tathāgatas, with their unhindered awakened eyes, penetratively realize, thoroughly know, that meritorious roots of virtue have such a nature, such a characteristic, and such content as is worth rejoicing, so also should I rejoice at the roots of virtue. Tathāgatas are really worthy of offerings; they have attained ultimate awakening. Just as the Tathāgatas, with their unhindered awakened eyes, penetratively realize, thoroughly know, that one should transfer such acts of merit toward the attainment of unsurpassed ultimate awakening, so also should I practice such transference.'"
>
> The Buddha praised Subhūti and said, "Very good. . . ."
>
> And even[188] this was said:[189] "Who does the transference? What is transferred? Where is the transference directed? With the three wheels free from discrimination, being free from any expectation, let me, equally with other living beings, transfer this root of virtue toward unsurpassed ultimate awakening (*anuttarā samyaksaṃbodhi*)."

The same sutra says (T. 6, vol. 331, 695c):

17a A bodhisattva *mahāsattva* ("great being"), who observes living beings suffering from all kinds of diseases, will make this vow: "I should make assiduous effort, without looking back on my physical life, cultivate the six kinds of perfection (*pāramitā*s), bring beings to maturity, ultimately purify the Buddha land, and quicken the consummate attainment of unsurpassed ultimate awakening. In our Buddha land all living beings should cleanse and purify their bodies and minds and be free from the suffering of any disease, even to the extent that no one hears the names of painful diseases. Making full use of these six kinds of perfection, I should cause every being to approach unsurpassed ultimate awakening."

Therefore, I am now going to do merit transference as is stated in the sutra, make a similar vow, come across the knowledge of emptiness in one life after another, in this world after that, cultivate the supreme truth of the Tathāgata's *dhyāna*, work together with all living beings to cultivate the means of great compassion, and never become weary throughout the future.

The ten gates of the *Treatise on Letting Zen Flourish to Protect the State* have been generally explained.

Basically, the Buddha-Dharma does not itself speak out; it assumes scriptural expressions to manifest its teachings. Originally *dhyāna* has no intent to introduce itself; it actualizes itself only through our self-concentration (*samādhi*). Therefore, the expressions by which people characterize Zen, such as "the hair of a tortoise" or "the horns of a hare," naturally reveal the living principle that is hard to be manifested, whereas the awakened truth of mind that is free from mind (*wuxin; mushin*) or from thought (*wunian; munen*), profoundly accords with the One Mind, the innermost shrine. The purpose of this treatise is to state this meaning of the awakened truth and to let the Buddha's teachings flourish.

I am afraid that there might be differences between the passages as they were quoted according to my understanding from the sutras, *śāstras*, and their commentaries, and the original texts themselves. I might also be mistaken in quoting their titles. The reason is that I have quoted them from memory. My mistakes may not be limited just to passages and my understanding of their meanings. I am afraid that there might be discord beween a truth and its expression. Notwithstanding all such possible mistakes, a certain revered ancient (unidentified) remarks thus:

> Since I quote without the original text near at hand, I might give a wrong title. But even if the title may be wrongly quoted, how could this mean the corruption of the content?

I hope my readers will be kind enough to correct wrong quotations, if there are any.

End of Fascicle Three

A Note on the Future

[By Eisai]

On 23 August, the eighth year of Kenkyū, *teishi* (*dingsi, hinoto-mi,* 1197)[190] a man named Zhang Guoan (Chō Kokuan) came from Hakata[191] Harbor, Chinzei (Kyushu), and related the following:

> In July of Qiandao (Kendō) the ninth year of the Great Song, Jōan the third year in Japan, *guisi* (*mizunoto-mi,* 1173), I reached Lin'anfu (the present capital), visited Lingyin (Rinnin) Temple, and personally met the presiding priest, Chan Master Fohai (Fohai Huiyuan; Bukkai Eon, 1103–76).[192] The master gave a sermon from the high seat, and said to me, "Twenty years after I die, the Dharma will pervade the entire world. As it is said, the sun after rising goes to the west; in the west it inevitably enters the western mountains. Then the tide surges to return to the east. On returning east, it necessarily flows and empties into the eastern sea. So, how can the Buddha-Dharma that advances to the east not reach the land of Japan? This being the case, there will be an elder monk from the eastern sea who will come to the west and transmit the Chan principle. This will never be false. You may return to your native place and tell others what I have said. Now I see you; you also see me. On the thirteenth of January next year, I shall quit the world. When you come here next time, you will hear my name alone. Please keep in mind what you have heard today. Favored by my karma from my former lives, I have seen you and talked about the per- 17b
> vasion of the Buddha-Dharma in Japan. You may remember this and try not to forget it."
>
> I, Guoan, myself took leave of the master and went to my native place. In April the next year I crossed the sea to China,

> and on coming to the temple asked about the master. I was told that he had passed away peacefully on the thirteenth of January, just as the master had told me the previous year.[193] Chan Master Fozhao[194] received the imperial mandate, succeeded the seat, and held a feast for the priests in answering obligations from the state. I, Guoan, attended the assembly and stated my wishes to show gratitude to the previous master. Chan Master Fozhao praised this, and said, "You have come traveling across the sea from afar, to repay the master's favor."

Now, Chan Master Fohai was a man who had seen the truth of no-birth. He knew what was coming in the future very well. I, Eisai, myself have already been there, had the Dharma transmitted to me, and returned home. Unworthy as I am, there already was a coincidence. I wonder who Master Fohai could have predicted except for me. No other person crossed the sea. Of the ignorant person who had arrived there, however, what could be expected? May a person of wisdom look into the matter! It was eighteen years after Chan Master Fohai made the prediction (in 1173) when I crossed the Sea of Penglai (Hōrai)[195] to return home [in 1191]. How . . .[196] the marvelous prediction was! Turning my thoughts to the future, I am convinced that the principle of the Zen school will never diminish or die out. Fifty years after I leave the world, this school will certainly flourish most vigorously. Prompted by this thought, I, Eisai, write this.

End of A Note on the Future

[Postcript] 17b14

[By Kōhō Tōshun, Compiler of the *Treatise on Letting Zen Flourish to Protect the State*]

The three fascicles of the *Treatise,* which have undergone copying several times, cannot be exempt from the ambiguity of the printing process, such as the difficulty of distinguishing certain characters. This is much more so the case as these texts have passed through many years.

I once collected several copies of the old [Kanmon] edition to make a revised one. I also examined the original expressions of the sutras and *śāstra*s quoted in the text. I discovered that letters and phrases that had been left out or were erroneous were many more than one or two, so I revised them. Of those that I had had no means to check, I marked them as doubtful.

Now I have come to the end of the work. Although I lack the ability to do it well, it may not be that I have supplied not even one missing word out of ten thousand. I was afraid the print might be blotted out if I were to continue storing [the text] in a case. This was why I put it into the engraver's hands. I hope what remains incomplete in the present edition will undergo further correction by later people.

[Written] in the spring, the second month of An'ei, *tsuchinoe-inu* (1778), sincerely noted by Bhikṣu Tōshun, Descendant of the Founding Master of Kenninji.

Appendix

List of Works Cited in the *Treatise on Letting Zen Flourish to Protect the State*

The number before each title shows the order in which the text is first cited in this translation of the *Treatise*. These numbers also appear in the endnotes to ease identification and cross-referencing. Each listing includes all or some of the following information: English title used in the translation; English title in full, when applicable; Sanskrit title, when applicable (* asterisk denotes provisional Sanskritization); romanized Chinese and/or Japanese title; name of author or translator; date of publication, when known; and collection reference number.

1. *Sixfold Prajñāpāramitā Sutra; The Buddha's Teaching in a Scripture Called the Sixfold Perfection on the Ground of the Great Vehicle; Mahāyāna-yuktiprajñāpāramitā-sūtra; Dashengliquliuboluomiduojing; Daijōrishu-ropparamittakyō*
Translated by Prajñā, 788, ten fascicles
Taishō Vol. 8, No. 261

2. *Mahāprajñāpāramitā Treatise; A Commentary on the Buddha's Teaching in a Scripture Called Perfection of the Knowledge of Emptiness; Mahā-prajñāpāramitā-śāstra; Dazhidulun; Daichidoron*
Translated by Kumārajīva, 405, one hundred fascicles
Taishō Vol. 25, No. 1509

3. *Chan School Monastic Rules; Monastic Rules for the Chan School; Chan-yuanqinggui; Zen'onshingi*
Compiled by Zongze (Sōsaku), 1103, ten fascicles
Zokuzōkyō 2–16

4. *Vinaya in Four Divisions; The Collection of Monastic Precepts in Four Divisions; Dharmaguptaka-vinaya; Sifenlü; Shibunritsu*
Translated by Buddhayaśas with Buddhasmṛti, 410–12, sixty fascicles
Taishō Vol. 22, No. 1428

5. *Brahmā Net Sutra on the Bodhisattva Śīla; The Buddha Vairocana's Teaching on the Moral Conduct of Bodhisattvas in a Scripture Called the Brahmā Deity's Net; Fanwangpusajiejing; Bonmōbosatsukaikyō*
Translation ascribed to Kumārajīva, but believed to be a Chinese work of the Liu Song dynasty, 420–79, two fascicles
Taishō Vol. 24, No. 1484

6. *Mahāparinirvāṇa Sutra; The Buddha's Teaching in a Great Vehicle Scripture Called Great Death; Mahāparinirvāṇamahāyāna-sūtra; Dabanniepanjing; Daihatsunehangyō*
Translated by Dharmakṣema (385–433), forty fascicles
Taishō Vol. 12, No. 374
Beijing Tibetan Tripiṭaka Vol. 31, No. 788

7. *Mahāsāṃghika Vinaya; Monastic Precepts of the Mahāsāṃghika School; Mahāsāṃghika-vinaya; Mohesengqilü; Makasōgiritsu*
Translated by Faxian and Buddhabhadra, 416–8, forty fascicles
Taishō Vol. 22, No. 1425

8. *Buddha Treasury Sutra; The Buddha's Teaching in a Scripture Called the Buddha's Treasury of the Dharma; Buddhakoṣadharmavyañjana; Fozangjing; Butsuzōkyō*
Translated by Kumārajīva, three fascicles
Taishō Vol. 15, No. 653
Beijing Tibetan Tripiṭaka Vol. 31, No. 791

9. *Sutra of the Benevolent King; The Buddha's Teaching in a Scripture Called the Benevolent King's Inquiry on Perfection of the Knowledge of Emptiness; *Kāruṇikārājaprajñāpāramitā-sūtra; Renwangwenbanruoboluomijing; Ninnōmonhannnyaharamitsukyō*
Translated by Kumārajīva (344–413), two fascicles
Taishō Vol. 8, No. 245

10. *Mahāprajñāpāramitā Sutra; The Buddha's Teaching in a Great Vehicle Scripture Called Perfection of the Knowledge of Emptiness; Mahāprajñā-pāramitā-sūtra; Dabanruoboluomiduojing; Daihannyaharamittakyō*
Translated by Xuanzang, 660–3, six hundred fascicles
Taishō Vols. 5–7, No. 220

11. *Great Dharma Torch Dhāraṇī Sutra; The Buddha's Teaching in a Scripture Called the Dhāraṇī of the Great Dharma Torch; Dafajutuoluonijing; Daihōkodaranikyō*
Translated by Jñānagupta (561–600), twenty fascicles
Taishō Vol. 21, No. 1340

12. *Supreme Deity King's Prajñāpāramitā Sutra; The Buddha's Teaching in a Scripture Called the Supreme Deity King's Proposition of the Perfection of the Knowledge of Emptiness; Shengtianwangbanruoboluomijing; Shōtennō-hannyaharamitsukyō*
Translated by Upaśūnya, 565, seven fascicles
Taishō Vol. 8, No. 231

13. *Sutra of Forty-two Sections; The Buddha's Admonitions in Forty-two Sections; Sishierzhangjing; Shijūnishōkyō*
A complete text was quoted at the beginning of the *Baolinzhuan* (*Hōrinden*), a Chan school's record of transmission compiled in the Tang dynasty around 801. The text cited here is a recompiled version of the preceding text of the same title, Taishō Vol. 17, No. 784.
Translated into Chinese by Kāśyapa-Mātaṅga and Dharmarakṣa, ca. first century C.E.
Zokuzōkyō 1–59
English translation by Heng-ching Shih, in the volume *Apocryphal Scriptures* (Numata Center, 2005)

14. *Sutra of Śūraṃgama Practices; The Buddha's Teaching in a Fully Developed Scripture Called the Bodhisattvas' Myriad Practices of Heroic Advance for Attaining the Cause, the Tathāgata's Secret on the Buddha's Uṣṇīṣa; Shoulengyanjing; Shuryōgonkyō*
Believed to be a Chinese compilation, ten fascicles
Taishō Vol. 19, No. 945

15. *Official Document Presented to the Emperor; Chishō-daishikyō*
Enchin (814–91), who studied in China for five years (851–55), brought to completion the Tendai esoteric teaching. The whereabouts of this text are unknown.

16. *Sutra on the Abiding of the Dharma; The Buddha's Prediction on His Deathbed of the Abiding among Latter-day People of the Dharma He Had Propagated; Folinniepanjifazhujing; Butsurinnehankihōjūkyō*
Translated by Xuanzang, one fascicle
Taishō Vol. 12, No. 390

17. *Middle Treatise; Piṅgala's Commentary on Nāgārjuna's Verses on the Root Middle; Madhyamaka-kārikā; Zhonglun Qingmuzhu; Chūron Shōmokuchū*
Nāgārjuna's *Mūlamadhyamaka-kārikā,* with a commentary by Piṅgala.
Translated by Kumārajīva, 409, four fascicles
Taishō Vol. 30, No. 1564

18. *Elucidatory Comments; An Elucidation of and Brief Comments on Master Zhiyi's Treatise: The Profound Meaning of the Saddharmapuṇḍarīka-sūtra; Tiantaizong Fahuaxuanyishiqian; Tendaishū Hokkegengishakusen*
Jingxi Zhanran (Keikei Tannen, 711–782), twenty fascicles
Taishō Vol. 33, No. 1717

19. *Lotus Sutra; The Buddha's Teaching in a Scripture Called the Living Dharma White Lotus Flower; Saddharmapuṇḍarīka-sūtra; Miaofalianhuajing; Myōhōrengekyō*
Translated by Kumārajīva, 406, seven fascicles
Taishō Vol. 9, No. 262

20. *Solutions for Propagation; A Commentary on Master Zhiyi's Great Calming and Contemplation (Mohezhiguan), with the title Giving Solutions to Problems in Helping and Propagating the Great Practices of Calming and Contemplation; Tiantaizong Zhiguanfuxingzhuanhongjue; Shikanfugyōdenguketsu*
By Zhanran, ten fascicles
Taishō Vol. 46, No. 1912

21. *Calming and Contemplation: Their Meaning and Examples; Meaning and Examples of Master Zhiyi's Calming and Comtemplation; Zhiguanyili; Shikangirei*
By Zhanran, two fascicles
Taishō Vol. 46, No. 1913

22. *Words and Phrases in the Lotus Sutra; Miaofalianhuajing Wenju; Myōhōrengekyō Mongu*
By Zhiyi (Great Master Tiantai), twenty fascicles
Taishō Vol. 34, No. 1718

23. *Genealogy; Saichō (Great Master Dengyō)'s Passage: A Bloodline Genealogy of the Transmission of the Teachings of the Buddha-Dharma Personally Attained; Dengyōdaishifumon: Saichōsen Naishōbuppōsōshōkechimyakufu*
By Saichō (Great Master Dengyō, 765–822), who presented this text to Emperor Saga in 819, one fascicle
Dengyō Daishi Zenshū (Shiga, 1926), Vol. 1, pp. 199–248

24. *Notes to the Words and Phrases; Notes to Master Zhiyi's Commentary on the Lotus Sutra: The Wenju (Mongu); Miaole-dashi Fahuawenjuji; Myōrakudaishi Hokkemonguki*
By Zhanran (Miaole; Myōraku; Tannen), thirty fascicles
Taishō Vol. 34, No. 1719

25. *Sutra of Pleasure and Garlands; The Buddha's Teaching in a Scripture Called A Chapter on Using Pleasure and Garlands as a Means for Attaining Awakening; Āryastrīvivartavyākaraṇa-sūtra; Leyingluozhuyanfangbianpinjing; Rakuyōrakushōgonhōbenbonkyō*
Translated by Dharmayaśas, 407–15, one fascicle
Taishō Vol. 14, No. 566
Beijing Tibetan Tripiṭaka Vol. 34, No. 857

26. *Commentary on the Mahāvairocana Sutra;* 1) *Darijing Shu; Dainichi Kyō Sho,* twenty fascicles; 2) *Zhenyanzong Darijing Yishi; Shingonshū Dainichikyō Gishaku,* fourteen fascicles
A commentary on Śubhākarasiṃha's (637–735) Chinese translation of the

Mahāvairocanābhisaṃbodhivikurvitādhiṣṭhānavaipulyasūtrendrarāja-dharmaparyāya
By Yixing (683–727)
1) Taishō Vol. 39, No. 1796; 2) *Zokuzōkyō* 1–36

27. *Mañjuśrī Inquiry Sutra; The Buddha's Teaching in a Scripture Called Mañjuśrī's Inquiry; Wenshushiliwenjing; Monjushirimonkyō*
Translated by Saṃghavarman, 518, two fascicles
Taishō Vol. 14, No. 468

28. *The All-pleasing: A Commentary on the Rules of Discipline; Buddhaghoṣa's Commentary on the Vinaya-piṭaka Called Samantapāsādikā ("Affording Help to All"); Shanjianlü; Zenkenritsu*
Translated by Saṃghabhadra, 488, eighteen fascicles
Taishō Vol. 24, No. 1462

29. *Great Calming and Contemplation; The Great Calming (Śamatha) and Contemplation (Vipaśyanā) of Tiantai; Tiantaizong Mohezhiguan; Tendaishū Makashikan*
Zhiyi's lectures recorded by Guanding (561–632), 594, twenty fascicles
Taishō Vol. 46, No. 1911

30. *Sutra of the Brahmā Called Excellent Thinker; The Buddha's Teaching in a Scripture Called the Responses of the Brahmā Deity Viśeṣacinti ("Excellent Thinker") upon Inquiry; Āryabrahmaviśeṣacintiparipṛcchānāmamahāyāna-sūtra; Siyifantiansuowenjing; Shiyakubontenshomonkyō*
Translated by Kumārajīva, four fascicles
Taishō Vol. 15, No. 586
Beijing Tibetan Tripiṭaka Vol. 33, No. 827

31. *Diamond Sutra; The Buddha's Teaching in a Scripture Called the Diamond-cutting Perfection of the Knowledge of Emptiness; Vajracchedikāprajñāpāramitā-sūtra; Jingangbanruoboluomijing; Kongōhannyaharamitsukyō*
Translated by Kumārajīva, one fascicle
Taishō Vol. 8, No. 235

32. *Great Tang Dynasty Record of the Western Regions; Datangxiyuji; Genjōki Daitōsaiikiki*

By Xuanzang, 646, twelve fascicles
Based on the author's travels in Central and South Asia from 630–646, undertaken with the objective of visiting the original homeland of the Buddha and the sites where he lived and taught.
Taishō Vol. 51, No. 2087
English translation by Li Rongxi (Numata Center, 1996)

33. *Similarities and Dissimilarities of the Teaching Forms; A Collection of Similarities and Dissimilarities Among the Various Buddhist Schools' Teaching Forms; Chishō-daishi Shokekyōsōdōishū*
By Enchin, 891, one fascicle
Taishō Vol. 74, No. 2368

34. *Brief Commentary on the Ten Wheels Sutra; Shenfang Shilunjing lüeshu; Shinbō Jūrinkyōryakusho*
By Shenfang (Shinbō)
Text not identified. Quoted in Enchin's *Similarities and Dissimilarities of the Teaching Forms,* see number 33.

35. *Vimalakīrti Sutra; The Buddha's Teaching in a Scripture Called Instructions of the Layman Vimalakīrti; Vimalakīrtinirdeśa-sūtra; Jingmingjing / Weimajiesuoshuojing; Jōmyōkyō / Yuimakitsushosetsukyō*
Translated by Kumārajīva, three fascicles
Taishō Vol. 14, No. 475
Beijing Tibetan Tripiṭaka Vol. 34, No. 843
English translation by John R. McRae (Numata Center, 2005)

36. *Treatise on Teaching Time Polemics; Annen Kyōjisōron*
By Annen (d. 889–98), one fascicle
Taishō Vol. 75, No. 2395

37. *Song Dynasty Biographies of Eminent Monks; Biographies of Eminent Buddhist Sangha Members of the Great Song; Zanning Dasonggaosengzhuan; Sannei Daisōkōsōden*
Compiled by Zanning (Sannei, 919–1002), 982, thirty fascicles
Taishō Vol. 50, No. 2061

38. *Buddha-contemplation Samādhi Sutra; The Buddha's Teaching in a Scripture Called the Sea of Samādhi with Contemplation on the Buddha; Foshuoguanfosanmeijing; Bussetsukanbutsuzanmaikyō*
Translated by Buddhabhadra (368–421), ten fascicles
Taishō Vol. 15, No. 643

39. *Notes to the Latter-day World Dharma Lamp; Notes to the Lamp of Dharma for the Latter-day World; Dengyōdaishi Mappōtōmyōki*
Ascribed to Saichō (Great Master Dengyō), one fascicle
Dengyō Daishi Zenshū, Shiga 1926, Vol. I
English translation by Robert Rhodes, *The Candle of the Latter Dharma* (Numata Center, 1994)

40. *Bequeathed Teaching Sutra; The Buddha's Final Admonitions on His Deathbed for the Practice of Penance; Foyijiaojing / Fochuibanniepanshilue-shuojiaojejing; Butsuyuikyōgyō / Butsusuihatsunehanjiryakusetsukyōkaikyō*
Translated by Kumārajīva, one fascicle
Taishō Vol. 12, No. 389
English translation by J. C. Cleary, in the volume *Apocryphal Scriptures* (Numata Center, 2005)

41. *Essentials for Chan Practice; Xiuchanyaojue; Shuzenyōketsu*
Given by Buddhabhalliya, a Dhyāna master from Northern India, as responses to questions by Mingxun of Chanlinsi in the Western Capital.
Translated by Huizhi, 677, one fascicle
Zokuzōkyō 2-15, 419: Vol. 110, 834b

42. *Sutra on Contemplation of Samantabhadra; The Buddha's Teaching in a Scripture Called Contemplation of the Dharma of Bodhisattva Samanta-bhadra ("Wholly Auspicious")'s Practice; Samantabhadrabodhisattvadhyāna-caryādharma-sūtra; Guanpuxianpusaxingfajing / Puxianguan; Kanfugen-bosatsugyōhōkyō / Fugenkan*
Translated by Dharmamitra, Liu Song dynasty, 424, one fascicle
Taishō Vol. 9, No. 277

43. *Sutra on the Most Wondrous Supreme Dhyāna; Zuimiaoshengdingjing; Saimyōshōjōkyō*

Compiled in China toward the end of the Six Dynasties period, one fascicle
This text is found in the appendix to Shindai Sekiguchi's *Tendai Shikan no Kenkyū*.

44. *Vaipulya Sutra; The Buddha's Teaching in a Scripture of the Great Vaipulya ("Extensive") on Dhāraṇī; Vaipulya-sūtra; Dafangdengtuoluonijing; Daihōdōdaranikyō*
Translated by Fazhong, Northern Liang dynasty, four fascicles
Taishō Vol. 21, No. 1339

45. *Bodhisattva Garland Sutra; The Buddha's Teaching in a Scripture Called Bodhisattvas Honored with the Formless Garland upon Attaining Awakening; Pusayingluojing; Bosatsuyōrakukyō*
Translated by Buddhasmṛti, 376, thirteen fascicles
Taishō Vol. 16, No. 656

46. *Sutra of Supra-sunlight Samādhi; The Buddha's Teaching in a Scripture Called the Samādhi that Illuminates Beyond the Sun; Chaorimingsanmeijing; Chōnichimyōzanmaikyō*
Translated by Nie Chengyuan, Western Jin dynasty (240–300)
Taishō Vol. 15, No. 638

47. *Profound Meaning of the Lotus Sutra; The Profound Meaning of the Saddharmapuṇḍarīka-sūtra; Miaofalianhuajingxuanyi; Myōhōrengekyōgengi*
By Zhiyi, recorded by Guanding, ten fascicles with two parts each
Taishō Vol. 33, No. 1716

48. *Collection of Records from the Ancestral Mirrors; Zongjinglu; Sugyōroku*
Compiled by Yongming Yanshou (Yōmyō Enju, 904–75), 961, one hundred fascicles
Taishō Vol. 48, No. 2016

49. *Sutra of Treasure Clouds; The Buddha's Teaching in a Scripture Called the Mahayana Treasure Clouds; Ratnamegha-sūtra; Dashengbaoyunjing; Daijōhōunkyō*
Translated by Maṇḍarāsana (?) and Saṃghapāla, Liang dynasty, 503, seven fascicles
Taishō Vol. 16, No. 659

50. *Instructions and Admonitions on Observing Restraints; Instructions and Admonitions for Newly Ordained Sangha Members on Observing Restraints (Saṃvara); Daoxuanlishi Jiaojielüyi; Dōsenrisshi Kyōkairitsugi*
By Daoxuan (Dōsen, 596–677), one fascicle
Taishō Vol. 45, No. 1897

51. *Sutra of Perfect Awakening; The Buddha's Teaching in a Scripture of Penetration Called Perfect Awakening; Yuanjuexuiduoluoliaoyijing; Engakushūtararyōgikyō*
The extant scripture is regarded to have been composed in China; the foreword quoted by Eisai is not found in the extant scripture.
Translation ascribed to Buddhatrāta, Tang dynasty, one fascicle
Taishō Vol. 17, No. 1824

52. *Commentary on the Middle Treatise; Sanlunzong Jicang: Zhonglunshu; Sanronshū Kichizō: Chūronsho*
Jizang (Kichizō, 549–623), ten fascicles
Taishō Vol. 42, No. 1824

53. *Foreword to the Brahmā Net Sutra; A Foreword to the Bodhisattvas' Moral Precepts in the Brahmā Net Sutra; Fanwangjing xu; Bonmōkyō jo*
Found in the *Rinzaishūseiten;* this text differs from the text listed at number 5

54. *Afterword to the Mahāparinirvāṇa Sutra; Dabanniepanjing houfen; Daihatsunehangyō gobun*
Translated by Jñānabhadra, Tang dynasty, two fascicles
Taishō Vol. 12, No. 377

55. *Sutra of Bodhisattva Samudrajñāna; The Buddha's Teaching in a Scripture Called Bodhisattva Samudrajñāna ("Sea-Wisdom")'s Exposition of the Dharma; Haihuipusasuoshuojing; Kaiebosatsushosetsukyō*
Translated by Zhiyan, Tang dynasty
Quoted in *A Collection of Passages from Various Scriptures on Mahayana Bodhisattva Practices; Dashengxiuxingpusaxingmenzhujingyaoji; Daijōshugyōbosatsugyōmonshokyōyōshū*
Taishō Vol. 17, No. 847

56. *Sutra of Ratnakumāra; The Buddha's Teaching in a Scripture Called Ratnakumāra Devī Paripṛcchā; Baotongzijing / Baotonfurensuowenjing; Hōdōjikyō / Hōdōfujinshomonkyō*
Included in *A Collection of Passages from Various Scriptures on Mahayana Bodhisattva Practices* (see number 55, above)
Taishō Vol. 17, No. 847

57. *Biography of Prince Shōtoku; The Biography in Calendar Form of Prince Shōtoku; Shōtokutaishidenryaku*
Compilation ascribed to members of the Taira clan, ca. 992, two fascicles
Dainihon Bukkyō Zensho Vol. 112

58. *Single Mind Moral Precept by Great Master Dengyō (Saichō); Documents for Reporting and Narrating the Single Mind Moral Precept; Dengyōdaishi-isshinkai; Denjutsu-isshinkaimon*
Compiled by Kōjō (d. 858), three fascicles
Taishō Vol. 74, No. 2379

59. *Postscript to A Treatise on the Contemplation of Mind; Tiantai Guanxin-lun Aopi; Tendai Kanjinron Ōhi*
The *Treatise*, authored by Zhiyi, is extant (Taishō Vol. 46, No. 1920, one fascicle) but the *Postscript* is not.

60. *Reasons for the Rise of the Chan School; Chanzongxingqi / Dazangjinggan-muzhiyaolu; Zenshūkōyu / Daijōkyōkōmokushiyōroku*
Given at the end of the *Records of Important Items in the Buddhist Tripiṭaka*, Vol. 8, compiled by Chan Master Foguo Weibai, end of the Northern Song dynasty
Shōwa Hōbō Sōmokuroku (*General Index of the Shōwa Dharma Treasure*) Vol. 2, 770a

61. *Longer Record of the Buddha's Words I; A Great Work in the Buddha's Former Lives (Mahāpadāna), in the Longer Record of the Buddha's Words I; Dīrghāgama; Zhang'ahanjing / Dabenjing; Jōagongyō / Daihongyō*
Translated by Buddhayaśas and Buddhasmṛti, twenty-two fascicles
Taishō Vol. 1, No. 1

62. *Sutra on Handing Over a Lotus Flower; The Buddha's Teaching in a Scripture Called Handing Over a Lotus Flower in Greeting; Āryakuśala-mūlaparidhara-sūtra; Huashoujing; Keshukyō*
Translated by Kumārajīva, ten fascicles
Taishō Vol. 16, No. 657
Beijing Tibetan Tripiṭaka Vol. 28, No. 769

63. *Sutra on the Great Drum of the Truth; Mahābherīhārakaparivarta-sūtra; Dafagujing; Daihōkukyō*
Translated by Guṇabhadra, 435–43, two fascicles
Taishō Vol. 16, No. 270
Beijing Tibetan Tripiṭaka Vol. 35, No. 888

64. *Flower Ornament Sutra; The Buddha's Teaching Extensively Expounded in a Scripture Called Buddhāvataṃsaka, [Samādhi named] Adorning the Buddha with a Flower Garland; Buddhāvataṃsaka-sūtra; Dafangguangfo-huayanjing; Daihōkōbutsukegongyō*
1) Translated by Buddhabhadra, Jin dynasty, 418–20, Taishō Vol. 9, No. 278, sixty fascicles
2) Translated by Śikṣānanda, Tang dynasty, 695–99, Taishō Vol. 10, No. 279, eighty fascicles

65. *Heap of Jewels Sutra; Mahāratnakūṭadharmaparyāyaśatasāhasrikā-grantha; Dabaojijing; Daihōshakukyō*
Taishō Vol. 11, No. 310, 120 fascicles, 49 sections
Fascicle 52, section 12, translated by Xuanzang, Tang dynasty
Fascicle 62, section 16, translated by Narendrayaśas, Northern Qi dynasty
Fascicle 92, section 25, translated by Bodhiruci, Tang dynasty

66. *Laṅkāvatāra-sūtra; The Buddha's Teaching in a Scripture Called Entering Laṅkā; Lengkajing; Ryōgakyō*
Translated by Guṇabhadra, 443, four fascicles
Taishō Vol. 16, No. 670

67. *Mahāvairocana Sutra; Sutra of Great Sun; Mahāvairocanābhisaṃbodhi-vikurvitādhiṣṭhānavaipulyasūtrendrarājadharmaparyāya; Zhenyanzong Darijing; Shingonshū Dainichikyō*

Translated by Subhākarasiṃha and Yixing, Tang dynasty, seven fascicles
Taishō Vol. 18, No. 848

68. *Scripture on the Explication of Underlying Meaning; Gambhīrārtha Saṃdhinirmocana-sūtra; Foshuo Jiejiejing; Bussetsu Gesetuskyō*
Translated by Paramārtha, Chen dynasty, one fascicle
Taishō Vol. 16, No. 677
Beijing Tibetan Tripiṭaka Vol. 29, No. 774
English translation by John P. Keenan (Numata Center, 2000)

69. *Sutra of the Jain Satyaka's Instruction; Satyakanirgranthaputranirdeśa-sūtra / Bodhisattvagocaropāyaviṣayavikurvaṇa-nirdeśa; Dasazheniganzisu-oshuojing; Daisasshanikenshishosetsukyō*
Translated by Bodhiruci, Wei dynasty (508–38), ten fascicles
Taishō Vol. 9, No. 272
Beijing Tibetan Tripiṭaka Vol. 32, No. 813

70. *Sutra of Moonlight Samādhi; Samādhirājacandrapradīpa-sūtra / Ārya-sarvadharmasvabhāvasamatāvipañcitasamādhirājanāmamahāyāna-sūtra; Yuedengsanmeijing; Gattōzanmaikyō*
Translated by Narendrayaśas, Northern Qi dynasty, 557, ten fascicles
Taishō Vol. 15, No. 639
Beijing Tibetan Tripiṭaka Vol. 32, No. 795

71. *Sutra of Examining through Divination; Sutra of Examining the Retribution of Good and Evil Conduct through Divination; Zhanchashan'e'ye-baojing; Sensatsuzen'akugōhōkyō*
Although this translation is ascribed to Bodhipradīpa (?), Sui dynasty (589–618), it is believed to have been produced in China; two fascicles
Taishō Vol. 17, No. 839

72. *Sutra of the Diamond Samādhi; Jingangsanmeijing; Kongōzanmaikyō*
Translator's name is lost; the text appeared in the Northern Liang dynasty; one fascicle
Taishō Vol. 17, No. 273

73. *Sutra of King Longevity; The Buddha's Teaching in a Scripture Called King Longevity (Dīghiti); Zhangshouwangjing; Chōjuōkyō*

Translator unknown, Western Jin dynasty (256–316), one fascicle
Taishō Vol. 3, No. 161

74. *Sutra of the Bodhisattva Precepts for Practicing Good; Pusashanjiejing; Bosatsuzenkaikyō*
This is another version of the *Bodhisattvabhūmi,* attributed to Maitreya (Asaṅga).
Translated by Guṇavarman, nine fascicles
Taishō Vol. 30, No. 1580

75. *Demonstration of Consciousness Only; Chengweishilun; Jōyuishikiron*
Translated by Xuanzang, ten fascicles
Taishō Vol. 31, No. 1585
English translation by Francis H. Cook, in *Three Texts on Consciousness Only* (Numata Center, 1999)

76. *Treatise on Awakening Confidence; Treatise of the Great Vehicle that Advocates Awakening Confidence in the True Self; Dashengqixinlun; Daijōkishinron*
1) Taishō Vol. 32, No. 1666, one fascicle: Translation attributed to Paramārtha, Liang dynasty. The authorship ascribed to Aśvaghoṣa has not been confirmed.
2) Taishō Vol. 32, No. 1667, two fascicles: Translated by Śikṣānanda, Tang dynasty.

77. *Blue Cliff Record; Collection of Chan Records: The Blue Cliff; Biyanlu; Hekiganroku*
A collection of one hundred cases (*kōans*) for attaining awakening and related verses by Master Xuedou Chongxian (Setchō Jūken, 980–1052), with critical remarks by the compiler Yuanwu Keqin (Engo Kokugon, 1063–1135), ten fascicles
Taishō Vol. 48, No. 2003

78. *Eye and Treasury of the True Dharma; Zhengfayanzang; Shōbōgenzō*
A collection of cases (*kōans*) for attaining awakening, compiled by Dahui Zonggao (Daie Sōkō, 1089–1163), three fascicles
Zokuzōkyō 2–23

79. *Jingde Records of Transmission of the Lamp; Jingdechuandenglu; Keitoku-dentōroku*
Compiled by Daoyuan (Dōgen), 1040, the first year of the Jingde (Keitoku) era, thirty fascicles
Taishō Vol. 51, No. 2076

80. *An Essential Understanding of Dhyāna Practice; Chanfayaojie; Zenpōyōge*
Translated by Kumārajīva, two fascicles
Taishō Vol. 15, No. 616

81. *Sutra of Moral Conduct; Śīla-sūtra; Jiejing; Kaikyō*
Unidentified text.

82. *Sutra of Words of Truth on Great Acts; The Buddha's Teaching in a Scripture Called Words of Truth and Their Concrete Examples; Fajupiyu-jing; Hokkuhiyukyō*
Translated by Faju and Fali, Jin dynasty, 290–306, four fascicles
Taishō Vol. 4, No. 211

83. *Sutra Treasury of Miscellaneous Jewels; The Buddha's Teaching in a Scripture Called A Treasury of Miscellaneous Jewels; Zabaozangjing; Zōhōzōkyō*
A collection of one hundred thirty-one stories.
Translated by Kinkara and Tanyas, Wei dynasty, 472, ten fascicles
Taishō Vol. 4, No. 203

84. *Commentary on the Diamond Sutra by the Dharmalakṣaṇa School; A Commentary on the Diamond Sutra by Great Master Ci'en Ji of the Concept-analysis (Dharmalakṣaṇa) School; Faxiangzong Ci'en-dashi Ji Jingang-banruojinghuishi; Hossōshū Jion-daishi Ki Kongōhannyakyōeshaku*
By Ci'en Ji (Jion Ki, 632–82), three fascicles
Taishō Vol. 40, No. 1816

85. *Commentary on the Diamond Sutra; Commentary on the Diamond Sutra by Huizhao (Eshō) of Zizhou (Shishū); Zizhou Huizhao Jingangjingshi; Shishū Eshō Kongōkyōshaku*
By Huizhao (650–714), a disciple of Xuanzang
Unidentified text.

86. *Sutra on Attaining the Mudrā that Effects the Strength of Confidence; Āryaśraddhābalādhānāvatāramudrānāmamahāyāna-sūtra; Xinliruyinfa-menjing; Shinrikinyūinhōmonkyō*
Translated by Dharmaruci, Wei dynasty, ten fascicles
Taishō Vol. 10, No. 305
Beijing Tibetan Tripiṭaka Vol. 34, No. 867

87. *Bodhisattva Stages; Bodhisattva Stages of the Observance of Samādhi; Yogācārabodhisattvabhūmiḥ; Yujiashidilun Pusadi; Yugashijiron Bosatsuji*
Translated by Xuanzang, fascicles thirty-five to fifty of one hundred total fascicles
Taishō Vol. 30, No. 1579

88. *Exposition of the Ten Stages; Daśabhūmikavibhāṣā-śāstra; Shizhupipo-shalun; Jūjūbibasharon*
Attributed to Nāgārjuna; translated by Kumārajīva, seventeen fascicles
Taishō Vol. 26, No. 1521

89. *Buddhist Monastic Traditions of Southern Asia: A Record of the Inner Law Sent Home from the South Seas; Tang Yijingsanzang Datang Nanhai-jiguineifazhuan; Tō Gijōsanzō Daitō Nankaikikinaihōden*
By Yijing (Gijō Sanzō, 635–713), Tang dynasty, 691, four fascicles
Taishō Vol. 54, No. 2125
English translation by Li Rongxi (Numata Center, 2000)
See also J. Takakusu, trans. *A Record of the Buddhist Religion as Practised in India and the Malay Archipelago (671–695) by I-tsing* (New Delhi: Munshiram Manoharlal, 1982, reprint)

90. *Sutra of Golden Light; The Buddha's Teaching in a Scripture Called the Gold Brilliance, Supreme King of All the Scriptures; Suvarṇaprabhāsotta-marāja-sūtra; Zuishengwang Jinguangmingjing; Saishōō Konkōmyōkyō*
Translated by Yijing, Tang dynasty, ten fascicles
Taishō Vol. 16, No. 665

91. *Sutra of the Buddhas' Names; Fomingjing; Butsumyōkyō*
Translated by Bodhiruci, twelve fascicles
Taishō Vol. 14, No. 440

92. *Contemplation Sutra; Sutra of Contemplation on the Buddha Amitāyus; Amitāyurdhyāna-sūtra; Guanwuliangshoujing; Kanmuryōjukyō*
Translated by Kālayaśas, 424–42, one fascicle
Taishō Vol. 12, No. 365
English translation by Hisao Inagaki, in the volume *The Three Pure Land Sutras* (Numata Center, 2003, Revised Second Edition)

93. *Invitation of Bodhisattva Avalokiteśvara; The Sutra of the Dhāraṇī Pronounced to Invite Bodhisattva Avalokiteśvara to Suppress Damage from Poisoning; Qingguanshiyinpusaxiaofuduhaituoluonijing; Shōkanzeonbosatsushōfukudokugaidaranijukyō*
Translated by Dharmanandiya, Eastern Jin dynasty, one fascicle
Taishō Vol. 20, No. 1043

94. *Treatise on the Treasury of Analyzed Concepts of Buddhism; Abhidharmakośavyākhyā-śāstra; Apidamojushelun; Abidatsumakusharon*
By Vasubandhu, translated by Xuanzang, thirty fascicles
Taishō Vol. 29, No. 1558

95. *Three Teachings Pointing to Where to Return; Kōyadaishi Kūkai Sangōshīki*
By Kūkai (Kōbō Daishi, 774–835), three fascicles
Kōbō-daishi Zenshū Vol. 9, pp. 324–58, Mikkyō bunka kenkyūsho, 1978

96. *Sutra of the Original Practice; Fobenxingjijing; Butsuhongyōjikkyō*
Unidentified text. Passages quoted by Eisai cannot be located in the *Sutra of the Collection of the Buddha's Original Practices* (Taishō Vol. 3, No. 190), translated by Jñānagupta, Sui dynasty, sixty fascicles

97. *Sutra on the Prince Coming into Being with Auspicious Responses; Taiziruiyingbenqijing; Taishizuiōhonkikyō*
Translated by Zhiqian, Wu dynasty (223–53), two fascicles
Taishō Vol. 3, No. 185

98. *Record of the Transmission of the Dharma Treasury; Fufazangyinyuanzhuan; Fuhōzōinnenden*
Translated by Kinkara and Tanyas, Wei dynasty, six fascicles
Taishō Vol. 50, No. 2058

99. *Essentials of the Single Vehicle; Ichijōyōketsu*
By Genshin, Eshin'in (942–1017), Yokawa, Mount Hiei, three fascicles
Taishō Vol. 74, No. 2370

100. *Sutra on the Excellence of Donation of a Lamp Fire; Āryapradīpadānīya; Foshuoshidenggongdejing; Bussetsusedōkudokukyō*
Translated by Narendrayaśas, Qi dynasty, one fascicle
Taishō Vol. 16, No. 702
Beijing Tibetan Tripiṭaka Vol. 34, No. 871

101. *An Approach to Truth through the Samādhi Called No Polemics; Wuzhengsanmeifamen; Musōzanmaihōmon*
By Nanyue Huisi (515–77), two fascicles
Taishō Vol. 46, No. 1923

Notes

1 I.e., the Zen school. The term *busshin* is derived from *butsugoshin* ("core or heart of the Buddha's words"), in Sanskrit, *buddhapravacanahṛdaya*, a term used as the subtitle of the text in the *Laṅkāvatāra-sūtra* [66].

2 The western part of present-day Okayama Prefecture.

3 Emperor Kōrei was the seventh in succession from Emperor Jinmu, according to the records on divine rule by mythological emperors in the two earliest histories of Japan, the *Kojiki* (*Records of Ancient Matters*), compiled in 712 C.E., and the *Nihonshoki* (*Chronicles of Japan*), compiled in 720. Both these early histories were compiled by imperial order for clearly political purposes.

4 The eastern part of present-day Okayama Prefecture.

5 The western part of present-day Tottori Prefecture.

6 Present-day Fukuoka Prefecture, Kyushu.

7 In Japanese, *rakan*, "attainers of awakening among Śākyamuni's disciples."

8 Zhizhe, i.e., Zhiyi (538–597), also called Great Master Tiantai, systematized the Tiantai school's teachings after deep thought and practice. In the *Treatise on Letting Zen Flourish to Protect the State* Eisai quotes from Zhiyi's three representative works: *Words and Phrases in the Lotus Sutra* [22], *Great Calming and Contemplation* [29], and *Profound Meaning of the Lotus Sutra* [47].

9 This text is dated the ninth of the eighth month of the first year of Baoqing, 1205 C.E.

10 The northern part of Kyushu.

11 Bodhisattvas (lit., "awakening [*bodhi*] beings [*sattva*s]") are those who attain awakening but forego their own entrance into nirvana in order to help other beings attain awakening, and they constitute the spiritual ideal of the Mahayana. The bodhisattva *śīla* are a set of moral precepts for Mahayana followers, both lay and monastic. Eisai, however, believed that the precepts for monks should be the same as those for the early disciples (*śrāvaka*s) as indicated in Buddhist Vinaya texts such as the *Vinaya in Four Divisions* [4]. See also notes 30 and 31.

[12] Tōdaiji, the head temple of the Kegon school in Nara, housed a gigantic Buddha statue, built by order of Emperor Shōmu in 752 C.E., which had burned down in 1180.

[13] The southeastern part of present-day Yamaguchi Prefecture.

[14] The original edition of the *Treatise* was printed in the sixth year of Kanmon, 1666. See the Translator's Introduction, p. 56.

[15] What Eisai means by "Mind" here is the original nature of the ordinary mind, which is no-mind. It also means the *shin* ("essence" or "heart") of the *busshin-shū,* the "school of the Buddha's mind."

[16] I.e., Me, in that the mind that is me is not any mind that is me.

[17] In the following phrases describing Mind, Eisai draws from a variety of sources. The term "best vehicle" (*śreṣṭhayāna; zuishangsheng; saijōjō*) first appears in the *Diamond Sutra* [31] (T. 8: 750c). See the *Laṅkāvatāra-sūtra* [66] for the terms "ultimate reality" (*paramārtha; diyiyi; daiichigi*) (T. 16: 483b) and "unsurpassed awakening" (*anuttarā samyaksaṃbodhi; wushangputi; mujōbodai*) (T. 16: 488a). The *Mahāprajñāpāramitā Treatise* [2] (T. 25: 519a) has: "In the contemplation of the true characteristics of all that have their own characteristics there obtains perfection of the knowledge of emptiness." The term "one true mode of being" (*dharmadhātu; yizhenfajie; ichishinhokkai*) is found in the *Demonstration of Consciousness Only* [75] (T. 31: 48a). "The calm self in heroic advance" (*śūraṃgama samādhi; lengyuansanmei; ryōgonzanmai*) is the title and main theme of an early Mahayana sutra, the *Śūraṃgamasamādhi-sūtra,* translated by Kumārajīva (Taishō vol. 15, no. 642, two fascicles); English translation by John McRae published under the title *Śūraṅgama Samādhi Sutra* (Numata Center, 1998).

[18] The following two terms are from fascicle one of the *Baolinzhuan* (*Hōrinden;* originally ten fascicles, seven fascicles extant), an early history of the Dharma transmission of the Chan school, compiled in 801 by Zhiju (Chiko). The phrase "eye and treasury of the True Dharma" (*saddharmacakṣukośa?; zhengfayanzang; shōbōgenzō*) is supposedly quoted in this Chan text from the *Mahāparinirvāṇa Sutra* [6], though the sutra (T. 12: 617b) speaks only of "transmission of the True Dharma." See the *Hōrinden-yakuchū,* a Japanese translation of the *Baolinzhuan* with annotation by Ryōshō Tanaka (Tokyo: Uchiyamashoten, 2003), pp. 37–8. The phrase "sublime mind (or heart, *hṛdaya*) of nirvana" is also from the *Baolinzhuan,* where the Buddha cites it as one of the synonymous phrases of what he transmits to Mahākāśyapa. See the *Hōrinden-yakuchū,* p. 30.

[19] The term "three wheels" (*sanlun; sanrin*) is from a passage in *Attending to the Lotus Sutra* (*Fahuayouyi; Hokkeyūi*) (Taishō vol. 34, no. 1722, 634c) by Jizang (Kichizō; 549–623): "The Buddha expounded the *Lotus Sutra*

as he wanted to turn the threefold Dharma wheel: 1) the root Dharma wheel, 2) the teachings of branches and knots, and 3) absorbing the knots to return to the root." For "eight treasuries," see note 75. The term "four trees" (*sishu; shiju*) refers to the comparison of *śrāvaka*s, *pratyekabuddha*s, bodhisattvas, and Buddhas in Chapter V of the *Lotus Sutra* [16], "Medicinal Herbs" (T. 9: 20ab), where *śrāvaka*s are likened to small herbs, *pratyekabuddha*s to medium herbs, and bohisattvas to the best herbs; bodhisattvas are compared to trees and Buddhas to great trees. See also Hakūju Ui's *Bukkyō-jiten* (Tokyo: Tōsei-shuppansha, 1953). "Five vehicles" (*wucheng; gojō*), among various classifications of the vehicles for liberation, refers to the two worldly vehicles of humans and gods and the three supramundane vehicles of *śrāvaka*s, *pratyekabuddha*s, and bodhisattvas-Buddhas.

20 The term "truth of mind" (*cittadharma; xinfa; shinbō*) usually means either *citta* and *dharma*, i.e., mind and what is not mind, or the *dharma* (phenomenon) that is called *citta* (mind). The Sanskrit term *cittadharmatā* (*xinfaxing; shinhosshō*), meaning the original, supramundane nature of the mind, would be a more precise analog for "truth of mind." This double use of the term *cittadharma / cittadharmatā* finds its reason in the way the "mind of a sentient being" (*sattvacitta; zhongshengxin; shujōshin*) is explained as twofold in the *Treatise on Awakening Confidence* [76]. See also note 118.

21 The term "golden ascetic" for Mahākāśyapa comes from fascicle forty-six of the *Sutra of the Original Practice* [96], where the Buddha said to the monks (T. 3: 869a), "Mahākāśyapa looks like a golden statue because, due to his virtuous conduct in former lives he was born into a well-off brahman family, wealthy to the extent that he never lacked for anything, of upright and fine features. He has been foremost in ascetic practice; he has been completely contented with anything while practicing morality since becoming a mendicant; he has attained arhatship; and therefore I have assured his attainment of Buddhahood."

22 According to Professor Seizan Yanagida, the term "special transmission independent of (or outside the) scriptural teachings" (*jiaowaibiechuan; kyōgebetsuden*) first appeared in the section on Master Shishuang Qingshu (Sekisō Keisho; 807–888), in fascicle six of the *Collection of the Chan Patriarchal Hall* (*Zutangji; Sodōshū*), compiled in Korea in 952 (Kyoto: Chūbun-shuppansha, 1972). In this text (p. 130b) Shishuang asks a disciple of Master Xuefeng Yicun (Seppō Gison; 828–887) what sort of opportunity for awakening Xuefeng offers his students. The monk replies, "The master tells us, 'What hasn't been, isn't, and won't be sung by any Buddha of the three times; what can't be disclosed in the twelve divisions of the Buddha's teachings has been specially transmitted in the ten directions independent of the scriptural teachings of the three vehicles. Having cited this for you, I find my mouth crushed!'" Shishuang involuntarily cries out,

"What's the use of your being here? You've already suffered having your head bent down."

In the *Laṅkāvatāra-sūtra* [66] (T. 16: 503ab), the Buddha expounds the twofold directives to the awakened truth: communication and principal aim. The latter is the principle by which practitioners get free of false discrimination, not falling into any of the alternatives of oneness and difference, both oneness and difference, and neither oneness nor difference; or of what surpasses the mind, ego-thought, and the thought-discerning faculty. This nondiscrimination is the noble mode of being personally attained and realized by past, present, and future Tathāgatas. The first directive, communication, refers to a diverse collection of sutra teachings, required for various purposes and taught according to sentient beings' capacities. Although such teachings are expressed in words, they are the self-expression of the principal aim, so they are in essence free from verbal expression. Verbal expression necessarily deviates from nondiscrimination.

Chan practitioners knew this well, and some referred to the danger of one's eyebrows falling off through speaking of suchness. In case twenty-seven of the *Blue Cliff Record* [77] (T. 51: 167c), the compiler Yuanwu Keqin admonishes anyone who wants to give expression to true reality to not spare not only their eyebrows but their very lives.

23 Vulture Peak (i.e., Mount Gṛdhrakūṭa), located northeast of the city of Rājagṛha in Magadha, India, meaning here Śākyamuni, who expounded many of his teachings there.

24 Cockfoot Ridge (i.e., Mount Kukkuṭapāda) in Magadha, India, meaning here Mahākāśyapa, who is said to have sequestered himself there. In the *Great Tang Dynasty Record of the Western Regions* [32], T. 51: 919bc, Xuanzang describes how Mahākāśyapa, knowing his time of death, ascended the mountain and hid himself among its three peaks, holding the Buddha's robe, which the Buddha's aunt Mahāprajāpatī had given him.

25 For a gloss on this phrase "support of the teaching of nirvana for monastic discipline" (*niepanfulü; nehanfuritsu*) and other similar expressions in the text, such as "the eternity of nirvana as the true support of morality" (p. 86), "the eternity of nirvana offers ultimate support to monastic discipline" (p. 110–11), and "the eternity of nirvana supports morality as its ultimate basis" (p. 159), see the passage from the *Mahāparinirvāṇa Sutra* [6] given in note 155.

26 As is expounded in the *Sutra of the Benevolent King* [9].

27 In the *Sutra of Maitreya's Descent and Attainment of Buddhahood (Milexiashengchengfojing; Mirokugenshōjōbutsukyō;* Taishō vol. 14, no. 454), it is said that five trillion, six hundred and seventy billion years after Śākyamuni's *parinirvāṇa* Bodhisattva Maitreya will appear in the world,

attain Buddhahood under a *pumnāra* tree, and without fail liberate humans and gods according to their capacities—lesser, middling, and greater—through his teachings at three Dharma meetings.

28 The "bubbling spring of ultimate reality" is cited as one of the five significances of the Buddhist sutras by Chengguan (Chōkan; 738–839), one of the great Tang dynasty scholars of the *Flower Ornament Sutra* [64], in a detailed commentary on his own commentary on the sutra, the *Collected Writings for Unfolding Meanings through Following the Commentary* (*Suishu Yanyichao; Zuisho Engishō*), Taishō vol. 36, no. 1736, 36a. In the phrase "for eons under a thousand Buddhas," Eisai refers to the thousand Buddhas who are expected to appear in the future lunar-mansion *kalpa;* see note 107.

29 The phrase "practicing *dhyāna* and investigating the Way" appears in the *Blue Cliff Record* [77], in two comments by Yuanwu (cases two and nine). The term *dhyāna* (*chan; zen*) is commonly translated as "meditation" but in a Zen context means "getting free from thought," the aim of Zen meditation. The Way (*dao; do*) refers to the Buddhist path of liberation.

30 The monastic precepts to be followed to avoid various offenses and transgressions, as enumerated in the *Vinaya in Four Divisions* [4], totals two hundred and fifty for monks; there are three hundred and forty-eight for nuns.

31 The threefold collection of purifying precepts are: 1) keeping the precepts of restraint (*saṃvara-śīla; shelüyijie; shōritsugikai*), including the ten weighty and forty-eight less weighty precepts; 2) practicing good acts; and 3) furthering people's aspiration for awakening. This is of a completely Mahayana nature. Saichō, founder of the Tendai school in Japan, wished to receive official approval for requiring new ordainees to adopt these Mahayana precepts of the *Brahmā Net Sutra on the Bodhisattva Śīla* [5], but only after his death did the government sanction this. A different set of the precepts of restraint in the threefold collection is given in another Mahayana text, the *Bodhisattvabhūmi* (*Pusadichijing; Bosatsujijikyō*), Taishō vol. 30, no. 1581, I, 10, consisting of the traditional precepts for the seven groups (*bhikṣu*s, *bhikṣuṇī*s, *śrāmaṇera*s, *śrāmaṇerī*s, *śikṣamānā*s, *upāsaka*s, *and upāsikā*s) of the Mahayana sangha.

According to the the *Brahmā Net Sutra* (T. 24: 1004b–1005a), the ten weighty transgressions that violate the precepts of restraint are: 1) killing, either taking the life of another or one's own life, 2) stealing, 3) committing obscenity toward oneself or others without compassion, 4) lying, 5) trading in intoxicants, 6) speaking of others' faults, 7) praising oneself while denigrating others, 8) being stingy and abusive toward alms-seekers, 9) being angry even with one who apologizes, and 10) slandering the Three Treasures (Buddha, Dharma, and Sangha). The precepts of restraint against these transgressions are called the bodhisattvas' ten *prātimokṣa* (lit., "what liberates one from transgressions"). The forty-eight less weighty transgressions include consuming intoxicants; eating meat or foods prepared with onions, garlic, etc.; seeing a sick person without helping them; possessing weapons for killing; rejecting Mahayana sutras and Vinayas as non-Buddhist; and so on (1005b–1009b).

The *Brahmā Net Sutra* also states that these precepts should be accepted equally by both monastics and lay practitioners, with no distinction in this regard, whether the practitioner is a king, prince, minister, or official; a monk, nun, or lay follower; a licentious person or a slave (1008b). One who has committed a transgression against any of the weighty precepts is said to be unable to give rise to the aspiration for awakening (*bodhicitta*) and will lose one's position as a king or monk (1004b). Beginners in the practice should recite the ten weighty and forty-eight less weighty precepts of restraint each *upoṣadha* day, the fortnightly meeting of the sangha (1008a). This was the practice Saichō wanted to institute for ordainees of the Tendai school. In this Eisai squarely parted from Saichō, saying that monks should firmly uphold the two hundred and fifty monastic precepts (see note 30), and laypeople should uphold the threefold collection of purifying precepts, especially the ten weighty and forty-eight less weighty precepts.

32 The phrase "last five hundred-year period" refers to the categorization of the time after the Buddha's *parinirvāṇa* into five five hundred-year periods, in which people's capacity for understanding the authentic teaching of the Buddha and attaining awakening progressively declines. This concept is seen in the "Moon Treasury" section, in fascicle fifty-five of the *Large Collection Sutra* (*Saṃnipata-sūtra; Dajijing; Daijikkyō*), Taishō vol. 13, no. 397, 363ab. In the first five hundred-year period, there are many who are able to attain to wisdom and liberation; in the second, many are able to practice *dhyāna* but not attain liberation; in the third, many are firm in hearing, reading, and reciting the Buddha's teachings but are not able to practice *dhyāna* or attain liberation; in the fourth, many are able to build stupas and temples but not to practice or study the teachings; the fifth and last five hundred-year period is a period of degeneration, when many people are contentious and argue about the Buddhist teachings. This corresponds to the "latter-day world" referred to by Eisai throughout this treatise, reflecting the widespread belief in *mappō* ("age of the decadent Dharma") in medieval Japan.

33 Tathāgatas, lit. "one who comes from thusness (*tathāta*)," are those who have realized the true nature of reality, i.e., Buddhas.

34 "The awakened truth of Zen that supports people in keeping the precepts": see notes 25 and 155 for similar expressions, where Eisai identifies *chan* (*zen*) with the eternity of nirvana.

35 The word "means"—correction number 1.

36 The *uṣṇīṣa,* a protuberance on the top of the head, is one of the thirty-two distinguishing marks of a Buddha, along with a lock of hair between the eyebrows (*ūrnā*), the sign of a thousand-spoked wheel on the soles of the feet, etc.

37 The word "having"—correction number 2.

38 "The principle of Zen" (*zenshū*)—By this term, Eisai seems to mean not only the Zen principle but also the Zen school and practitioners of Zen.

39 The "four kinds of restraint" are to have a mind free from thoughts of obscenity, murder, theft, and the falsehood that one has attained awakening. Toward the end of fascicle six of the *Sutra of Śūraṃgama Practices* [14], the Buddha finished expounding these four kinds of restraint, and now, in fascicle seven, he goes on with the present exposition.

40 The Chinese version of the *sitātapatra-dhāraṇī* appears in the *Sutra of Śūraṃgama Practices* [14], Taishō vol. 19, no. 945, pp. 134–6. Three Sanskrit versions—one corrected Nepalese text and two texts restored from the Chinese—together with their Japanese translations were published in the article *"Ryōgonshu to Byakusangaidarani,* Comparative Studies of Restored Sanskrit Texts" (Kyoto: Rinzaishū Myōshinjiha Education Research Bulletin No. 1, April 2003), by Professor Toshihiko Kimura of Shitennoji International Buddhist University, Osaka. The text is in three parts; the first part mentions worshiping bodhisattvas, *śrāvaka*s, the Three Treasures, and the Five Tathāgatas as well as the Hindu gods Brahmā, Indra, Viṣnu, Nārāyaṇa, and Mahākāla (Śiva). The second part mentions that all the gods worship the goddess called Tathāgata Uṣṇīṣa Sitātapatra ("White Umbrella"; *sita,* "white"; *ātapa,* "causing pain," "heat"; *ātapatrā* [n., f.], "heat protector," "a large umbrella"), and that she destroys ghosts and demons, eliminates enemies' mantras, and protects reciters of the *dhāraṇī* from nightmares, poison, weapons, fire, and water. The third part invokes all the goddesses to protect reciters. The *dhāraṇī* deifies a large white umbrella in the belief that just as the white umbrella protects its holder from the afflicting heat of the sun, this *dhāraṇī* will bring about calm and composure to the reciter.

41 For understanding the phrase, "divine . . . mantras uttered by my heart-Buddha (*xinfo; shinbutsu*)," (T. 19: 133a, I, 17), two expressions that precede this in the quoted text, the *Sutra of Śūraṃgama Practices* [14], offer help (T. 19: 133a, II, 6–8): "the unsurpassed *sitātapatra-dhāraṇī* (or *sitātapatra-mantrapadāni*), which are beams from the protuberance (*uṣṇīṣa*) of my Buddha's head"; "the heart-mantras uttered by the heart-Buddha that is of the unseen nature of the protuberance on the Tathāgata's head and unconditioned, and that issues beams from the *uṣṇīṣa* while [the

Tathāgata is] sitting in a jewel lotus flower." The term "heart-Buddha" sounds strange but seems to have something to do with "heart (*hṛdaya*)-mantras. The Chinese word *xinfo* also suggests another term, "mind-Buddha," as what the compilers of the sutra may have meant. In this case it means "the mind as Buddha," and this is the interpretation adopted by Hajime Nakamura, et al., *Bukkyōgo-daijiten,* vol. II (Tokyo: Tokyo-shoseki, 1975).

42 A *yojana* is an Indian unit of distance, sometimes equated to the distance that can be traveled in one day.

43 Chishō, i.e., Enchin (814–891) went to Tang China and studied both exoteric and esoteric Buddhism from 853–858. He established an altar for *goma* (i.e., *homa,* burnt offering) ritual at Onjōji, and became the fifth head priest of Enryakuji on Mount Hiei. See Hajime Nakamura, et al., *Bukkyō-jiten* (Tokyo: Iwanami shoten, 1992). In the *Treatise* Eisai quotes from his *Official Document Presented to the Emperor* [15] and *Similarities and Dissimilarities of the Teaching Forms* [33].

44 Jikaku, i.e., Ennin (794–864), first studied under Saichō, went to Tang China from 838–847, and established the basis for Tendai esoteric Buddhism. He was the third head priest of Enryakuji on Mount Hiei. His record of his nine years in Tang China seeking the Dharma, the *Nittōguhōjunreikōki,* is well known. See Nakamura, et al., *Bukkyō-jiten* (Tokyo: Iwanami shoten, 1992).

45 The text has Śrāvastī here.

46 The eight forms of being of the Buddha include his birth, suffering, attainment of awakening, and passing away (*parinirvāṇa*). According to the *Treatise on Awakening Confidence* [76], T. 32: 581a, the eight forms of being are: 1) leaving the Tuṣita Heaven, 2) entering a human womb, 3) abiding in the womb, 4) leaving the womb, 5) becoming a mendicant, 6) attaining awakening, 7) turning the wheel of the Dharma, and 8) entering nirvana.

47 The word "answer"—correction number 3.

48 The *Elucidatory Comments* [18] is a commentary on Zhiyi's *Profound Meaning of the Lotus Sutra* [47] (see note 8) by Jingxi Zhanran (Keikei Tannen), also known as Great Master Miaole (Myōraku). Zhanran (711–782) was considered the sixth patriarch of the Tiantai school founded by Zhiyi. Before he became a monk at the age of thirty-eight, he had studied the Tiantai teachings for twenty years. Besides this text, Eisai quotes from three other of Zhanran's commentaries on Zhiyi's works, *Solutions for Propagation* [20], *Calming and Contemplation: Their Meaning and Examples* [21], and *Notes to the Words and Phrases* [24].

49 Actually, this quote is from fascicle eighteen, 472b, in the Northern version and fascicle sixteen, 715a, in the Southern version of the *Mahāparinirvāṇa Sutra* [6].

50 The word "respecting"—correction number 4.

51 Also by Zhanran. See note 48.

52 I.e., Zhiyi. See note 8.

53 I.e., "everything that has form is empty of its self-nature."

54 The *Jingde Records of Transmission of the Lamp* [79], fascicle twenty-five, about State Master Tiantaishan Deshao (891–972), cites the following record (T. 51: 407c):

> There was a transmitter of Tiantai Zhizhe's teaching named Yiji, who frequently told the master (Deshao), "Zhizhe's teachings have become remote as the years have gone by. I am afraid many of them will be lost. Now the Xinluoguo is equipped with many of his books. Without the master's compassionate power, who could afford to bring them here?" The master reported this to King Zhongyi of the Wuyueguo. The king dispatched a messenger with a letter from the master to the country, the messenger made copies there and, fully equipped, returned. Nowadays the copies prevail.

55 Daoxuan, i.e., Dōsen (also Daorui; Dōei; 702–760). He received transmission of the Northern school of Chan from Puji (651–739). In 736 he came to Japan in response to a request by two monks, Fushō and Yōei, who had come to Tang China from Japan, and stayed at the Dai'anji Saitoin in Nara. Versed in Kegon and Tendai teachings, he had influence on Saichō through his disciple Gyōhyō (see note 56). See Nakamura, et al., *Bukkyō-jiten* (Tokyo: Iwanami shoten, 1992).

56 Gyōhyō (727–797) was ordained along with seven hundred others in 741 at the imperial court, and accepted the precepts and Chan practice under the guidance of Daoxuan of the Dai'anji (see note 55). Later he lived at the Sūfukuji in Shiga, Ōmi Province. Toward the end of his life he retired to the Hisoji in Yamato Province and transmitted the Chan truth to Saichō (see note 41). See Ui, *Bukkyō-jiten* (Tokyo: Tōsei-shuppansha, 1953).

57 Dengyō, i.e., Saichō (766 or 767–822) was the founder of the Tendai school in Japan. At the age of twelve he became a disciple of Gyōhyō (see note 56) of the Kokubunji, Ōmi Province; he was ordained at age fourteen and took the name Saichō. In 785 he entered Mount Hiei, where he built a hut to live in and began reading Buddhist scriptures such as the *Lotus Sutra* [19], the *Sutra of Golden Light* [90], and the *Heart Sutra* (*Prajñāpāramitā-hṛdaya-sūtra; Banruoboluomiduoxinjing; Hannyaharamitashingyō;* Taishō vol. 8, no. 251), and studying various other scriptures and treatises, especially the three great treatises by the Tiantai master Zhiyi (see note 8).

Three years later he consecrated his hut as a temple, naming it the Ichijōshikan-in (later known as the Konponchūdō). In 794 he held a large offering service at the temple, attended by Emperor Kanmu (r. 781–806) and learned priests of the major temples of Nara. After that he was appointed to serve the imperial inner court as a priest, and his temple was ranked as a state-protecting *dōjō* (*bodhimaṇḍa*, "seat of awakening"). In 804, according to an imperial order by Kanmu to promote the study of the Tiantai school, Saichō went to Tang China. There he received the Tiantai transmission from Daosui and Xingman, the Chan transmission from Xiaoran, the bodhisattva *śīla* (precepts) from Daozui, an esoteric method from Shunxiao and others, and returned the following year, in 805. In 806 he received public approval for his Tendai school from the imperial court. Toward the end of his life he wanted to establish a system in which practitioners would be ordained in the Mahayana *śīla* to be followed by twelve years of study and practice at Mount Hiei. Though this system was not instituted during his lifetime due to opposition from other Buddhist schools in Nara, it was publicly approved after his death. See Ui, *Bukkyō-jiten* (Tokyo: Tōsei-shuppansha, 1953). In the *Treatise* Eisai quotes from Saichō's *Genealogy* [23] and *Single Mind Moral Precept* [58] as well as from the *Notes to the Latter-day World Dharma Lamp* [39] attributed to him.

58 The word "second"—correction number 5. The phrase "fifty-third year of King Mu" (in the Kanmon-Yanagida version and the Kōhō Tōshun Taishō version) has been corrected to "fifty-second year of King Mu," following two sources: 1) the biography of the monk Tan Wusui (Don Musai) of Wei in fascicle twenty-three of Daoxuan's *Continued Biographies of Eminent Monks* (*Xugaosengzhuan;* Taishō vol. 50, no. 2060, 624c–625a); and 2) the middle fascicle of the *Separate Biography of Monk Falin* (*Hōrin*) *of Tang* (Taishō vol. 50, no. 2051, 207b).

59 The word "bodhisattvas"—correction number 6.

60 The word "bodhisattvas"—correction number 7.

61 The word "become"—correction number 8.

62 The word "these"—correction number 9.

63 The Tōji in Kyoto represents the Kongōbuji on Mount Kōya.

64 The Tendai school is represented by the Enryakuji on Mount Hiei.

65 The "eight schools" are the six schools of the Nara period (710–94), Hossō, Jōjitsu, Kegon, Kusha, Ritsu, and Sanron; and the two schools of the Heian period (795–1191), Shingon and Tendai. These were the major schools of Buddhism in Japan.

66 Kāśyāpa-Mātaṅga is an Indian Buddhist who came to Luoyang, China, in 67 C.E.

67 Vajrabodhi (671–741) came to China in 720.

68 The word "rare"—correction number 10.

69 Annen (841–889 or 898), was ordained by Ennin (see note 44) in the bodhisattva *śīla* in 859. After Ennin died, he studied exoteric and esoteric Buddhism under Henjō. In 884, he became a *denbō-dai-ajari* ("great *ācārya* [teacher] for transmission of the esoteric truth") and lived at a temple called the Godai-in which he had had built on Mount Hiei.

70 The four attainments are the four stages of spiritual accomplishment of *śrāvaka*s: stream-enterer (*srota-āpanna*), once-returner (*sakṛdāgāmin*), non-returner (*anāgāmin*) and arhat. The ultimate of the four attainments is arhatship.

71 Taigong Wan (Taikō Bō), a title of honor presented to Lushang of the Zhou (Shū) dynasty.

72 According to a story described in the *Mahāparinirvāṇa Sutra* [6] (T. 12: 450a–451a), Siddhārtha, while a bodhisattva in a former life, was deeply moved upon hearing a demon (*rākṣasa*) cite the first half of a verse deep in the Himālayas, and sought to hear the second half by offering himself to the demon as a reward. This is alluded to by Eisai in saying that even "half a verse" on the Dharma was not belittled even though it was recited by a demon.

73 Eisai refers here to the *Collection of Records from the Ancestral Mirrors* [48], T. 48: 497a.

74 The king of Pengcheng told the priests that he would take refuge in a holy person as his master someone who, as the result of having attained awakening, could manifest such miracles as making water gush from under their left shoulder and flames from under their right shoulder, fly up high into the sky, emit beams of light, and shake the earth. Master Niutou Farong criticized the king's view, saying he was afraid that if he were to attain such powers he would be going against the Dharma and that, in such a case, a magician would be a Buddha. Awakening is the transformation of wisdom, and has nothing to do with mere changes of form, such as the difference between male and female or whether men or women have fine or ugly features or clothing. This story in the *Collection of Records from the Ancestral Mirrors* [48] does not appear elsewhere, such as in the biography of Master Farong in Daoxuan's *Continued Biographies of Eminent Monks* (Taishō vol. 50, no. 2060), compiled around 645; in the section of the *Collection of the Chan Patriarchal Hall,* fascicle three, that introduces Master Niutou Farong; or in the *Jingde Records of Transmission of the Lamp* [79], fascicle four.

Meanwhile, these three texts all introduce Farong as a master deeply respected not only by humans but also by animals and even plants in the unity of all beings. According to the *Collection of the Chan Patriarchal Hall,* Daoxin, the Fourth Patriarch of Chan, drawn by some omens he had observed from far away, came to see Master Farong deep in the mountains, surrounded by beings that were all friendly to him. After the Fourth Patriarch taught Master Farong how everything was empty of their characteristics, it is said that no ghosts were able to see the master to bring offerings. Nevertheless, when Master Farong had to leave the mountain, all the animals and plants, it is said, grieved upon being separated from him.

Master Farong is now regarded as the author of the *Jueguanlun* (*Zekkanron*), an early Chan text unearthed from Dunhuang. See the English translation by Gishin Tokiwa, *A Dialogue on the Contemplation-Extinguished* (Kyoto: Institute for Zen Studies, 1973).

75 According to the *Sutra of the Bodhisattva Abiding in the Womb* (*The Buddha's Teaching in a Scripture Called the Bodhisattva Descending from Tuṣita Heaven, Abiding in the Mother's Womb, and Expounding the Truth Extensively; Pusachutaijing; Bosatsushotaikyō*) translated by Zhu Fonian (Taishō vol. 12, no. 384, 1058b), the eight treasuries of the Buddha's teachings are: 1) the teaching expounded when he was still in his mother's womb, 2) the teaching expounded during the period immediately after his departure from human life, 3) the teaching of the Great Vehicle, 4) the teaching of *śīla* and *vinaya,* 5) the teaching from each of the ten bodhisattva stages, 6) miscellaneous teachings, 7) the teaching of the *vajra* treasury, i.e., the esoteric teaching, and 8) the teaching of the Buddha treasury (i.e., teachings by all the Buddhas).

76 The "four grave offenses" are the four *pārājika* offenses that result in expulsion from the sangha. The "five grave transgressions" are 1) patricide, 2) matricide, 3) killing an arhat, 4) causing a schism in the sangha, and 5) causing blood to flow from the body of a Buddha.

77 In Chapter II, "The Tathāgata's Indestructible Body," of the *Mahāparinirvāṇa Sutra* [6] (Taishō vol. 12, no. 374, fasc. 3, 383c–4a; Taishō vol. 12, no. 376, by Faxian, 666c–867a; Tibetan vol. 31, no. 788, 47b–49a), the story of the monk Buddhadatta (*datta,* "given") and King Bhavadatta (*bhava,* "samsaric being") goes as follows:

> In the past, immeasurable *kalpa*s ago, in this same city of Kuśinagara there appeared a Buddha, Tathāgata, World-honored One named Nandivardhana ("Pleasure-increasing"). In those days the land was as extensive, rich, and comfortable as the Land of Bliss, Sukhāvatī. The people prospered and knew no famine. The Buddha abided in the world, teaching people for immeasurable years, and under the twin *śāla* trees he entered *parinirvāṇa.* After this the Buddha's authentic teachings remained for immeasurable *koṭi*s of years and forty more years before the teachings were extinguished.
>
> Then there was a precept-keeper monk named Buddhadatta. He had many followers surrounding him to hear his lion's roar extensively expounding the

nine scriptures. He caused others to restrain from keeping servants, cows, buffalo ("sheep" in no. 374), as prohibited by the monastic rules.

There were many ill-behaved monks who, on hearing Buddhadatta's exposition, decided to kill him. They gathered, took weapons in hand, and went straight to Buddhadatta. The king of the land, Bhavadatta, heard of this and in order to protect the Buddha's teachings he went immediately to save the preacher from harm. He engaged in fighting the ill-behaved monks. The king was attacked with swords, spears, diamond-pointed weapons, and arrows; no place on his body, even as small as grains of mustard seed, was left unpierced.

Buddhadatta saw this, and praised the king, "A protector of the Buddha's authentic teachings should be like you. You will be the vessel of truth for innumerable *kalpa*s." The king, hearing the monk's words, died and was reborn in the land of Akṣobhya ("Immovable") Buddha. His men, whose hearts were transported with joy, continued to fight, all determined to attain awakening, and after death were reborn in the Buddha land of Akṣobhya.

The monk Buddhadatta also, after the king's death, died and was reborn in Akṣobhya Buddha's presence as his chief disciple. The king became the second disciple (according to the Faxian and Tibetan versions; in no. 374 the king becomes the chief disciple).

The authentic teachings, when about to be hidden, should be protected in this way. The one who was King Bhavadatta was me (Śākyamuni). The monk Buddhadatta was Kāśyapa Buddha, who has entered *parinirvāṇa*. The fruit of protecting the authentic teachings in this way is immeasurable. I have gained the indestructible body and the Dharma body.

78 According to Professor Seizan Yanagida, the phrase "not setting up any words" (*buliwenzi; furyūmonji*) first appeared in the opening remarks of a Tang dynasty Chan text, mid-eighth century, *On the Genealogy from Buddha to Buddha* (*Xuemailun; Kechimyakuron*), one fascicle, the sixth of *Bodhidharma's Six Gates* (*Shaoshilumen; Shōshitsurokumon*), Taishō vol. 48, no. 2009. The passage in question (T. 48: 373b) goes:

> The three worlds [of desire, form, and no-form] that have been made to arise return together to one mind; one Buddha through mind transmits mind to another Buddha, setting up no words.

The text goes on to say that since no words are set up by Buddhas for transmission—only mind—not even words like *buddha, bodhi,* or nirvana are set up as something to be transmitted (ibid.). But this does not mean that the ordinary sentient mind is the ultimate truth for transmission. The mind that grasps itself and others as actual phenomena does not realize the original nature of mind, which is one, beyond grasping (374a, c). No one other than the Buddhas realized this empty nature of mind (376a). Thus "setting up no words" also means not setting up even the concept of "mind" as transmitter or transmitted, and this is called the transmission of mind through mind from one Buddha to another.

79 "Perfect rank" (*yuanwei; en'i*), one of the terms beginning with "perfect" that were frequently used since Zhiyi, means the rank of the "perfect teaching" (*yuanjiao; engyō*), one point of which includes all the other points in itself. See also Yanagida's headnote for the *kundoku* text, *Nihon-shisōtaikei*, vol. 16 (Tokyo: Iwanami-shoten, 1972), p. 39.

80 "Perfect and immediate awakening" (*yuandun; endon*) means the nature of the practice whose first stage is at once both no different and different from the remaining stages, as the waxing or waning moon is both no different and different from the full moon.

81 The "sixfold immediacy" of awakening (*luji; rokusoku*) is a series of six concepts which stand for six stages through which the mind of awakening (*bodhicitta; putixin; bodaishin*) attains ultimate awakening, introduced by Zhiyi in the latter half of fascicle one of his *Great Calming and Contemplation* [29], T. 46: 10bc. He introduces this along with two other important themes for promoting and deepening practitioners' understanding of the mind of awakening: the "four noble truths" (*catvāryārya-satyāni*) and the "fourfold grand vow" (*sihongshiyuan; shiguzeigan*).

According to Zhiyi, practitioners need to be freed from lack of confidence and excess of pride at each stage of practice. One needs to be confident 1) in ultimate reality or reason being immediate to every moment of one's mind (*liji; risoku*), 2) in the immediacy of reason through literary knowledge (*mingziji; myōjisoku*), 3) in one's knowledge through the practices of contemplation (*guanxingji; kangyōsoku*), 4) in one's practice through the realization of approaching ultimate awakening (*xiangsiji; sōjisoku*), 5) in approaching ultimate awakening through the revelation of suchness (*fenzhonji; bunshinsoku*), and 6) in ultimate awakening through attainment (*jiujingji; kukyōsoku*).

82 "An ancient one," namely, Master Zhiyi, quoted from the *Great Calming and Contemplation* [29], T. 46: 80c.

83 The phrase "the former is a clumsy crossing"—correction number 11.

84 The phrase "and the latter a clever crossing"—correction number 12.

85 I.e., the self-nature of everything, which is empty of itself.

86 The three modes of reality (*sandi; santai*) are: empty (*śūnya*), provisional (*prajñapti*), and the middle (*madhya*).

87 The practice of *nembutsu* is the recollection of Amitābha Buddha's vow by reciting his name.

88 The word "after"—correction number 13.

89 *Dhyāna* as one of the six *pāramitās* (perfections).

90 *Samādhi* as one of the three *śikṣās*, or basic Buddhist learnings.

[91] Chōnen (938–1016), a priest of the Tōdaiji, Nara, studied Sanron and Shingon teachings; in 983 he went to Song China and was accorded a cordial reception by Emperor Taizong (r. 976–97), made a pilgrimage to Wutaishan (Godaisan) and so on, and returned to Japan in 987, bringing home five thousand volumes of a newly printed Tripiṭaka and a Buddha image. See Nakamura, et al., *Bukkyō-jiten* (Tokyo: Iwanami shoten, 1992).

[92] "*Sangaku*" means the three basic Buddhist learnings (*śikśā*s): morality (*śīla*), concentration (*samādhi*), and wisdom (*prajñā*).

[93] The phrase "the nondiscriminating *dhyāna* of the Tathāgatas," as well as "the Tathāgata's *dhyāna*" (see note 96) are drawn from the *Laṅkāvatāra-sūtra* [66], T. 16: 492a. Eisai considers this to represent one of the core concepts of Chan/Zen. See the quote from the *Laṅkāvatāra-sūtra* at the end of Fascicle Two of the *Treatise,* p. 151.

[94] Emperor Toba (r. 1107–41), after leaving the throne, out of his faith in the Buddha-Dharma, visited the Tennōji in Osaka to make offerings in its Nembutsu hall, November 12, 1149.

[95] The word "school"—correction number 14.

[96] The Tathāgata's *dhyāna* is considered to include all three of the basic Buddhist learnings (*śikṣā*s) of morality (*śīla*), concentration (*samādhi*), and wisdom (*prajñā*). The concept appears in the *Laṅkāvatāra-sūtra* [66], T. 16: 492a; see also note 93.

[97] Concerning "the foreword to the *Sutra of Perfect Awakening*" [51], the extant foreword does not include the passage quoted here.

[98] The *Foreword to the Brahmā Net Sutra* [53], included in the *Rinzaishū-seiten* as the *Foreword to the Bodhisattvas' Moral Precepts;* this text differs from the *Brahmā Net Sutra on the Bodhisattva Śīla* [5].

[99] The three evil paths are the three lower realms of hell, hungry ghosts, and animals into which sentient beings may be reborn.

[100] The five components of the Tathāgata's being are the three learnings (*śikśā*s) of morality (*śīla*), concentration (*dhyāna*), and wisdom (*prajñā*), plus liberation and the realization of liberation.

[101] Cited in the *Rinzaishūseiten.* See note 98.

[102] The word "Master"—correction number 15.

[103] The *Postscript to A Treatise on the Contemplation of Mind* (*Tiantai Guanxin-lun Aopi; Tendai Kanshinron Ōhi,* Taishō vol. 46, no. 1920, 584), is not extant.

[104] The word "selected"—correction number 16.

[105] The term "seal of the mind" expresses the nonduality between the concepts of the mind as a seal for stamping and the mind as the mark stamped with the seal. It carries the same meaning as "transmitting mind through mind" (*yixinchuanxin; ishidenshin*), i.e., the realization that there is no transmitter or recipient, just the transmission of mind itself. See also note 78 on "not setting up any words."

[106] The word "lineage"—correction number 17.

[107] The passage quoted here is not found in the *Longer Records of the Buddha's Words* [61]. In the *Great Root Sutra* (*Mahāpadāna-suttanta; Dabenji; Daihongyō;* Taishō vol. 1, no. 1; *Dīghanikāya* II), Śākyamuni cites the names of the six Buddhas who appeared in the world before him: three in the past *kalpa* and three in the present auspicious *kalpa* (*bhadrakalpa*). However, the Buddha makes no reference to the name of the past *kalpa* or to the appearance of one thousand Buddhas.

What constitutes the source of Eisai's quote is seen in the *Account of the Three-Kalpa Three-Thousand Buddhas* (*Sanjiesanqianfo-yuanqi; Sangōsanzenbutsu-engi;* Taishō vol. 14, no. 446, 364c–365a), a passage quoted from another sutra, the *Sutra on Contemplation of the Two Bodhisattvas Bhaiṣajyarāja and Bhaiṣajyarājasamudgata* (*Guanyaowangyaoshangerpusajing; Kanyakuōyakujōnibosatsukyō*), translated by Kālayaśas in the Liu-Song dynasty, 424–442; Taishō vol. 20, no. 1161. In the *Account of the Three-Kalpa Three-Thousand Buddhas,* Śākyamuni refers to the threefold one thousand Buddhas and their appearances in the world in the past "*kalpa* of supernal manifestations (*vyūhakalpa; zhuangyanjie; shōgongō*)," the present "auspicious *kalpa* (*bhadrakalpa; xianjie; gengō*)," and the future "lunar-mansion *kalpa* (*nakṣatrakalpa; xingxiujie; seishukugō*)." In the Taishō Tripiṭaka the *Account* is followed by the *Sutra of the Names of One Thousand Buddhas in the Past Kalpa of Supernal Manifestations* (*Guoquzhuangyanjieqianfomingjing; Kakoshōgongōsenbutsumyōkyō*). After the title, before the text of the sutra, where the translator's name would usually appear, there is a note that reads: "The translator's name is missing. This is gleanings from the *Kaiyuan (Kaigen) Buddhist Text Catalogue,* recorded in the *Liang (Ryō) Catalogue.*" Sengyou (Sōyū) of Liang, the compiler of the *Liang Catalogue,* includes the *Account* in his *Śākya Genealogy* (*Shijiapu; Shakafu*), Taishō vol. 50, no. 2040, 9c.

The Sanskrit term "*vyūhakalpa,*" here assumed to be the original for "*zhuangyanjie; shōgongō,*" has not been confirmed in any available Sanskrit text, including the *Mahāvastu* and the *Dharmasaṃgraha.* For the meaning of "*vyūha*" I consulted Franklin Edgerton's *Buddhist Hybrid Sanskrit Dictionary* (Delhi: Motilal Banarsidass, 1972, reprint).

[108] The word "as"—correction number 18.

[109] The stupa called "Plenty of Children" refers to the Bahuputraka shrine,

called either the Bahuputraka *caitya* (Duozita; Tashitō) or the Bahuputraka *nyagrodha* (Duozishu; Tashiju), a banyan or Indian fig tree located on the road between Rājagṛha and Nālandā, which served as a shrine for people who prayed for sons. According to the *Mahāvastu* ("Stories of Great Events," a Sanskrit collection of the Buddha's legends edited by E. Senart in three volumes, Paris, 1882–97), the Licchavis presented this shrine together with three others to the Buddha and his sangha for their use (Vol. I, p. 300). In the chapter "Mahākāśyapa's Event of Entering Ascetic Life," Mahākāśyapa tells Ānanda how he left the householder life to practice under the guidance of the Buddha, met him in Rājagṛha at the Bahuputraka shrine, was accepted as a disciple, attained arthatship in eight days, offered a seat for the Buddha by spreading out his cotton under-robe on the ground under a tree, and the Buddha gave him an under-robe in return (Vol. III, pp. 50–5).

Concerning the "Bahuputraka shrine," see footnotes to the term in the corresponding pages in J. J. Jones's English translation, *The Mahāvastu* (London: Pali Text Society, 1973, Vol. I; 1978, Vol. III). The same story of Mahākāśyapa's first meeting the Buddha appears in fascicle forty-six of the *Sutra of the Original Practice* [96], where Bahuputraka is described as a shrine deity and as a tree (T. 3: 866ab).

110 The *Tiansheng Records of the Expanding Lamp* (*Tianshengguangdenglu; Tenshōkōtōroku*) compiled in 1036, thirty fascicles, *Zokuzōkyō* 8–306c, says:

> When the Buddha preached the Dharma on Vulture Peak, heavenly beings presented flowers to him. The Buddha held a flower in his hand and showed it to the audience. Kāśyapa smiled. Then the Buddha said, "I am entrusting Mahākāśyapa with the eye of the Dharma that is pure and clean. . . ."

This story has its antecedent in the *Sutra of the Original Practice* [96], fascicle four (T. 3: 668b):

> Then Dīpaṃkara, the Tathāgata, *arhan, samyaksaṃbuddha,* knew my mind, and smiled thereupon. An attending *bhikṣu* stood up from his seat, adjusted his robe, uncovered his right shoulder, paid sublime homage to the Buddha, and said: "For what reason, Most Exalted One, did the Tathāgata smile?" The Buddha Dīpaṃkara told the *bhikṣu:* "You, my mendicant, have seen how this young man [Bodhisattva Megha] (*megha,* "cloud") honored me with the seven stalks of lotus flowers he held, and then threw himself face down with hair spreading out on the muddy ground to make a bridge for me to tread upon. Because of this, this young man will, after an innumerable *kalpa,* attain awakening and be called Śākyamuni, the Tathāgata, *arhan, samyaksaṃbuddha,* provided with the Tathāgata's ten epithets, no different from me.

111 "He also composed a verse"—Here Eisai follows descriptions in the *Jingde Records of Transmission of the Lamp* [79], T. 51: 206a and 205b. To this he adds the place names "Bahuputraka shrine" and "Vulture Peak" in

order, possibly according to the *Tiansheng Records of the Expanding Lamp, Zokuzōkyō* 8–306c and 306a.

[112] A *saṃghāṭī* robe is one of the three larger outer garments of a *bhikṣu* (monk).

[113] A *śrāvaka* (lit. "word-hearer") refers to the original disciples of the Buddha who directly heard him teach, and more generally to a Buddhist mendicant whose practice consists in listening to the Buddha's teachings. A *pratyekabuddha* ("solitary awakened one") is a Buddhist practitioner who attains awakening through a direct understanding of the Buddha's teachings, in particular the teaching of dependent origination, and who does not teach or guide others. Both *śrāvaka*s and *pratyekabuddha*s, as part of the Hinayana vehicle, are distinguished from the Mahayana ideal of the bodhisattva.

[114] Eisai composes the following sections on the Chan/Zen school Dharma transmission according to the contents of fascicle three of the *Jingde Records of Transmission of the Lamp* [79].

[115] Eisai follows the dates given in the *Jingde Records of Transmission of the Lamp* [79], fasc. 3, T. 51: 219a. According to the notes of correction later inserted in the *Jingde Records,* Bodhidharma reached Guangfu in Putong the first year of Liang, not the eighth year (527), and visited Luoyang in November of the same year, the first year of Zhengguang (Shōkō), not Taihe, the tenth year of Wei (486), as is given here in the *Treatise*. This means that the correct date is the year of *gengzi* (*kōshi; kanoe-ne*), 520.

[116] "Listen to my verse"—this is what is referred to below as Bodhidharma's Dharma transmission verse. According to the *Jingde Records of Transmission of the Lamp* [79], fasc. 3, T. 51: 219c, the verse reads:

> I've originally come to this land,
> To transmit the Dharma and help the lost.
> A single flower opens in five leaves;
> The forming of seeds will naturally succeed.

[117] Eisai refers here to a passage in fascicle eighty-six of a collection of rules of practice and oral traditions of the Tendai school, compiled by the Mount Hiei priest Kōshū (1311–1348), entitled *Bundles of Leaves Collected in the Valley Mist* (*Keiranshūishū,* originally three hundred fascicles; one hundred and thirty fascicles extant). The passage (T. 76: 779c) reads:

> As has been transmitted, Bodhidharma, foreseeing the time of death, said this in verse:
>
> When one ceases to sense trickling in the jade pond,
> Getting some mysterious light at the bottom of the waves,
> There one knows impermanence.

> Then one should listen to the drum of the human skull,
> Count the number, and know on what date to die.

This was brought by a former sea captain in the days of Song named Hansheng (Hanshō) and was entrusted to Holy Priest Yōjin of Chinzei (Kyushu). The personal tradition transmitted thereafter says:

> By the jade pond is meant the mouth, by the bottom of the waves are the eyes, and by listening to the drum of the human skull is meant that at the time of the mouse on the final day of a year, one may extend both one's hands to cover both ears and hit the head, counting the number of the monthly days of the next year. When the sound of hitting ceases to be heard, that shows the date of one's death.

Further ways of practice cannot be cited here.

118 By "oneness" or "the single gate" of the mind, the monk seems to have meant the sentient being as mind is originally nothing other than the Buddha as no-mind. The source of this view is sought in the *Treatise on Awakening Confidence* [76], where the mind of a sentient being (*sattva-citta*), as yet unawakened, is explained to have two gates or modes of being: 1) the original, true mode (*tathatā*) of the mind and 2) the arising-perishing mode (samsara) of the mind. The true mode of the mind is the awakened mode of being, free of mind. The arising-perishing mode of the mind concerns how an unawakened being comes to attain awakening into the original true mode of being. Speaking of the "oneness of the mind" presupposes the above two gates. Speaking of "oneness" or "a single gate" without reference to the two gates fails to be real. The original, true mode of the mind is beyond oneness as well as twoness; it is "nothing," of "no gate."

119 The following verse is an adaptation from the biography of Xuanzang (Genjō), in fascicle one (T. 51: 2a) of the *Biographies of Eminent Buddhist Sangha Members in the Great Tang Who Visited the Western Districts to Seek the Teachings of the Buddha-Dharma* (*Datangxiyuqiufagaosengzhuan; Daitōsaiikiguhōkōsōden;* Taishō vol. 51, no. 2066), by Yijing (Gijō, 635–713).

120 Concerning the Chinese characters for these two questions, footnote number two in the Taishō text has: "The Kanmon text had a headnote that read, 'All nine characters were possibly incorrectly transcribed.'"

121 The word "calligraphy"—correction number 19.

122 In Eisai's expression, "through directly pointing to the source of the mind," the "source of the mind" means "the mind that is originally the Buddha" (*xin benlai shi fo; kokoro honrai kore butsu*), an expression by Huangbo Xiyun (Ōbakū Kiun, c. eighth–ninth centuries), according to the *Record at Wanling* (*Wanlinglu; Enryōroku*), Taishō vol. 48, no. 2012-B, 385b. In the *Essentials of the Transmission of Mind* (Taishō vol. 48, no. 2012-A;

English translation by John McRae published in this volume, pp. 1–42), Huangbo quotes the Sixth Patriarch, Huineng (T. 48: 384a):

> Just when one reaches this occasion, one knows how the patriarch has come from the west, directly pointing to the human mind, and how seeing one's nature, getting awakened to it, resides in no verbal exposition.

And this (T. 48: 383a):

> You should simply eliminate the ratiocination of the ordinary [mind] and the [enlightened] realm of the sage—there is not any separate Buddha outside of the mind. The patriarch [Bodhidharma] came from the west to point out directly that all persons are in their entireties the Buddha.

123 The two lines "It also says in effect:/Vimalakīrti remained silent" were lacking in the Kanmon version and added by Kōhō Tōshun.

124 The two lines "The *Laṅkāvatāra-sūtra* says/The Tathāgatas' nondiscriminating *dhyāna*" were lacking in the Kanmon version and added by Kōhō Tōshun.

125 This quote is not found in the *Mahāprajñāparamitā Sutra* [10], but a similar expression is found in T. 7, fasc. 531, 727c.

126 The *Mahāparinirvāṇa Sutra* [6], T. 12: 520b has, "The Tathāgata never expounds the Dharma." The line quoted here is found in the *Laṅkāvatāra-sūtra* [66], T. 16: 499c.

127 The passage quoted by Eisai here is from the first version of the *Commentary on the Mahāvairocana Sutra* [26], the *Dainichikyō Sho* (Taishō vol. 39, no. 1796), brought back by Kūkai. It is not found in the second version, the *Dainichikyō Gishaku* (*Zokuzōkyō* 1–36), brought back by Ennin. There are slight differences between the two versions. Eisai quotes from the *Dainichikyō Gishaku* at three other places in the text, pp. 90–1, 103–4, and 154. This is the only quote from the *Dainichikyō Sho*.

128 The word "Confidence"—correction number 20.

129 The three schools are the Huayan (Kegon), Faxiang (Hossō), and Tiantai (Tendai).

130 The Kanmon version has: "Originally...obtained is called seeing the Buddha-Dharma."

131 This four-line passage, beginning with "As soon as you estimate it. . . ," is from the *Extensive Record of Great Master Xuansha Zongyi of Fuzhou* (*Fuzhou Xuansha Zongyi Dashi Guanglu; Fukushū Gensha Sōitsu Daishi Kōroku*), *Zokuzōkyō* 2–31, 190a, a text in three fascicles of Xuansha Shibei (Gensha Shibi, 835–908), originally compiled between 900 and 907 by Zhiyan (Chigon), recompiled in 1080 by Sunjue (Sonkaku), reprinted in

1325 in three fascicles, and printed in Japan in 1690. However, Eisai may possibly have quoted the passage from the *Eye and Treasury of the True Dharma* [78], *Zokuzōkyō* 2–23, 59c. The expression of the original four sentences is the same in both the *Extensive Record* and the *Eye and Treasury*. The third sentence given here by Eisai is a shortened form of the last two sentences of the original, which read:

> If you let movement and quietude die out (*min; bin*), you will fall through and be lost (*luokongwang; rakukūbō*). If you accept (*shou; shū*) both movement and quietude, you will squander your Buddha-nature.

132 In his comment on case nine of the *Blue Cliff Record* [77], T. 48: 149c, Yuanwu says, "Now tell me how you would grasp it. When doing like this won't do, and not doing like this won't do either, what will you do?"

133 The expression "an arrow that has left the bow is not bound to return" is from fascicle two of Xuansha's *Extensive Record* (*Zokuzōkyō* 2–31, 190b) (see note 131, above), where it appears in the following context: "The manner of a man of the Way is like fire that melts ice and never causes freezing, or like an arrow that has left the bow, never bound to return." Yuanwu used this as a comment on the opening words of case thirty-seven of the *Blue Cliff Record* [77], T. 48: 175a: "Panshan said, 'In this triple world there is no Dharma,'" meaning that there is no Dharma, no Buddha, nothing that has its own characteristics. Panshan Baoji (Banzan Hōshaku; dates unknown) was a disciple of Mazu Daoyi (Basu Dōitsu; 709–788).

The phrase "none of the thousand sages would be able to grasp it" appears in Yuanwu's foreword to case thirty-eight of the *Blue Cliff Record* [77], T. 48: 175c: "If we speak about the immediacy of awakening, it will leave no sign or trace. None of the thousand sages would be able to grasp it."

134 In his comment on case nine of the *Blue Cliff Record* [77] (see also note 132), Yuanwu used the expression "the final day of the year-end" to mean a closing date for settling the accounts of one's life.

135 When Taiyuan Fu was lecturing on the boundless and responsive nature of the Dharma body (*dharmakāya*), a Chan practitioner in the audience laughed at him. Fu asked the practitioner why he had laughed. The Chan practitioner said that Fu could lecture on the quantity level of the Dharma body but did not see the Dharma body itself. To Fu's further questioning on what he should do, the Chan practitioner said that he should stop lecturing for a while and go sit in a quiet room, and then he would necessarily see the Dharma body for himself. Fu followed this advice and one night, while sitting in a quiet room, on hearing the gong marking the fifth watch of the night he suddenly attained awakening.

Later, Fu went to Master Xuefeng Yicun (Seppō Gison; 822–908) and practiced with him, not leaving to take up residence in any temple. That is why he was called Fu Shangzuo (Jōza, "Elder Monk"). See also fascicle nineteen of the *Jingde Records of Transmission of the Lamp* [79], T. 51: 359c–360a.

136 The word "seek"—correction number 21.

137 "An ancient man of Chan"—Eisai refers here to Muzhou Daozon (Bokujū Dōshō; 780?–877?), a Dharma heir to Huangbo Xiyun (Ōbakū Kiun), according to the *Chanmenniansongji* (*Zenmonnenjushū*) 16, a record of Chan masters' words and comments in verse compiled in Korea, 1226. It seems Eisai knew of this through some other source, but his contemporary source is no longer extant.

138 Luoshan Daoxian (Razan Dōkan; dates unknown), a Dharma heir to Yantou Quanhuo (Gantō Zenkatsu; 826–885).

139 Shishuang Qingzhu (Sekisō Keisho; 807–888), a Dharma heir to Daowu Yuanzhi (Dōgo Enchi; 769–835).

140 The phrase "make one moment ten thousand years" is from the *Inscription on the Confident Mind* (*Xinxinming; Shinjinmei*), in fascicle nineteen of the *Jingde Records of Transmission of the Lamp* [79], T. 51: 457b:

> The Dharma world of suchness has neither self nor other.
> To whom accord is pressing, let me just say, "Be nondual."
> Being nondual, all are the same, leaving none uncontained.
> The wise in the ten directions all enter this principal aim.
> The principal aim being neither short nor long, one moment is ten thousand years.

(A variant translation of the passage appears in the English translation by Osamu Yoshida, published under the title "The Faith-Mind Maxim," Taishō vol. 48, no. 2010, in the volume *Three Chan Classics,* Numata Center, 1999).

In response to Luoshan's question,"When arising and perishing don't cease, what shall I do?", Shishuang said, "Have the container fit the lid," meaning for Luoshan not to separate himself from arising and perishing. Luoshan could not accord with this response and left Shishuang to go to Yantou, who responded "What is it that arises and perishes?" At this, Luoshan could be one with arising and perishing.

141 Yantou Quanhuo (Gantō Zenkatsu) a Dharma heir along with Xuefeng Yicun (Seppō Gison) to Deshan Xuanjian (Tokusan Senkan; 782?–865).

142 In his comment on case two of the *Blue Cliff Record* [77], Yuanwu cites the first two lines of the *Inscription on the Confident Mind* (see note 140) with Master Zhaozhou Congshen's (Jōshū Jūshin; 778–897) critical remarks on them. The lines read:

> The ultimate Way is not hard to attain, though it dislikes selection.
> Only take care not to hate or love, and the Way will be thoroughly clear.

Zhaozhou says, "As soon as there is any word, that's a selection. I don't abide even in being clear." Yuanwu comments (T. 48: 141c): "Tell me where Zhaozhou abides. Do apprehend the aim of the steelyard hook. Never cling to the measurement marks on the beam."

143 To "throw a pepper seed onto the tip of a needle"—in Chapter I, part two, of the *Mahāparinirvāṇa Sutra* [6], fasc. 2, T. 12: 372c, a lay devotee named Cunda-Karmāraputra expresses in verse his joy at having the opportunity to offer a meal to the Buddha. Tradition holds that the Buddha did accept the meal, which proved to be his last. In this Mahayana scripture, however, the Buddha continues discoursing about the meaning of his passing into *parinirvāṇa*. In the verse Cunda compares the rarity and difficulty of receiving a human life and encountering a Buddha to that of throwing a pepper seed onto the tip of a needle or a blind tortoise ascending from the depths of the sea through a hole in a piece of wood floating on the surface.

144 Fascicle eighty of the *Book of Jin* (*Shinjo,* one hundred and thirty fascicles) cites the following episode with Wang Huizi (Ō Kishi), the son of Wang Xizi (Ō Gishi):

> Huizi, who styled himself Ziyou (Shiyū) . . . once resided in Shanyin (San'in). One night it stopped snowing and cleared up for the first time. The moon looked clean and bright, and made all in the four quarters appear bright. Drinking alone, he recited a poem by Daikui (Daiki), who was then in Shan (Zhe). Immediately Huizi boarded a ship and arrived there. After a night he approached the hermitage but he stopped at the gate and returned [home]. When someone asked him the reason [for this], Huizi said, "I went there while in a joyful mood. When the mood was gone, I left. Why did I have to see [Daikui] by all means?"

(Quoted from the Zhonghuashuju text, Beijing, 1974, p. 2103.)

145 Tianhuang Daowu (Tennō Dōgo; 748–807), a Dharma heir to Shitou Xiqian (Sekitō Kisen; 700–791).

146 Said by Tianhuang Daowu (Tennō Dōgo) to Longtan Chongxin (Ryūtan Sōshin; dates unknown), Deshan Xuanjian's (Tokusan Senkan) master, who requested from him instruction on the essentials of the mind.

147 Qinglin Shiqian (Seirin Shiken; d. 904), a Dharma heir to Dongshan Lianjia (Tōzan Ryōkai).

148 The following passages on the practice of zazen are considered an abbreviated form of material found in the extant text of the *Chan School Monastic Rules* [3] fasc. 8, *Zokuzōkyō* 2–16, 460c. However, according to Seizan Yanagida, this passage on the manner of practicing zazen was added to the *Chan School Monastic Rules* in 1202, after Eisai wrote and made public the *Treatise* in 1198. Professor Yanagida surmises that Eisai must have seen the same material in another source.

149 The word "Thus"—correction number 22.

150 The word "back"—correction number 23.

151 In the Tang dynasty a monk named Wuzhe (Mujaku) learned the Huayan (Kegon) teachings from Dharma Master Chengguan (Chōkan; 738–839), and in the second year of Dali (Daireki; 767) he went to Wutaishan (Godaisan) to see the region of holy persons. In May he reached the Huayansi (Kegonji) on the mountain. Then he went to a cave called Jingangku (Kongōkutsu) where after a nap he heard an old man admonishing a cow to take water. The old man invited Wuzhe to tea at his own temple nearby. After drinking a cup of tea brought by a young boy, fourteen or fifteen years old, and conversing for awhile, Wuzhe wanted to leave. Then the old man recited a verse he had composed, quoted by Eisai here in the *Treatise*. With deep thanks, Wuzhe parted from the old man. The latter instructed the boy to accompany Wuzhe down the mountain. The boy recited a verse: "The face with no hatred upon it is offering a gift./The mouth with no hatred in it breathes out fragrant scent./The mind with no hatred in it is a rare treasure./Being neither defiled nor disgraced, one is truly constant." After the verse was over, and while he was still enraptured, Wuzhe suddenly lost sight of both boy and temple and saw only the mountain, forest, earth, and rocks. Wuzhe later secluded himself on this mountain and died there (T. 50: 836c–837b).

152 The word "confidence"—correction number 24.

153 The source of this quote from the *Commentary on the Diamond Sutra by the Dharmalakṣaṇa School* [84] (Taishō vol. 40, no. 1816) by C'ien (Jion) has not been identified.

154 The source of this quote from the *Commentary on the Diamond Sutra* [85] by Huizhao (Eshō) of Zizhou (Shishū) has not been identified.

155 The *Mahāparinirvāṇa Sutra* [6] has this passage by the Buddha (T. 12, XXII, 493b):

> Bodhisattvas hear of the great nirvana that has been unheard of. No *śrāvaka*s or *pratyekabuddha*s have ever heard that the Buddha has the eternity-delight self-purity that is never extinguished, that the Buddha-nature of the Three Treasures is beyond any discriminative characteristics, and that those who have committed the fourfold transgressions or found fault with the Mahayana scriptures, transgressors of the five grave sins, and those who have no aspiration (*icchantika*s), when giving rise to the aspiration to attain awakening (*bodhicitta*), are all equipped with Buddha-nature. But now in this scripture they can hear of it. This is my so-called hearing of what has been unheard of.

This seems to be what was meant by the Tiantai (Tendai) concept of "the eternity of nirvana as the true support for morality."

[156] These are two groups of the monastic precepts. The "five definitive distinctions of sin" include the 1) *pārājika,* 2) *saṃghāvaśesa,* 3) *pāyattika* and *pātayantika,* 4) *pratideśanīya,* and 5) bodily and verbal transgressions, which include *aniyata, śaikṣadharma,* and *adhikaraṇaśamathā.* See the quote from the *Chan School Monastic Rules* [3] in Gate I, p. 76, for a complete description of these Sanskrit terms.

The "seven groups of transgressions" include 1) *pārājika,* 2) *saṃghāvaśesa,* 3) *sthūlātyaya* ("coarse transgressions," i.e., attempted *pārājika* and *saṃghāvaśesa*), 4) *pāyattika* and *pātayantika,* 5) *pratideśanīya,* 6) bodily transgressions (*duṣkṛta*) and 7) verbal transgressions (*durbhāṣita*).

[157] "Four phrases concerning *yāna* (vehicle) and *śīla* (precepts) [with which one is either relaxed or firm]"—In the *Mahāparinirvāṇa Sutra* [6] the Buddha takes up the problem of how monks' and bodhisattvas' seeking liberation and keeping precepts are to be related to one another after the Buddha's passing into *parinirvāṇa,* for during his lifetime it was the Buddha who provided practitioners with precepts. According to the scriptural context, the term *yāna* seems to mean *niryāṇa* ("going forth," "final liberation"). The Buddha says there can be relaxation or slacking of *yāna* but not *śīla,* for a bodhisattva's not slacking in upholding the precepts in the mind of the Mahayana is what is meant by the "original precept" (T. 12: 400c). In the *Great Calming and Contemplation* [29], T. 46: 39ab, Zhiyi classifies the relation between *yāna* and *śīla* into four: 1) being firm with both *yāna* and *śīla,* 2) being firm with *yāna* and relaxing with *śīla,* 3) being firm with *śīla* and relaxing with *yāna,* and 4) relaxing with both *yāna* and *śīla.*

[158] The word "should"—correction number 25.

[159] "A sutra," unidentified. The quote cited in the *Great Calming and Concentration* [29] (T. 46: 20a) is found in the *Treatise on the Core of Analysis of Buddhist Concepts Taken Up for Meditation* (*Saṃyuktābhidharmahṛdaya-śāstra; Zaapitaxinlun; Zōabidonshinron*), translated by Saṃghavarman et al., Taishō vol. 28, no. 1552. In this text Dharmatrāta took up Dharmaśrī's *Treatise* for meditation. The *Treatise on the Core of Analysis* (T. 28, IX, 949c) may be the sutra referred to here.

[160] Devadatta was a Buddhist who died the death of a *pratyekabuddha* after going through the suffering of hell because of his grave transgressions. See also vol. II, *"Saṅghabhedavastu"* ("Matters of Disunion in the Sangha") of the *Mūlasarvāstivādavinayavastu* (*Matters of Discipline with the Original Advocates of the Existence of All; Genbenshuoyiqieyoubupinaye; Konponsetsuissaiububinaya*), translated by Yijing, Taishō vol. 24, no. 1450, pp. 147–50.

[161] Udraka Rāmaputra was a non-Buddhist master practitioner of *dhyāna* in the days of Śākyamuni. See also Aśvaghoṣa's *Buddhacarita,* XII, verse

84 and others, translated by E. H. Johnston (Delhi: Motilal Banarsidass, 1972).

162 The word "also"—correction number 26. The Taishō text had the word *fei* (*hi, arazu*), "not" here, which has been replaced by the word *yi* (*yaku, mata*), "also," according to the context.

163 According to the *Bequeathed Teaching Sutra* [40] (T. 12: 1110c), on his deathbed the Buddha said, "After I die you may respectfully make much of *prātimokṣa* (i.e., liberation from all self-afflicting passions through the practice of *śīla*), . . . for that is your great master."

164 The word "applying"—correction number 27.

165 The word "delusive"—correction number 28.

166 In his *Sutra of the Jeta Grove Drawings* (*Zhiyuantujing; Gionzukyō;* two fascicles, Taishō vol. 45, no. 1899, 883a–895c), Daoxuan (596–667) includes a detailed description according to tradition of the structures of the Jetavana residence built by Sudatta for the Buddha, but no drawings are found in the extant text. Daoxuan's own title for the text, *Drawings of the Jetavana Anāthapiṇḍikārāma* or *Anāthapiṇḍadasyārāma* (*Drawings of the Jetavana Piṇḍada-vihāra; Zhishugeiyuantu; Gijugyūenzu*), lacks the word *jing* (*kyō*), i.e., *sutra,* which is included in the title by the author of the Foreword as well as in the closing title of each fascicle.

167 See the *Mahāsāṃghika Vinaya* [7], T. 22: 262b. The Vinaya text says that the Tathāgata visited monks' cells once every five days in order to know 1) whether or not his disciples were attached to things of the world, 2) whether or not they indulged in secular discussions, 3) whether or not they overindulged in sleep to the detriment of practice, 4) whether or not they looked after sick monks, and 5) so that newly ordained young monks might rejoice at the sight of the Tathāgata.

168 See also a passage from the *Chan School Monastic Rules* [3], quoted previously in Gate VII, p. 148.

169 The word "holds"—correction number 29.

170 The extant text of the *Bequeathed Teaching Sutra* [40] does not include this passage. It is found in Zhiyi's *Smaller Tiantai Text of Calming and Contemplation* (*Tiantaixiaozhiguan; Tendaishōshikan;* Taishō vol. 46, no. 1915) which quotes it from another, unspecified sutra (T. 46, IV, 465b).

171 The word "Hakata"—correction number 30.

172 Dongjing (Tokei), i.e., Kaifeng (Kaifū), the capital of Northern Song.

173 When Eisai, then twenty-eight years old, was about to leave for Song China.

[174] Lizhou (Reishū) in Sichuan Province.

[175] A year before Eisai, then fifty, returned to Japan.

[176] Master Zhiyi was said to have had spiritual experiences at Guoqing (Kokusei) Temple.

[177] I.e., the *vajrāsana,* the place where Siddhārtha attained awakening under the *bodhi* tree.

[178] During the reign of Emperor Taizong (Taisō).

[179] The source of this quote and one on the following page is unidentified. The *Sutra of the Original Practice* [96] does not include these passages.

[180] See also another passage about Upagupta and the nun from the *Mahāprajñāpāramitā Treatise* [2] quoted in Gate III, pp. 104–5.

[181] *Repa* or *ripta-lepa,* "what sticks or adheres."

[182] Daosheng (Dōshō; d. 434), of the Eastern Jin (Shin) dynasty. After becoming a Buddhist mendicant, Daosheng went to Lushan (Rozan) and lived deep in the mountains for seven years. He later practiced under the guidance of Kumārajīva. From his reading of a Chinese version in six fascicles of the *Nirvana Sutra* (*Niepanjing; Nehangyō;* Taishō vol. 12, no. 376), translated in 418 by Faxian (Hokken), Daoxuan believed in the scriptural standpoint that an *icchantika* (i.e., one who lacks the aspiration to attain awakening) can indeed attain awakening, though Faxian's version of the sutra did not contain any passage to support this point. Contemporary Buddhist scholars faulted Daosheng for this lack of scriptural support for his view. Later a more comprehensive version of the *Nirvana Sutra,* translated in 422 by Dharmakṣema (Taishō vol. 12, no. 374), included the very passage that Daosheng had suggested. In the eleventh year of Yuanjia, of Song of the Southern Dynasties, at Lushan, Daosheng was near the end of giving a Dharma talk when he suddenly saw the strands of a whisk (*fuzi; hossu*) in his hand fall thick and fast to the ground. Daosheng then sat upright, adopted a stern countenance, leaned on the table, and died. See the *Biographies of Eminent Monks* (*Gaosengchuan; Kōsōden*) compiled by Huijiao (Ekō; 497–554), Taishō vol. 50, no. 2059, 366bc–367a.

Genshin, in his *Essentials of the Single Vehicle* [99] (T. 74: 361a), praised Daosheng by calling him a *ninshibosatsu* ("bodhisattva who endured death"), meaning that Daosheng said he had long endured death before his view that *icchantika*s could attain awakening could be demonstrated, but when scriptural support for this view finally appeared, he passed away.

[183] The quoted passage is not found in the *Mahāprajñāpāramitā Treatise* [2].

[184] The Pure Land practices of *chengming* (*shōmyō*) ("calling the name of Amitābha Buddha") and *nianfo* (*nembutsu*), "recalling the vow made by

Amitābha Buddha while he was a bodhisattva for the actualization of a Land of Bliss (Sukhāvatī) for ordinary beings" or "chanting the Buddha's name," essentially the same practice as *chengming*.

185 Namely, Hakozaki Shrine in Hakata, Kyushu.

186 Correction number 31. Eisai mistakes this text, *An Approach to the Truth through the Samādhi Called No Polemics* [101] for a sutra (*jing; kyō*), when the word *famen* (*hōmon*) in the title, *Wuzhengsanmeifamen* (*Musōzanmaihōmon*) indicates otherwise.

187 The word "evil"—correction number 32.

188 The words "And even"—correction number 33.

189 The passage that follows here is not found in the extant text. It seems to be Eisai's interpolation.

190 A year before Eisai wrote the *Treatise*.

191 The last syllable "ta"—correction number 34.

192 Fohai Huiyuan (Bukkai Eon) was the successor to Yuanwu Keqin (Engo Kokugon; 1063–1135).

193 Fohai died in 1176 not 1174, as indicated here.

194 Fozhao Deguang (Busshō Tokukō; 1121–1203) was a Dharma heir to Dahui Zonggao (Daie Sōkō; 1089–1163). One of Fozhao's Dharma successors was Dainichibō Nōnin, who is discussed in the Translator's Introduction, pp. 48, 49–50, 52–3.

195 "Sea of Penglai" (Hōrai) refers to the Bohai (Bokkai) Sea, which extends between the two peninsulas of Shandong and Liaodong in the northeastern part of China. An ancient belief held that a fabled abode of immortals called Mount Penglai (Hōraisan) existed in the midst of this sea.

196 Here a character is missing.

A UNIVERSAL RECOMMENDATION FOR TRUE ZAZEN

Translator's Introduction

The author of this text, Eihei Dōgen, was born in Kyoto in 1200 C.E. His family was of the noble class: his father, Koga Michichika, was a minister of the imperial court and his mother was the daughter of the regent Fujiwara Motofusa. While still a young child, Dōgen lost both parents—his father died when Dōgen was just two years old, and five years later his mother died. It is not difficult to imagine that the tragic events of Dōgen's childhood gave him a powerful experience of the impermanence of existence and led him to seek true awakening and total peace. Five years after his mother's death, at the age of twelve, he renounced secular life. The following year, in 1213, he took the tonsure and received ordination in the bodhisattva precepts at Mount Hiei.

At Mount Hiei Dōgen first studied the Tendai teachings, and met Myōan Eisai, who had brought the teachings of the Linji (Rinzai) school of Chan to Japan. He continued his studies under Eisai's disciple, Myōzen Ryōnen, eventually receiving *inka,* the certificate of confirmation of spiritual attainment conferred from Zen master to disciple.

In 1223, Dōgen traveled to China, seeking the true Awakened Way. Two years later, in 1225, he met Tiantong Rujing (1163–1228) and entered a course of intensive meditation practice (zazen) under him. During the summer retreat of that year he realized the complete dropping off of body and mind during zazen and received formal confirmation in the Dharma from Rujing. He returned to Japan in 1227, with "the grave thought of propagating the Dharma and saving sentient beings." He stayed first at the Kenninji in Kyoto, then the capital. In 1233 he founded the Kannondōri-in (Avalokiteśvara Benefactory Hall) at the site of the former Gokurakuji (Supreme Bliss Temple) in the Kyoto suburb of Uji.

In 1243 Dōgen left Kyoto and went to live deep in the mountains of Echizen Province (present-day Fukui Prefecture). He founded the Daibutsuji (Great Buddha Temple), renaming it Eiheiji (Perpetual Peace Temple) two years later. Dōgen passed away in 1253. His transformational work continues even today through his spiritual legacy that has been maintained and transmitted by many generations of Zen practitioners.

Dōgen is regarded by Japanese Buddhist historians as the founder of the Japanese Sōtō Zen school. However, the full scope of his contribution to the Buddhist tradition has long been underestimated. He was a truly great reformer of Japanese Buddhism. By his time Buddhism in Japan had undergone both evolution and involution. Scholasticism and ritualism dominated within the traditional Buddhist institutions. At the same time, several new Buddhist movements had evolved, such as the Pure Land (Jōdo) and Nichiren schools founded respectively by Hōnen (1133–1212) and Nichiren (1222–1282), near-contemporaries of Dōgen. New schools struggled for ascendancy and legitimacy within the existing state-supported Buddhist institutions, often facing imperial sanction.

Facing this tumultuous situation, Dōgen advocated the single Awakened Way, which went far beyond the narrow sectarian boundary of the Sōtō school. He stressed the significance of practice through maintaining awakening with the body, and revealed the path of "pure sitting" (*shikantaza*), which requires no other goal or activity. At the same time Dōgen upheld the idea of universal salvation on the basis that all beings are endowed with Buddha-nature. He thus embraced both the rigorous path of early Buddhist practice and the comprehensive ideals of the Mahayana (Great Vehicle).

Text of *A Universal Recommendation for True Zazen*

In 1227, at the midpoint of his career, Dōgen returned from China, having found an answer to his long-standing question: Why does one need to practice, if, as is taught in the Mahayana tradition, all beings have Buddha-nature and are thus originally enlightenened? Dōgen realized that the path of seeking *bodhi* (awakening), the path of practice, was at the same time the method of saving all beings, the bodhisattva path. This work, *A Universal Recommendation for True Zazen* (*Fukanzazengi*), was written in part in response to a request from his followers. This was Dōgen's first turning of the wheel of the Dharma and also his last will and testament, as he continued to refine the text until the end of his life.

In this work Dōgen offers a unique message of the essence of the Awakened Way in its utmost aspiration, profound perspective, and penetrating purity. Here, Dōgen recommends to all the most direct and simplest way to unsurpassed awakening and unconditioned peace. He reveals the way to living one's life in harmony with the entire world in the ten directions (the four cardinal directions, the four intermediate directions, and the zenith and nadir, i.e., everywhere), beyond the bounds of the three times (past, present and future, i.e., all times). The way demonstrated by Dōgen is truly the purest practice of unified cultivation and verification. Cultivation and verification are necessary to get free of one's karma and must not be defiled by delusion and desire.

The title *Fukanzazengi* reveals Dōgen's intent in writing this work. *Fukan* ("universal recommendation") reflects his assurance and aspiration that all beings shall become Buddhas, i.e., awakened, and realize the awakened world, based on his conviction that "all are Buddha-nature." Dōgen was convinced that zazen (lit., *za,* "seated," *zen,* "meditation," *zen* being a transliterated form of the Sanskrit term *dhyāna*) is the most useful, universal form of practice for this purpose, having no discriminations, no requirements, and no fabrications. This method puts a stop to acquired habits (karmas). *Gi* ("true form and norm") expresses the true essence and meaning of zazen, not just in its limited sense as the practice of seated meditation. In this respect, it points to the paramount truth or ultimate meaning (*paramārtha*), which puts the body, mind, and world in perfect order, free of discrimination and in total harmony beyond any boundaries.

The title itself thus demonstrates the dropping off of body and mind—the dropping away of all karmas of the three actions of body, speech, and mind, both new actions and the karmic results of old actions. It is at once the realization of freedom *from* body and mind and freedom—the free use—*of* body and mind in perfect perspective and full function. Zazen stops all karmas and allows one to see the existential root of original purity and harmony. Here cultivation itself becomes verification. Thus, the "dignified form (i.e., the awakened form and norm) itself is Buddha."

Though brief, the text can be seen as having four parts: 1) essence, 2) form, 3) function, and 4) existence.

1. Essence: Pure zazen manifests in a true (original, absolute) existential form having four hallmarks: *penetration, freedom, purity,* and *locus*. These four correspond respectively to the four key elements of Dōgen's spiritual system, as mentioned previously: the single Awakened Way, the practice of maintaining awakening with the body, "pure meditation" (*shikantaza*) requiring no other aim or activity, and the ideal of universal salvation. The body and mind in zazen are likened to a bowl of water that has been allowed to settle and become still, without turbulence and turbidity, which then reflects reality without distortion. This is called "sitting (calm)" and "becoming clear." Or it is likened to a top spinning in perfect balance and full function. Cultivation—the unconditioning and reconditioning of karmas through zazen—is the verification of the true nature of our existence and our free use of it.

The four hallmarks of zazen are not just one's subjective experience in sitting but objective reality. True existential form is the limitless interrelation of dependent origination. The law of dependent origination (*pratītyasamutpāda*)—all phenomena (*dharmas*) come into being through a confluence of causes and conditions—works universally, *penetrating* throughout space and time. *Freedom* (*priyadhāman*, a Sanskrit cognate word meaning "beloved domain") consists in familiarizing oneself with this *dharma* (norm and form) in knowing and acting. *Purity* is found in this, in transcending limited understanding and action. The *locus* of realization is here and now.

2. Form: The concrete method of zazen is putting body, mind, and world in the best, absolute order, not limited by distorted, discriminated states. "Fathomless" (*hishiryō*, "no thought-measure") is the state before conceptual thought and beyond perceptual boundaries—that is, freedom from measures and the free use of them. It is a world totally penetrated, "all in one and one in all," by dependent origination. It is full functioning, with body, mind, and world in total oneness. Each action works with the entire world. This calm, clear, unlimited, and unmoved state is maintained regardless of one's outward disposition of sitting, standing, walking, or lying down. It is the most stable, wakeful, and peaceful state in the free, full function of totality. This function is no mere outer appearance of "meditation" but the cultivation and verification of the unconditioned peace (nirvana) and unsurpassed awakening (*bodhi*) of universal truth beyond boundaries and bonds.

Here zazen is not mere meditation practice with relative means and ends, with signs and symbols, with desires to gain merit and designs to become a Buddha, or in outward forms and norms. It is instead pure freedom, the dropping off of all these. It is "pure meditation" (*zen = dhyāna*)" or "devoted sitting" (*shikantaza*) which engages in no mental or physical fabrications, whether of conceptualization or conduct.

3. Function: This is the full function beyond all physical and mental limitations. Sublime functioning at the very source cannot be understood or attained by supernatural faculties, much less by discriminating or weighing thoughts. If one sits singleheartedly in the Buddha-seal (zazen), stopping all mental fabrication, one returns home to the original state of Buddha-nature and actualizes the Awakened Way. As we have been so fortunate as to receive a rare and precious human life and encounter the Dharma, we should not waste a single moment but constantly strive in pure zazen and realize limitless light and life (insight and action) fully and freely.

All the actions of the Buddhas and ancestors derive from this state of pure zazen in limitlessness. Many examples of masters who passed away while sitting or standing, or even at a prescribed time, have been recorded in Zen literature. In the Chinese Chan tradition, Juzhi always used his finger to respond to questions. There are yet other examples dating further back, to the roots of Zen in Indian Buddhism. On Ānanda's response to Kāśyapa's calling him, Kāśyapa bade Ānanda to take down the banner staff, indicating that his teaching was completed. Āryadeva was admitted as Nāgārjuna's disciple when he placed a needle onto the surface of water in a bowl proffered by Nāgārjuna. Kāśyapa did not raise his mallet to admonish Mañjuśrī for going out to propagate the teachings during the rainy season (summer) retreat, when monks were forbidden to leave, on hearing the Buddha ask, "Which (of the limitless) Mañjuśrīs do you expel?" Qingyuan's whisk, Zhaozhou's fist, Teshan's stick, and Linji's shout were all methods employed by these Zen masters to catalyze students' attainment of awakening.

4. Existence: Dōgen returned home from China "emptyhanded, knowing only that the eyes are horizontal and the nose vertical." He realized intimately that the realization of Buddha-nature is the very fact, right here and now, of the dropping off of body and mind in zazen itself. It is the realization (awakening and actualization) of the limitless Dharma.

This point is underscored in the *Bendōwa* (*Lecture on the Wholehearted Practice of the Way*), where Dōgen says:

> Though this Dharma is abundantly endowed, it never develops without cultivation; it can never be attained without verification.

And this:

> As verification is already cultivation, it has no end. As cultivation is verification, it has no beginning.

And in this passage from the *Genjōkōan (Realization of the Universal Truth)*:

> When Zen Master Baochi was using his fan, a monk came and asked, "The wind-nature abides constantly everywhere and pervades everywhere. Why should the master need to use a fan?"

> The master said, "You only know that the wind-nature is ever-abiding, but you have not yet realized the truth of its all-pervasiveness."
>
> The monk asked, "What is the truth of its all-pervasiveness?"
>
> At this the master just used his fan.
>
> The monk bowed.

When we realize the universal truth of universal unity in principle and practice as the net of Indra, or "the entire world in the ten directions as a ball of clear crystal," we can appreciate and use all the treasures of our treasure house—the universe—at will.

Note on the Translation

The present translation is based on Ekō Hashimoto's *Fukan-zazen-gi no Hanashi* (*Discourse on the Universal Recommendation for True Zazen*) (Tottori, Japan: Daijuji, 1977). This version of the text includes many new readings and interpretations based on detailed references to Dōgen's other works, especially to the earlier version of the text written in Dōgen's own hand (Chinese version) published in the first year of Tempuku, 1233, as well as the *Zazengi* (*Standard Method of Zazen*) (Japanese version in the *Shōbōgenzō; Eye and Treasury of the True Dharma*), the *Zazenshin* (*Zazen Lancet*), and the *Bendōhō* (*Methods for the Wholehearted Practice of the Way*). There are many corrections of popular readings and interpretations based on textual critique, word analyses, text comparsions, and references, etc. grounded in Hashimoto's lifelong study of the Dharma and zazen practice. Any translators and serious practitioners should study and practice with his text.

I referred to the following translations of the text when I first prepared this manuscript two decades ago:

Carl Bielefeldt, in *Dōgen's Manuals of Zen Meditation* (Berkeley and Los Angeles: University of California Press, 1988).

Francis Dōjun Cook, in *How to Raise an Ox* (Los Angeles: Center Publications, 1978).

Heinrich Dumoulin, in *Monumenta Nipponica,* Vol. 14, Nos. 3–4 (Tokyo: Sophia University, 1958–59).

Harry Gort and Kōshin Kawagishi, *A Universal Guide on the Right Way to Zazen* (Tokyo: Seigan-in, 1972).

Reihō Masunaga, *Introduction to Fukanzazengi* (Tokyo: Seishin Shobō, 1956); in *The Sōtō Approach to Zen* (Tokyo: Layman Buddhist Society Press, 1958), pp. 101–5; and in *Zen for Daily Living* (Tokyo: Shunjūsha, 1964).

Norman Waddell and Masao Abe, "Dōgen's *Fukanzazengi* and *Shōbōgenzō Zazengi*" in *The Eastern Buddhist,* Vol. VI, No. 2 (October 1973), pp. 121–6; and "The Universal Promotion of the Principles of Zazen" in *On Zen Practice,* Vol. II, edited by Taizan Maezumi and Bernard Tetsugen Glassman (Los Angeles: Zen Center of Los Angeles, 1977), pp. 13–16.

Yūhō Yokoi and Brian Daizen Victoria, in *Zen Master Dōgen* (New York: Weatherhill, 1976).

A recent Internet search turned up numerous translations and references in English and other languages. There seem to be many secondary translations from other translations, not from the original Japanese. I have listed several of the English versions here, in the belief that more is not necessarily better and in the interest of not spreading misconceptions and misunderstandings. Readers should closely compare different versions so as to determine the most accurate renderings, even if they cannot read the original Japanese text or critical studies and expositions.

Thomas Cleary, in *Shōbōgenzō: Zen Essays by Dōgen* (Honolulu: University of Hawaii Press, 1986).

Jiyu Kennett, in *Selling Water by the River: A Manual of Zen Training* (New York: Pantheon Books, 1972).

Gudo Nishijima and Chodo Cross, in *Master Dōgen's Shōbōgenzō,* Book I (London: Windbell Publications Ltd., 1998).

Shohaku Okamura, in *Shikantaza: An Introduction to Zazen* (Tokyo: Sōtōshū Shumucho, 1985).

Sōtō Zen Text Project, "Universally Recommended Instructions for Zazen," in *Sōtō School Scriptures for Daily Services and Practice* (Tokyo: Sōtōshū Shumuchu, 2001).

Kazuaki Tanahashi, in *Enlightenment Unfolds: The Essential Teachings of Zen Master Dōgen* (Boston: Shambhala Publications, 2000).

Yasuda Joshu Roshi and Anzan Hoshin Roshi, "*Fukanzazengi:* How Everyone Can Sit," in *Progress into the Ordinary* (Ottawa, Canada: Great Matter Publications, 1986).

A UNIVERSAL RECOMMENDATION FOR TRUE ZAZEN

by

Eihei Dōgen

In exhaustive pursuit, the root of the Way is perfectly penetrating. 1a
Why should you assume cultivation and verification? The supreme vehicle moves freely. Why should you consume striving and skill? Much more, its entirety is far beyond the realm of dust. Who would believe in the measures of sweeping? It never departs from right where you are. Why should you require the steps of cultivation?

And yet, if there is even the slightest discrepancy, you become separated as far apart as heaven and earth. If the slightest liking or disliking arises, the mind is lost in confusion. Even though you may achieve the insightful power of glimpsing the [Buddha's] ground, taking pride in your understanding and enjoying enlightenment; even though you may generate the aspiration of pressing on to heaven, attaining the Way, and clarifying the mind; even though you may roam around the boundary of this realm, reaching the point of putting your head in, still you largely lack the life-path of liberation.

Moreover, the trace of six years' upright sitting by the innately awakened [Śākyamuni Buddha] at Jetavana must be observed. And the fame of nine years' facing the wall by the transmitter of the mind-seal [Bodhidharma] at Shaolin Temple must be heard. If the ancient sages were like this, why should you, a person of today, not exert yourself?

Therefore, you must stop comprehending the conduct of investigating words and chasing discourses. You must learn to step backward to turn your light around to reflect on yourself. Mind and body will naturally fall away and your original face will manifest itself. If you wish to attain suchness, devote yourself to suchness at once.

Now, in entering into Zen, a quiet room is suitable. Eat and drink in moderation. Abandon all relations and put all concerns to rest, not thinking of good and bad, not entertaining right and wrong. Still the driving of your heart, mind, and consciousness. Stop the measuring of memories, ideas, and meditations. No design, even that of becoming a Buddha, should be harbored. How can it (i.e., Zen) be concerned with sitting or lying down?

The usual practice is to spread out a thick mat and place a cushion upon it. Then sit in the full or half cross-legged position. In the full cross-legged position, place your right foot on your left thigh and your left foot on your right thigh. In the half cross-legged position, simply press your right thigh with your left foot. Wear your robes and sashes loosely but neatly and orderly.

Next, rest your right hand on your left foot, and place your left palm on your right palm, [both facing upward], with the thumb-tips supporting each other.

Now, sit upright, leaning neither to left nor right, neither forward nor backward. You must align your ears over your shoulders and keep your nose in line with your navel. Rest your tongue against the upper palate, lips and teeth closed. You must always keep your eyes open. Breathe through your nose subtly and silently.

Maintaining the proper bodily alignment, exhale deeply once and rock to the left and right. Settle into the solid, steadfast seated *samādhi*. Fathom the unfathomed state. How do you fathom the
1b unfathomed state? Fathomless! Such is the essential art of zazen.

What is here called zazen is not learning mere meditation. It is the Dharma gate of pure peace and bliss. It is the cultivation and verification of ultimate awakening. Here, the universal truth is realized, and nets and cages are totally absent.

If you realize this tenet completely, you are like a dragon obtaining water and a tiger reclining on the mountain. You will surely know that the True Dharma will naturally manifest itself, and dullness and distraction will drop off.

When you rise from sitting, move slowly and rise calmly and carefully. Never act hastily or violently.

Observe and appreciate that transcending the ordinary and going beyond the holy, passing away while sitting and dying while standing, all depend solely on this power. The transforming ability of a finger, a staff, a needle, and a mallet, or the verifying utilization of a whisk, a fist, a stick, and a shout at a critical moment cannot readily be realized by the discrimination of measuring thoughts.

How can they be known even by the cultivation and verification of supernatural faculties?

These are the dignified forms beyond sounds and colors. Are they not the rules before knowledge and views? Therefore, you should not be concerned whether you are a person of lofty intellect or lowly foolishness, nor discriminated as being a sharp person or a dull one. If you strive singlemindedly, that itself is the realization of the Way. Cultivation and verification by nature does not defile. Going forward then is totally calm and constant.

All the Buddhas, whether in this world or in other quarters, in the western heaven (India) or the eastern earth (China), equally held the Buddha-seal and altogether enjoyed the supreme style. They were fully devoted to this total sitting (*shikantaza*) and were totally installed in this unmoved state. Even though there are a thousand differences and a million nuances, they engaged devotedly in practicing zazen and realizing the Way.

Why should you forsake the seat of your own home and stray into the dusty realms of other countries? If you make a single misstep, you will mistakenly pass it by while directly facing it. You have ultimately obtained the functional essence of a human body. Never let the light and shadow (i.e., day and night) pass in vain. You have embraced and engaged in the essential function of the Buddha's path. Who could enjoy the spark of a flintstone aimlessly?

Furthermore, form and substance are like dew on a blade of grass, and fleeting life is as a flash of lightning, instantly emptied and immediately lost.

May respectable Zen practitioners constantly learn the right form and never doubt the true dragon.

Urgently strive for the Way that points directly to the right target, revere the unfabricating and unconditioned person, fit into the awakening (*bodhi*) of the Buddhas, and rightly inherit the *samādhi* of the ancestors. Practice in such a way constantly and you will never fail to realize suchness. The treasure house will open by itself, and you will appreciate and use it at will.

ADVICE ON THE PRACTICE OF ZAZEN

Translator's Introduction

Keizan Jōkin (1268–1325) was one of the main patriarchs of Japanese Sōtō Zen, generally considered second in importance only to Dōgen (1200–1253), founder of the school. Keizan established the prestigious Sōjiji in Ishikawa Prefecture, and wrote more than two dozen works on the Sōtō approach to Buddhist theory and practice. For a comprehensive study of Keizan's life and works in light of critical theory, see Bernard Faure, *Visions of Power: Imagining Medieval Japanese Buddhism,* translated by Phyliss Brooks (Princeton, NJ: Princeton University Press, 1996).

Keizan was born in Echizen Province (present-day Fukui Prefecture), where several decades earlier Dōgen had established Eiheiji, which became the center of the Sōtō sect. He studied with Tettsū Gikai, a leading Sōtō figure at Eiheiji and Dōjiji. He also trained under Ejō, Dōgen's main disciple, and Jakuen, a Chinese monk who was one of Dōgen's followers. In addition, he came in contact with Rinzai Zen scholars and with representatives of the Tendai, Shingon, Pure Land (Jōdo), and Shugendō Buddhist schools and movements on Mount Hiei and in his travels in the mountain provinces.

In absorbing these various influences and teachings—including esoteric and exoteric teachings, the Pure Land notions of self-power and other-power, the idea of sudden and gradual enlightenment, zazen practice and *kōan* study, and traditional and independent practices—and in assimilating popular rituals, Keizan developed a highly integrative and popularizing approach. This eclectic attitude helped transform the Sōtō school from a conservative monastic institution to a mass movement that spread throughout the northern and northeastern provinces. Keizan was largely responsible for giving Sōtō an appeal based on faith and devotion as well as meditation, and he advocated a close relationship with the common people in funeral and memorial services, and through social activities and construction projects.

Keizan was chronologically the Sōtō school's fourth patriarch (after Dōgen, Ejō, and Tettsū), but his significance for the development of the sect is recognized as being much greater. While Dōgen is known as *kōso* (founder), Keizan is known as *taiso* (progenitor). Similarly, Dōgen is affectionately referred to as the "father" of the sect, and Keizan as its "mother." Like Dōgen, who became a monk at a young age, Keizan entered Eiheiji at age thirteen, where he came in contact with Tettsū and Ejō. At eighteen, he studied with Jakuen at Hōkyōji, and later traveled to the center of Tendai and Rinzai Zen Buddhism on Mount Hiei. Still unfulfilled in his religious quest, Keizan returned to train with Tettsū at Daijōji Temple, which Tettsū had converted from Shingon to Zen. Keizan attained a spontaneous enlightenment (*kenshō*) at age twenty-seven upon reflecting on the famous saying of the Chinese patriarch Mazu (Baso), "Everyday mind is itself the Way."

After that, Keizan systematically studied Dōgen's *Shōbōgenzō* (*Eye and Treasury of the True Dharma*), the foundational text for Sōtō thought and practice, and composed his first work, the *Denkōroku* (*Record of the Transmission of the Light*), a sectarian biography written in Japanese of the fifty-three patriarchs in the Sōtō lineage, from Śākyamuni to Ejō, which remains one of the main sources for biographical studies of Dōgen. Keizan stayed at numerous temples, including Dōkokuji. He made the Shingon Yōkōji temple into a leading center of Zen studies, and transformed the Ritsu temple Shōgakuji (whose patriarch Jōken he converted to Sōtō) into Sōjiji, which came to rival Eiheiji as the main Sōtō training site. Keizan's invaluable role in Japanese religious history was commemorated in 1909 when he was awarded the title Jōsai Daishi ("Great Teacher") by Emperor Meiji.

In addition to this text, the *Zazenyojinki* (*Advice on the Practice of Zazen*), and the *Denkōroku,* Keizan's main works include the *Keizanshingi* (*Keizan's Monastic Rules*), *Keizangoroku* (*Keizan's Recorded Sayings*), *Zazensangonsetsu* (*Theory of Zazen for Three Types of People*), and *Shinjinmeinentei* (*Reflections on the Notion of Faith*).

Although Keizan is known for a generally eclectic approach to Zen, *Advice on the Practice of Zazen,* an instructional guide to zazen practice for monks and laymen, uncompromisingly insists on the priority of "zazen only" (*shikantaza*). Consistent with the central standpoint of Dōgen, which was based on his training under his Chinese mentor Tiantong Rujing, Keizan stresses that a clear recognition of the meaning of impermanence is the key to attaining an enlightened nondiscriminatory perspective beyond all dualities through rigorous discipline and complete dedication to zazen. The practice of zazen, according to Sōtō theorists, is the one single method of attainment that has been followed by all Buddhists since the time of Śākyamuni.

Keizan's text is greatly influenced by a number of Dōgen's writings on zazen, including the *Fukanzazengi* (*A Universal Recommendation for True Zazen*), pp. 233–8 in this volume, *Hōkyōki* (*Memoirs of the Hōkyō Period*), *Shōbōgenzō zuimonki* (*Miscellaneous Talks*), *Bendōhō* (*Methods for the Wholehearted Practice of the Way*), and the *Zazengi* (*Standard Method of Zazen*), *Zazenshin* (*Zazen Lancet*), *Bendōwa* (*Lecture on the Wholehearted Practice of the Way*), and *Sammai ō zammai* (*The Samādhi that is the King of Samādhis*) fascicles of the *Shōbōgenzō*. In *Advice on the Practice of Zazen,* Keizan pulls together a variety of key philosophical doctrines and practical recommendations from Dōgen's thought. The central doctrines include *shinjin datsuraku* (the dropping off of body and mind), *jijiyū zammai* (self-fulfilling *samādhi*), *honshō myōshu* (the identity of original realization and marvelous practice), and *hishiryō* (non-thinking beyond thinking and not-thinking). There are numerous specific recommendations for zazen practice, such as: regulations for posture and breathing exercises; requirements for the meditation cushion and place of practice; descriptions of the full- and half-lotus positions; techniques for focusing attention to eliminate mental distractions; methods for swaying on the meditation cushion and walking meditation; and recommendations for eating and personal associations.

An interesting contribution by Keizan is the clarification of the relation between zazen and the Buddhist ideals of teaching, practice, and realization as well as the goals of meditation, concentration, and wisdom in light of Dōgen's notions of the unity of being-time and the identity of practice-in-realization. Each of the three ideals and goals is based on zazen and thus inseparably connected to one another. None is an end in itself but all are varying perspectives of the dynamically integrated temporal unfolding of sustained zazen practice.

ADVICE ON THE PRACTICE OF ZAZEN

by

Keizan Jōkin, Monk of Tōkokuji

Zazen (seated meditation) allows people to directly enlighten the primordial mind and to abide peacefully in their original state. This is known as realizing one's original face, or manifesting the true nature of the primordial mind. Zazen is the dropping off of body and mind and remaining detached, whether seated or lying down. It is not concerned with good or evil, and transcends the distinctions of worldly and sacred delusion and enlightenment, sentient beings and Buddhas. It relinquishes the ten thousand things, renounces all conditions, casts aside everything, and does not rely on the six senses. 412a24

What is this that is nameless and cannot be identified with either body or mind? If you try to conceive of it, it is beyond thought; 412b
if you try to express it, words are exhausted. It appears both foolish and saintly. It is as high as the mountain and as deep as the ocean, yet discloses neither its full height nor depth. It is illuminatively unbound by conditions, displaying a radiance that cannot be discerned by the naked eye. It penetrates beyond thought and has a clarity above the entanglements of speech. It transcends both heaven and earth and is realized only by the entire person.

It is like an immeasurably perfected person who has experienced the greath death (*parinirvāṇa*) and has unobstructed vision and unhindered action. What dust defiles it, and what obstacle can block it? Clear water originally has neither front nor back, and empty space is not bound by inside or outside. Zazen has a pristine clarity that is self-illuminating prior to distinctions of form and emptiness, subject and object. It is eternal but has never been named. The Third Patriarch (Sengcan) [provisionally] referred to it as "mind," and Nāgārjuna [provisionally] referred to it as "body." It manifests the form of Buddha-nature and actualizes the body of all Buddhas. Like the full moon, it is without absence or excess. This mind itself is nothing other than Buddha. Self-illumination shines from the past through the present, realizing the transformation of Nāgārjuna [who manifested himself as the moon, symbolizing Buddha-nature] and attaining the *samādhi* of all Buddhas.

Mind originally is undifferentiated, and the body manifests various forms. Mind-only and body-only cannot be explained in terms of sameness or difference. Mind transforms itself and becomes body, and the manifest body has different forms. When one wave is generated, ten thousand waves appear; when mental discrimination arises, ten thousand *dharmas* appear. That is, the four elements and five *skandhas* interdependently originate, and the four limbs and five senses become manifest. Furthermore, the thirty-six parts [of the body] and the twelve conditions ceaselessly continue to appear. In explaining the interdependence of phenomena, the mind can be compared to ocean water and the body to waves. There are no waves without water, and no water without waves. Water and waves are inseparable, motion and stillness are indistinguishable. Therefore it is said, "The true man [who comprehends] life and death, coming and going, realizes the imperishable body of the four elements and the five *skandhas*."

Now, [practicing] zazen is directly entering into the ocean of Buddha-nature and manifesting the body of all Buddhas. The fundamental purity of the radiant mind is disclosed, and the original brightness shines forth without limit. There is no increase or decrease in the waters of the ocean, and the waves are never distracted in their course. Therefore, all Buddhas appear in the world for the singleminded function of causing sentient beings to realize Buddha[hood] and to attain and manifest enlightenment. Their incomparably tranquil and wondrous technique is known as zazen. It is also known as the self-fulfilling *samādhi,* or the king of all *samādhi*s.

If you abide tranquilly in *samādhi,* it directly enlightens the primordial mind and is the true gate to the attainment of the way of Buddhas. If you wish to enlighten the primordial mind, renounce discriminative knowledge and interpretation, cast away [the distinctions between] worldly and Buddhist principles, and remove
412c all attachments. If you manifest the One True Mind, the clouds of delusion will be dispersed and the mind will be as clear as the new moon. The Buddha said, "Listening and thinking are standing

outside the gate, zazen is sitting calmly in one's own home." How true! For listening and thinking perpetuate [one-sided] views, leaving the primordial mind in turmoil, just like being outside the gate. But zazen creates an all-pervasive restfulness, just like sitting calmly at home.

The attachments of the five desires all arise from ignorance, ignorance is due to a lack of clarity about the self, and zazen illuminates the self. For example, although the five desires may be removed, if ignorance is not yet removed that is not yet [the attainment] of a Buddha or patriarch. If you want to remove ignorance, the diligent practice of zazen is the key. An ancient said, "If distraction is removed tranquility arises, and if tranquility arises wisdom is attained, and if wisdom is attained the truth is clearly seen." If you want to remove distractions, you must be free from thoughts of [the distinction of] good and evil, and renounce all involvement in karmic relations. The most important concern is that the mind be free from thinking and the body free from acting. When distracting relations are ended mental disturbances are subdued, and when mental disturbances are subdued the unchanging body is manifest. You continuously realize its clarity as neither extinction nor commotion.

Therefore, you must not be involved in arts and crafts or healing and divination. Furthermore, song, dance, and music, debate and rhetoric, as well as the pursuit of fame and fortune must be completely avoided. Although eulogy and lyrical poetry can in themselves contribute to calming the mind, you must not indulge in writing them. The renunciation of literature and calligraphy is a priority for seekers of the Way, and is the most effective means of regulating the mind.

Do not wear clothing that is either elegant or tattered. Fine clothes give rise to greed as well as the fear of being robbed, and this becomes an obstacle to the pursuit of the Way. To refuse clothes if offered as alms has always been a praiseworthy practice since ancient times. Even if you already own such clothes, do not indulge in wearing them. If thieves come to steal the clothes, do not bother to chase after them or regret the loss. You should wear old clothes that have been washed and mended till completely clean. If you do not clean [and mend] the clothes you will get cold and sick, and that is also an obstacle to the pursuit of the Way. Although we should not be overly concerned with physical conditions, the lack of food, clothing, and shelter is known as the three insufficiencies, all of which are obstructive conditions.

Do not eat food that is either raw or tough, stale or spoiled, for intestinal rumbling is a discomfort for the body and mind and an obstacle to zazen. Do not indulge in eating fine food. That is not only an obstruction for the body and mind but indicates that you have not overcome greed. Eat enough food to maintain your vitality but do not relish it. If you try to sit in meditation after you have eaten until you are full, it can cause illness. Do not attempt med-
413a itation immediately after either a large or small meal; you must wait awhile to be ready to sit. Generally, mendicants and monks should eat sparingly. That means that they should limit their portions, for example, eating two parts of three and leaving the rest. The usual medicinal foods, such as sesame and yams, should be eaten. That is an effective means of regulating the body.

When sitting in meditation, you must not lean against a wall, support, or screen to prop yourself up. Do not sit in a place susceptible to wind and storm, or in a high and exposed spot, for that can lead to illness. When sitting in meditation, your body may feel hot or cold, tight or slack, stiff or loose, heavy or light, or you may feel abruptly awakened, all because the breath is not regulated and must be controlled. The method for regulating the breath is to keep your mouth open for a while, holding deep breaths and short breaths alternately until your breathing is gradually regulated and controlled for a period of time. When awareness comes, it means that breathing is spontaneously regulated. After this, let the breath pass naturally through the nose.

The mind may feel depressed or flighty, foggy or clear. Or, sometimes it may see outside the room or inside your body. Or, it may visualize the bodies of Buddhas or the forms of bodhisattvas, or it may formulate theories, or evaluate the sutra or *śāstra* literature. Such types of miraculous and unusual behavior result from a lack of regulating one's consciousness and breathing. When attachments such as this arise, focus attention on your lap. When the mind lapses into bewilderment, focus attention on the middle of your forehead (three inches above the center of the eyebrows). When the mind is distracted, focus attention on the tip of your nose or your lower abdomen (one and a half inches below the navel). As you remain seated, focus attention on the left palm. When sitting for a long time, although you will not necessarily reach a state of tranquility, your mind will on its own be freed from distraction.

Although the traditional precepts are instructions for illuminating the mind, you must not read, write, or listen to them too much, for that will cause mental disturbances. Generally, weariness of the body and mind is the cause of illness. Do not practice zazen in a place where there may be danger from fire, flood, storms, or robbers, or near the seashore, a liquor store, or brothel; or where you may meet a widow, virgin, or geisha. Do not visit the homes of kings, important officials, or powerful people, or associate with people who indulge in their desires or who gossip. Although attending a large congregation of monks or engaging in full-scale construction projects may be of great importance, you must avoid such practices in order to concentrate on zazen. Do not be attached to explanations and [intellectual activity], for a distracted mind and confused thinking will arise from them. Do not take pleasure [in attracting] crowds or seek out disciples. Do not be distracted by various sorts of practices or learning. Do not practice zazen where it is extremely light or dark, cold or hot, or in the vicinity of rowdy men and indecent women.

You must spend time in a monastery, among wise and compassionate people. Or, you must travel deep into the mountains 413b
and valleys, practicing concentration next to flowing streams amid the mountains or clearing the mind by sitting in meditation in a valley. You must carefully observe impermanence and never forget its significance, for this inspires the mind in the pursuit of the

Way. You must lay out a thick meditation cushion so as to be comfortable during zazen. The zazen area must be perfectly clean, and if you always burn incense and offer flowers, the good spirits who guard the Dharma, as well as Buddhas and bodhisattvas, will cast a protective aura around it. If you install an image of a Buddha, bodhisattva, or arhat there, no mischievous demons will be able to harm you. Always abide in great compassion and pity, and dedicate the immeasurable merit of zazen to all sentient beings. Do not develop pride, conceit, or self-righteousness, for these are the ways of non-Buddhists and ordinary people. Be concerned only with efforts to end attachment and realize enlightenment. The singleminded concentration of zazen is the most effective means of practicing Zen. You must always wash your eyes and feet, and act with dignity and compassion to keep body and mind tranquil. You must renounce both worldly attachments and any clinging to the pursuit of the Way.

Although you must not be stingy with the Dharma, do not offer explanations of it to anyone unless you are asked about it. Then, wait until the inquirer has asked three times and respond only if the fourth request is sincere. Of ten things you may wish to say, hold back nine. The method of followers of the Way can be likened to a winter fan waved around the mouth, or to a bell hanging in the air which does not wonder about the breeze blowing from all directions. Do not rely upon anyone in pursuing the Dharma, and do not overestimate yourself because of the Way—this is the most important consideration. Although zazen is not just a matter of teaching, practice, or realization, it encompasses all three ideals. That is, to evaluate realization only in terms of attaining enlightenment is not the essence of zazen; to evaluate practice only as following the true path is not the essence of zazen; and to evaluate teaching only as cutting off evil and practicing good is not the essence of zazen.

Although the establishment of teaching lies within Zen, it is not ordinary teaching. Rather, the Way of simple transmission through direct pointing is an expression demonstrated by the entire body.

It is speaking without phrases. At the point where thought and reason are exhausted, a single word conveys the totality of the world, and yet not a single hair is raised—isn't this the true teaching of the Buddhas and patriarchs? Although practice is realized [in Zen], it is the practice of non-action. The body functions spontaneously, the mouth does not chant esoteric doctrine, the mind is not preoccupied with thoughts, the six senses are naturally clear and unaffected by anything. This is not the sixteenfold practice of the Buddha's disciples, the twelvefold practice of dependent origination, or the myriad practices of the six stages of the bodhisattva. Because it is not doing any [particular] thing, it is known as acting as a Buddha. Only abiding tranquilly in the self-fulfilling *samādhi* of all Buddhas, or resonating in the four peaceful reposes of the bodhisattva—is this not the profound and marvelous practice of the Buddhas and patriarchs? Although realization is realized [in Zen], it is the realization of non-realization, the king of all *samādhi*s, the *samādhi* that realizes the unborn, comprehensive, and spontaneous wisdom, the gate to disclosing the Tathāgata's wisdom and the path of great tranquility and harmony. It transcends the distinction between sacred and mundane, goes beyond delusion and enlightenment—is this not the realization of original enlightenment?

Although zazen is not restricted to discipline (*śīla*), concentration (*samādhi*), or wisdom (*prajñā*), it encompasses all three goals. That is, although discipline is to prevent or stop evil, in zazen we observe the principle of complete nonduality, renounce the ten thousand things, put an end to all entanglements, abandon the distinction between Buddhist and worldly principles, forget attachments to the Way as well as to the world, and acknowledge nei- 413c
ther affirmation nor denial, neither good nor evil—so what is there to prevent or stop? That is the formless discipline of the primordial mind. Concentration is undivided contemplation. Zazen is the dropping off of body and mind, renouncing [the distinction between] delusion and enlightenment. It is neither motionless nor active, neither creative nor quiescent, and resembles both fool and saint,

mountain and ocean. No trace of movement or stillness originates from it. Concentration functions without form. Because it is formless, it is known as great concentration. Wisdom is discriminative awareness. In zazen, subject and object disappear on their own and mental discriminations are forever forgotten. The eye of wisdom pervades the body. Although it makes no discriminations, it clearly sees Buddha-nature. Originally without delusion, zazen cuts off conceptualization and remains unbound and clear. Wisdom is formless; because it is formless, it is known as great wisdom.

The teaching of all Buddhas, as expressed in their own lifetimes, is nothing other than what is included in discipline (*śīla*), concentration (*samādhi*), or wisdom (*prajñā*). Now, in zazen, there is no discipline that is not cultivated, no concentration that is not observed, no wisdom that is not realized. Overcoming suffering, attaining the Way, turning the wheel [of the Dharma], and the attainment of enlightenment all depend on its power. Supernatural powers and illuminating the Dharma are fully rooted in zazen. Studying Zen is also based on zazen.

If you want to practice zazen, you must first be in a quiet place and lay out a firm cushion. Do not let in either wind, smoke, rain, or dew. Keep a clean place to sit with plenty of room for your knees. Although ancient monks were reported to have sat on a diamond seat or on a huge rock, there were none who did not use a cushion. The place for sitting should not be too bright in the daytime or too dark at night, and must be kept warm in the winter and cool in the summer. That is the method [for zazen].

Renounce discriminative consciousness and terminate conceptualization. Do not try to gauge the activities of a Buddha or to judge good and evil. Make the most of your time as if your own life was at stake. The Tathāgata practiced zazen in an upright position, Bodhidharma sat with singleminded attention and no other concerns, Sekisō resembled a withered tree, and [Tiantong] Rujing was critical of those who sleep while doing zazen. Rujing counseled: "Attainment is reached through zazen only, not by burning incense, worship, repetition of the *nembutsu,* repentance, or reading or reciting sutras." Whenever you practice zazen, you must wear the *kesa* (*kaṣāya*) robe (except during the night and upon arising from sleep, as per the schedule). Do not neglect to do this. The cushion (twelve inches across, thirty-six inches in diameter) should not support the entire leg. It should extend from the middle of the leg to the base of the spine. That is the zazen method of the Buddhas and patriarchs.

You may sit in either the full-lotus or half-lotus position. The 414a
method for the full-lotus is to put the right foot on the left thigh and the left foot on the right thigh. Loosen your robe and let it hang neatly around you. Then, put your right hand on your left foot and your left hand on your right foot, keeping the thumbs together, close to the body at the navel. Sit perfectly upright without leaning left or right, forward or backward. The ears and shoulders, nose and navel must be perfectly aligned. The tongue should rest on the roof of the mouth and the breath pass through the nose. The mouth is closed but the eyes are left open. Having regulated the body so that it is neither stiff nor limp, breathe deeply through the mouth one time. Then, while sitting in concentration, sway your body [to the left and right] seven or eight times, going from a greater to smaller [range of motion]. Sit upright with lofty dedication.

So, how does one think of that which is beyond thinking? By non-thinking—that is the fundamental method of zazen. You must directly break through all attachments and realize enlightenment. If you want to rise from concentration [practice], put your hands on your knees and sway the body seven or eight times, going from a smaller to greater [range of motion]. Breathe through the mouth, put your hands on the ground, and simply raise yourself from your seat. Walk deliberately to the left or the right. If drowsiness threatens while sitting, always sway the body or open your eyes wide. Also, focus attention on the top of the head, the hairline, or the forehead. If you still do not feel awake, wipe your eyes or rub your body. If that still does not awaken you, get up from your seat and walk around in the correct manner. After walking about a hundred steps, your drowsiness should surely be overcome. The method [of walking meditation] is to take a half step with each breath. Walk as if you are not walking—calm and undistracted.

If you are still not awake after walking around in this way, rinse your eyes or cool off your head, or recite the preface to the bodhisattva vow. Or do any combination of these things so that you do not fall asleep.

You must consider the Great Matter of life and death and the swift changes of impermanence and ask yourself, "How can I sleep when the insight of the eye of the Dharma is not yet illuminated?" If drowsiness continues to threaten to overtake you, you must recite, "Because my karmic tendencies are so deeply rooted, I am now lost in the veil of fatigue—when will I awaken from my ignorance? I beg for the great compassion of the Buddhas and patriarchs to remove my suffering."

If your mind is distracted, focus attention on the tip of your nose or your lower abdomen and count the breaths coming in and out. If the distractions continue, then reflect on an instruction *kōan* for awakening, such as "What is it that thus comes?", "Does a dog have Buddha-nature?", "Unmon's Mount Sumeru" *kōan,* and "Dōshū's cypress tree in the garden" *kōan.* Artless dialogues such as these are suitable. If the distractions still persist, then medi-
414b tate by concentrating directly on stopping your breath or keeping your eyes shut. Or focus on the state prior to conception, before a single thought has been produced.

If you follow Buddhist practice, the twofold emptiness [of self and *dharmas*] spontaneously arises and mental attachments are necessarily dispersed. After emerging from concentration, to realize the majestic activities [of walking, standing, sitting, and lying down] without thought is the spontaneous manifestation of Zen enlightenment. When you actualize the undifferentiated differentiation of practice-in-realization, Zen enlightenment is spontaneously manifest. The primordial state before anything appeared, the condition prior to the formation of heaven and earth—the ultimate concern of the Buddhas and patriarchs is nothing other than this one thing.

Be still and calm, indifferent and free of passion, letting ten thousand years pass in an instant, like cool ashes or a withered tree, like incense burning without smoke in an ancient temple, or a piece of white silk. May this be realized!

Glossary

Amitābha ("Immeasurable Light"): A transcendental Buddha associated with great compassion, who resides over a blissful realm, or Pure Land, into which believers in his salvific power will be reborn. *See also* Pure Land.

Ānanda ("Joy"): The name of Śākyamuni's cousin, close disciple, and personal attendant who was renowned for his ability to recite all of the Buddha's sermons from memory.

anuttarā samyaksaṃbodhi: Unsurpassed, ultimate awakening or *bodhi*. *See also bodhi.*

arhat ("worthy one"): A saint who has completely eradicated the passions and attained liberation from the cycle of birth and death (samsara); the highest stage of spiritual achievement in the Hinayana. *See also* Hinayana; samsara.

Avalokiteśvara: A great bodhisattva who represents great compassion.

awakening. *See bodhi.*

birth and death. *See* samsara.

bodhi: Enlightenment; a state in which one is awakened to the inherent enlightened nature, or Buddha-nature, of all reality. *See also* Buddha-nature.

bodhicitta ("enlightenment mind"): The aspiration to achieve enlightenment.

Bodhidharma (470–543?): An Indian monk who came to China and became the First Patriarch of the Chan/Zen school. He is said to have spent nine years facing a wall in zazen at Shaolin Temple. *See also* Chan school; zazen.

bodhisattva ("enlightenment being"): One who has given rise to the profound aspiration (*bodhicitta*) to achieve enlightenment in order to help liberate all sentient beings from samsara; the spiritual ideal of the Mahayana. Bodhisattvas enter a course of practice of the six perfections and attain various stages on the way to Buddhahood. *See also* Mahayana; samsara; six perfections.

Buddhahood: The state of being or becoming a Buddha; the goal of the bodhisattva path.

Buddha-nature: The basic enlightened nature of sentient beings, which is chronically obscured by their ignorance and attachment to dualistic views. According to the Chan/Zen school, enlightenment is nothing other than the complete unfolding of one's inherent Buddha-nature. *See also* Chan school; enlightenment.

calming and contemplation: The two meditative practices of *śāmatha,* which entails calming the mind, stilling discursive thoughts, in order to prepare a stable base for the practice of *vipaśyana,* meditative insight into the nature of reality. Also called cessation and contemplation.

Chan school: A major school of East Asian Buddhism that developed in China in the sixth and seventh centuries, and was subsequently transmitted to Japan where it is known as the Zen school; so-called because of its emphasis on the practice of meditation (Skt.: *dhyāna;* Ch.: *chan;* Jp.: *zen*). The Chan/Zen school evolved new approaches to religious practice based on a lineal succession of Buddhas and patriarchs, in "a special transmission outside the scriptures"—direct transmission from master to disciple of the teaching and realization which does not rely on intellectual analysis or scriptural authority. The tradition traces its roots to an event related in the sutras, in which Śākyamuni Buddha, while teaching an assembly of followers, wordlessly raised a flower, upon which his disciple Māhakāśyapa smiled, indicating his realization of the Buddha's intent and teaching, without any verbal exchange. The Chan/Zen school emphasizes intensive meditation practice as the best means to a direct experience of enlightenment (*bodhi*) and realization of one's own Buddha-nature, which brings about the immediate transcendence of all dualistic conceptualization and a profound apprehension of ultimate reality. In the development of Chan Buddhism in China two approaches to the attainment of enlightenment came to be postulated—gradual, as the result of long practice, which was the approach adopted by the Northern school; and a sudden, spontaneous, direct experience of one's Buddha-nature, which was emphasized in the Southern school. *See also bodhi; dhyāna;* Buddha-nature; Māhakāśyapa; patriarchs; Rinzai sect; Śākyamuni; Sōtō sect; ultimate reality.

cultivation and verification: The oneness of practice or sitting meditation (zazen), which represents the aspect of cultivation, and realization, which represents the aspect of verification. These are considered two inseparable aspects of the Zen religious experience according to Sōtō sect masters Dōgen and Keizan. *See also* Sōtō sect; zazen.

dependent origination (*pratītyasamutpāda*): A basic Buddhist doctrine that all phenomena come into being only in dependence on causes and conditions and exist only as long as those causes and conditions prevail. Also called the law of causality.

Dharma body (*dharmakāya*): One of the three bodies, or manifestations of a Buddha, as ultimate reality or suchness. *See also* three bodies.

dharmadhātu: The Dharma realm, the sphere of ultimate reality or suchness. *See also* suchness; ultimate reality.

dharma: A phenomenon, thing, or element; the elements that make up the perceived phenomenal world.

dhyāna (Ch.: *chan;* Jp.: *zen*): Meditation, a state of meditative concentration and absorption. The primary practice of the Chan/Zen school. *See also* Chan school.

Dīpaṃkara: The name of a past Buddha.

eighteen realms: The six senses, their respective six objects, and the associated six consciousnesses. *See also* six consciousnesses; six sense objects; six senses.

emptiness (*śūnyatā*): A central and fundamental Buddhist teaching that all phenomena arise only in dependence on causes and conditions (dependent origination) and thus are "empty" of self-existence or inherent nature; nothing, therefore, has "real," independent, permanent existence. *See also* dependent origination.

enlightenment: A state in which one is awakened to the true nature of all reality; a direct experience of ultimate truth or ultimate reality. Also called *bodhi,* awakening. See also *bodhi.*

esoteric: A body of Mahayana Buddhist teachings that belong to the Esoteric Buddhist tradition, known in Japan as the Shingon or Mantra schools. Esoteric Buddhism is characterized by an emphasis on ritual practices, mantras, and secret teachings that are passed directly from master to disciple in a progression of spiritual stages. *See also* mantra.

five five hundred-year periods: Five periods that are predicted to occur after Śākyamuni's lifetime, which represent a gradual decline of the Buddhist teachings and practice. In the first period, attainment of enlightenment is possible; in the second, followers steadfastly practice meditation; in the third, followers eagerly listen to the Buddha's teaching; in the fourth, they engage in building stupas and temples; and in the fifth, followers engage in doctrinal disputes. These correspond to the three ages of the Buddhist teachings: the age of the Right Dharma, the age of the Semblance Dharma, and the final age of the Decadent Dharma, also known as the latter-day world (*mappō*). *See also* latter-day world.

five grave transgressions: 1) patricide, 2) matricide, 3) killing an arhat, 4) maliciously causing a Buddha to bleed, and 5) causing disharmony in the Buddhist order (sangha).

five *skandhas*: The five constituent elements or aggregates that make up what is experienced as one's personality or self: form (*rūpa*), feeling (*vedāna*), perception (*samjñā*), formations (*samskāra*), and consciousness (*vijñāna*).

four grave offenses: The four most serious offenses for Buddhist monks and nuns, which result in their expulsion from the sangha—1) killing, 2) stealing, 3) sexual activity, and 4) lying.

Four Noble Truths: The fundamental Buddhist teaching—1) the truth of suffering; 2) the truth of the cause of suffering; 3) the truth of the cessation of suffering; and 4) the truth of the eightfold path that leads to the cessation of suffering, i.e., right view, right thought, right speech, right action, right livelihood, right effort, right mindfulness, and right meditation.

Great Vehicle. *See* Mahayana.

Hinayana ("Small Vehicle"): A term used by Mahayana Buddhists to describe the teachings of early Buddhism, which had as its spiritual ideal the arhat. The two paths of Hinayana practice, that of *śrāvaka*s and *pratyekabuddha*s, are known collectively as the two vehicles. *See also* arhat; *pratyekabuddha; śrāvaka;* Mahayana.

icchantika: One who has no stock of good roots and thus no possibility of attaining Buddhahood.

kalpa: An eon, an enormously long period of time.

karma: Lit., "action," any act of body, speech, or mind, which leads to rebirth in samsara according to whether it is morally good, evil, or neutral. *See also* samsara.

kōan (Ch.: *gongan*): A conundrum or paradoxical phrase, story, or episode from the life of an ancient master used as an object of meditation, which cannot be grasped or solved by reason, thus forcing the practitioner to break through to another level of comprehension. Though not exclusive to it, *kōan* practice is especially emphasized in the Rinzai (Ch.: Linji) sect of Chan/Zen. *See also* Rinzai sect.

latter-day world (*mappō*): The final period of the Dharma, the age of the Decadent Dharma, in which authentic Buddhist teachings and practice are no longer available. *See also* five five hundred-year periods.

Mahākāśyapa: The disciple whom the Buddha designated as his successor, according to the Chan/Zen school. Also called Kāśyapa. *See also* Chan school.

Mahāsthāmaprāpta ("Possessed of Great Power"): A great bodhisattva who represents the wisdom of Amitābha. *See also* Amitābha.

Mahayana ("Great Vehicle"): A form of Buddhism that developed in India around 100 B.C.E. and which exalts as its religious ideal the bodhisattva, great beings who aspire to enlightenment on behalf of all sentient beings. *See also* bodhisattva.

Maitreya: The future Buddha, currently still a bodhisattva.

Mañjuśrī: A great bodhisattva who exemplifies transcendent wisdom.

mantra: A mystic or incantatory phrase or formula used in the rituals of Esoteric Buddhism. *See also* esoteric.

Māra: In Buddhist texts, the personification of death or evil; a symbol of the afflictions that hinder progress on the path to Buddhahood.

meditation. *See dhyāna; samādhi.*

nāga: A type of supernatural being in the form of a dragon or serpent.

nirvana: Liberation from samsara, a state in which all passions are extinguished and the highest wisdom attained; *bodhi,* enlightenment. *See also bodhi;* samsara.

One Vehicle: The Buddha vehicle, the Mahayana teaching that leads to complete enlightenment and attainment of Buddhahood, contrasted with the teachings of the two Hinayana vehicles. The One Vehicle includes and transcends all three vehicles of the *śrāvaka, pratyekabuddha,* and bodhisattva paths. *See also* three vehicles; two vehicles.

patriarchs: The lineage of masters in the Chan/Zen school, beginning with the First Patriarch, Bodhidharma, an Indian monk who, according to tradition, established the Chan teaching in China in the fifth century. *See also* Bodhidharma; Chan school.

prajñā: Nondiscriminating or transcendental wisdom, the understanding of the emptiness of all phenomena in their actual realities. One of the six perfections (*pāramitā*s) of a bodhisattva. *See also* bodhisattva; emptiness; six perfections.

pratyekabuddha ("solitary enlightened one"): One who has attained enlightenment through direct observation and understanding of the principle of dependent origination without the guidance of a teacher, and who does not teach others. One of the two Hinayana vehicles. *See also* dependent origination; Hinayana; two vehicles.

precepts: Vows concerning moral conduct (*śīla*) taken by lay Buddhists and monastics. The five basic precepts are: 1) not to kill, 2) not to steal, 3) not to commit adultery, 4) not to lie, and 5) not to take intoxicants. In addition, there are two hundred fifty monastic rules for monks and three hundred forty-eight for nuns. *See also śīla.*

Pure Land: A blissful, transcendent Buddha land or realm presided over by Amitābha Buddha, in which believers in his salvific power will be reborn. Also the name of a major East Asian Buddhist school which emphasizes the practice of worshiping Amitābha. *See also* Amitābha.

Rinzai sect (Ch.: Linji): Along with the Sōtō sect, one of the two main branches of Chan/Zen. Originating with the ninth-century Chinese master Linji, it was brought to Japan at the end of the twelfth century by Eisai and emphasizes the study and practice of *kōan*s. *See also kōan;* Sōtō sect.

Śākyamuni: The historical Buddha who lived in India in the fifth century B.C.E., and whose life and teachings form the basis of Buddhism.

samādhi: A meditative state of concentration, focusing the mind on one point; also a transcendent mental state attained by the repeated practice of meditative concentration.

Samantabhadra ("Universally Gracious"): A great bodhisattva who represents the ultimate principle, meditation, and the practice of all Buddhas. The embodiment of adherence to vows of great compassion.

samsara: The cycle of birth and death; transmigration or rebirth in the six realms of existence to which sentient beings are subject as a result of their actions (karma); the world of suffering, contrasted with the bliss of nirvana. *See also* karma; nirvana; six modes of existence.

sangha: The community of Buddhist monastics.

Śāriputra: One of the original disciples of the Buddha, called "foremost of the wise."

shikantaza: "Just sitting" or "pure sitting," a form of practice of zazen involving resting in a state of alert attention free of discursive thoughts, directed on no object, and attached to no particular content; the meditative practice emphasized in the Sōtō school of Zen. *See also* Sōtō school; zazen.

śīla: Moral conduct or the practice of the precepts; one of the six perfections. *See also* precepts; six perfections.

śīla, samādhi, and prajñā: The three practices of morality, meditation, and wisdom, which are also three of the six perfections. Also called discipline, concentration, and wisdom; morality, concentration, and wisdom. *See also* six perfections.

six consciousnesses: 1) Eye consciousness, 2) ear consciousness, 3) nose consciousness, 4) tongue consciousness, 5) body consciousness, and 6) the mental sense or intellect, which result from contact between the six senses and their respective objects. *See also* six sense objects; six senses.

six modes of existence: The six realms of samsaric existence into which sentient beings are reborn in accordance with their karma: the three higher realms of gods (*deva*s), *asura*s (demigods), and human beings; and the three lower realms of animals, hungry ghosts (*preta*s), and hell, which are also known as the three evil paths. *See also* karma; samsara.

six perfections (*pāramitā*s): Six practices, or qualities, perfected by bodhisattvas on the path to Buddhahood—1) generosity (*dāna*), 2) morality (*śīla*), 3) patience (*kṣānti*), 4) energy (*vīrya*), 5) meditation (*dhyāna*), and 6) wisdom (*prajñā*). *See also dhyāna;* bodhisattva; Buddhahood; *prajñā; śīla.*

six sense objects: The objects of perception associated with each of the six senses—1) form, 2) sound, 3) smell, 4) taste, 5) tactile objects, and 6) mental objects. *See also* six senses.

six senses: The six sense faculties of the 1) eyes, 2) ears, 3) nose, 4) tongue, 5) body, and 6) mind. Also called sense perceptions; sensory capabilities. *See also* six consciousnesses; six sense objects.

Small Vehicle. *See* Hinayana.

Sōtō sect (Ch.: Caodong): One of the two main branches of Chan/Zen Buddhism, along with the Rinzai (Ch.: Linji) sect; founded in China during the Tang dynasty and brought to Japan in the early thirteenth century by Eihei Dōgen. The Sōtō school emphasizes the practice of *shikantaza. See also* Rinzai sect; *shikantaza.*

śrāvaka ("auditor"): Originally, a disciple of the Buddha, one of those who heard him expound the teachings directly; later, the term came to refer to one of the two kinds of Hinayana followers, along with *pratyekabuddhas*, to distinguish them from followers of the Mahayana. *See also* Hinayana; Mahayana; *pratyekabuddha*; two vehicles.

suchness: Ultimate reality, the state of things as they really are, i.e., dependently arisen and empty of inherent, independent, permanent existence. Insight into the suchness of all phenomena is *prajñā,* transcendental wisdom. *See also* dependent origination; emptiness; *prajñā;* ultimate reality.

Tathāgata: An epithet for a Buddha, meaning one who has gone to (*gata*) and come from (*āgata*) suchness (*tathā*), i.e., the embodiment of the truth of suchness. *See also* suchness.

tathāgatagarbha: Lit., the "womb (*garbha*) of the Tathāgata," the inherent capacity for Buddhahood within all sentient beings. *See also* Buddhahood; Tathāgata.

ten directions: The four cardinal directions, the four intermediate directions, plus the zenith and nadir, i.e., all directions, everywhere.

three bodies: The three bodies in which a Buddha may appear—1) the Dharma body (*dharmakāya*), synonymous with ultimate truth or ultimate reality; 2) the reward body (*saṃbhogakāya*), a symbolic personification of the Dharma body that a Buddha assumes both as a reward for eons of ascetic practice and in order to expound the Dharma to bodhisattvas and others; and 3) the transformation body (*nirmāṇakāya*), an "incarnate" or "historically manifested" body of a Buddha such as Śākyamuni, which appears in the world to guide sentient beings in the manner best suited to their situations and abilities. *See also* Śākyamuni; ultimate reality.

three evil paths: The three lower samsaric realms of animals, hungry ghosts, and hell. Also called three lower realms; three evil modes of existence. *See also* six modes of existence.

three periods of time: Past, present, and future.

three poisons: Greed, anger, and delusion, all of which hinder the pursuit of enlightenment.

three refuges. *See* Three Treasures.

Three Treasures: The Buddha, the Dharma (the Buddhist teachings), and the Sangha (the community of Buddhist followers). Also called the "three refuges" because one becomes a Buddhist upon "taking refuge" in them.

three vehicles: The three Buddhist paths followed by *śrāvakas*, *pratyekabuddhas*, and bodhisattvas respectively. *See also* bodhisattva; *pratyekabuddha; śrāvaka.*

three worlds: The three realms of samsaric existence: the realm of desire (*kāmadhātu*), i.e., the world of ordinary consciousness accompanied by desires; the realm of form (*rūpadhātu*), in which desires have been eliminated but the physical body remains; and the formless realm (*ārūpyadhātu*), in which the physical body no longer exists. *See also* samsara.

Tripiṭaka: The three divisions or "baskets" (*piṭakas*) of the Buddhist canon: the Sutras, discourses and teachings of the Buddha; the Vinaya, codes of monastic discipline; and the Abhidharma, scholastic treatises on the Buddhist teachings.

two vehicles: The two Hinayana paths of *śrāvakas* and *pratyekabuddhas*. *See also* Hinayana; *śrāvaka; pratyekabuddha.*

ultimate reality: Ultimate truth, the state of things as they really are, suchness; the state of enlghtenment (*bodhi*), in which ultimate reality is apprehended. *See also bodhi;* suchness.

Vimalakīrti: A lay bodhisattva, subject and expounder of the *Vimalakīrti Sutra,* renowned for his great wisdom and spiritual accomplishment.

vinaya: Moral conduct or precepts, as practiced within the monastic community. Individual moral conduct is referred to as *śīla*. *See also śīla.*

Vinaya: Precepts and rules of conduct for monastics; along with the Abhidharma and the Sutras, one of the three divisions of the Tripiṭaka. *See also* Tripiṭaka.

Way (Ch.: Dao): The Buddhist path; the ultimate state of enlightenment, *bodhi*. *See also* Awakened Way.

zazen: Seated (*za*) meditation (*zen,* from *dhyāna*), the practice of sitting meditation emphasized in Zen Buddhism. *See also dhyāna.*

Zen school. *See* Chan school; Sōtō sect; Rinzai sect.

Bibliography

Essentials of the Transmission of Mind

Blofeld, John. *The Zen Teaching of Huang Po on the Transmission of Mind.* New York: Grove Press, 1958.

Suzuki, D. T. "Huang-po's Sermon, from 'Treatise on the Essentials of the Transmission of Mind' (Denshin Hoyo)," *Manual of Zen Buddhism.* New York: Grove/Atlantic, 1968 (reprint), pp. 112–19. A partial translation of the text.

A Treatise on Letting Zen Flourish to Protect the State

Tsunoda, Ryūsaku, William Theodore de Bary, and Donald Keene, comp. *Sources of Japanese Tradition.* New York: Columbia University Press, 1958. See Eisai's Foreword, in Chapter XII, "Zen Buddhism," pp. 235–6; and "Eisai: Preface to *Kōzen gokoku ron (Propagation of Zen for the Protection of the Country)*," pp. 241–3.

Yanagida, Seizan, trans. *Chūsei-zenke-no-shisō (Thoughts Expressed by Men of Zen in Medieval Japan), Nihon-shisō-taikei* No. 16, Tokyo: Iwanami-shoten, 1972.

A Universal Recommendation for True Zazen

Bielefeldt, Carl, trans. *Dōgen's Manuals of Zen Meditation.* Berkeley and Los Angeles: University of California Press, 1988.

Cleary, Thomas, trans. *Shōbōgenzō: Zen Essays by Dōgen.* Honolulu, HI: University of Hawaii Press, 1986.

Cook, Francis Dōjun, trans. "Fukan Zazengi, 'General Recommendations for Doing Zazen,'" *How to Raise an Ox.* Los Angeles: Center Publications, 1978, pp. 95–9.

Dumoulin, Heinrich, trans. "Allegemeine Lehren zur Förderung des Zazen von Zen-Meister Dōgen," *Monumenta Nipponica,* Vol. 14, Nos. 3–4 (Tokyo: Sophia University, 1958–59), pp. 430–6.

Gort, Harry, and Kōshin Kawagishi, trans. *A Universal Guide on the Right Way to Zazen.* Tokyo: Seigan-in, 1972.

Hashimoto, Ekō. *Fukan-zazen-gi no Hanashi (Discourse on the Universal Recommendation for True Zazen).* Tottori, Japan: Daijuji, 1977.

Kennett, Jiyu, trans. "Evening Service. Fuzanzazengi (Zazen Rules)," *Selling Water by the River: A Manual of Zen Training.* New York: Pantheon Books, 1972, pp. 231–3.

Maezumi, Taizen, and Bernard Tetsugen Glassman, trans."The Universal Promotion of the Principles of Zazen," *On Zen Practice,* Vol. II. Los Angeles: Zen Center of Los Angeles, 1977, pp. 13–16.

Masunaga, Reihō. *Introduction to Fukanzazengi.* Tokyo: Seishin Shobō, 1956.

—. *The Sōtō Approach to Zen.* Tokyo: Layman Buddhist Society Press, 1958, pp. 101–5.

—. *Zen for Daily Living.* Tokyo: Shunjūsha, 1964.

Nishijima, Gudo, and Chodo Cross, trans. *Master Dōgen's Shōbōgenzō,* Book I. London: Windbell Publications Ltd., 1998.

Okamura, Shohaku, trans. *Shikantaza: An Introduction to Zazen.* Tokyo: Sōtōshū Shumucho, 1985.

Sōtō Zen Text Project, trans. "Universally Recommended Instructions for Zazen," *Sōtō School Scriptures for Daily Services and Practice.* Tokyo: Sōtōshū Shumuchu, 2001.

Tanahashi, Kazuaki, trans. "Recommending Zazen to All People," *Enlightenment Unfolds: The Essential Teachings of Zen Master Dōgen.* Boston: Shambhala Publications, 2000, pp. 32–4.

Waddell, Norman, and Masao Abe. "Dōgen's *Fukanzazengi and Shōbōgenzō Zazengi,"* *The Eastern Buddhist,* Vol. VI, No. 2 (October 1973), pp. 121–6.

Yasuda Joshu Roshi and Anzan Hoshin Roshi, trans. *"Fukanzazengi:* How Everyone Can Sit," *Progress into the Ordinary.* Ottawa, Canada: Great Matter Publications, 1986.

Yokoi, Yūhō, and Brian Daizen Victoria, trans. "A Universal Recommendation for Zazen (Fukan Zazen-gi)," *Zen Master Dōgen.* New York: Weatherhill, 1976, pp. 45–7.

Advice on the Practice of Zazen

Anzan Hoshin Roshi, trans. "Zazen Yojinki," *The Art of Just Sitting: Essential Writings on the Zen Practice of Shikantaza, Second Edition.* John Daido Loori, ed. Somerville, MA: Wisdom Publications, 2004, pp. 41–50.

Cleary, Thomas, trans. and ed. "Keizan Jokin's *Zazen Yojinki,*" *Timeless Spring: A Soto Zen Anthology*. Tokyo and New York: Weatherhill, 1980, pp. 112–23.

Fauré, Bernard. *Visions of Power: Imagining Medieval Japanese Buddhism.* Princeton, NJ: Princeton University Press, 1996.

Index

B

C

D

E

O

P

S

T

U

V

W

X

Xiangtian Temple 177
Xiaoran 88, 220
Xiaozong, Emperor 63
Xinghua Cunjiang 132
Xingman 220
Xinluoguo 219
Xinwen Tanben 133
Xitang Zhizang 11
Xiuchansi 128, 177
Xu'an Huaichang 133, 150
Xuansha Shibei 230, 231
Xuanzang 95, 178, 179, 181, 195, 196, 199, 204, 206, 207, 208, 209, 214, 229
Xue'an Congjin 133
Xuedou Chongxian 206
Xuefeng Yicun 213, 231, 232

Y

Yama 36
Yamada-gun 182
Yamaguchi Prefecture 212
Yamato Province 219
yāna. *See* vehicle
Yanagida, Seizan 50, 56, 58, 213, 220, 223, 224, 233
Yantou Quanhuo 146, 147, 232
Yasuda Joshu Roshi 249
Yiji 219
Yijing 164, 181, 208, 229, 235
Yixing 198, 205
Yōei 219
Yōjin 229
Yōjō (*see also* Eisai) 63, 65
Yokawa 210
Yokoi, Yūhō 248
Yōkōji 260
Yongming Yanshou 201
Yōsai. *See* Eisai
"Yōsai and his problems developed in the *Kōzengokokuron*" 56
Yoshida, Osamu 232
Yuanling 11
Yuanwu Keqin 206, 214, 215, 231, 232, 233, 238
Yuchu 64
Yudhapati 95
Yuezhi (*see also* India) 97
Yunmen sect 136
Yu Ridge 72

Z

Zanning 102, 199
zazen (*see also* meditation, seated; sitting) 62, 87, 120, 233, 241, 243, 244–6, 247, 254, 255, 259, 261, 262, 265, 266, 267, 268, 269, 270, 271, 272–3
Zazengi 247, 261
Zazen Lancet. See Zazenshin
Zazensangonsetsu 260
Zazenshin 247, 261
Zazenyojinki. See Advice on the Practice of Zazen
zen (*see also chan; dhyāna*) 55, 76, 128, 215, 216, 243, 245
Zen (*see also* Zen school) 50, 51, 54, 65, 72–3, 83, 95, 102, 116, 119, 143–4, 151, 153, 163, 183, 186, 215, 225, 246, 253, 259, 260, 261, 270–1, 272, 274
  awakened truth of 78, 216
  essentials of 129, 142, 144
  master(s) 241, 246
  person(s) 112, 124, 125
  practice(s) 49, 50, 51, 52, 53, 82
  practitioner(s) 51, 53, 217, 242, 255
  principle(s) 55, 75, 79, 80, 82, 93, 99, 118, 137, 143, 144, 151, 217

A List of the Volumes of the BDK English Tripiṭaka (First Series)

Abbreviations

Ch.: Chinese
Skt.: Sanskrit
Jp.: Japanese
Eng.: Published title
T.: Taishō Tripiṭaka

Vol. No.		Title	*T.* No.
1, 2	*Ch.*	Ch'ang-a-han-ching (長阿含經)	1
	Skt.	Dīrghāgama	
3–8	*Ch.*	Chung-a-han-ching (中阿含經)	26
	Skt.	Madhyamāgama	
9-I	*Ch.*	Ta-ch'eng-pên-shêng-hsin-ti-kuan-ching (大乘本生心地觀經)	159
9-II	*Ch.*	Fo-so-hsing-tsan (佛所行讃)	192
	Skt.	Buddhacarita	
10-I	*Ch.*	Tsa-pao-ts'ang-ching (雜寶藏經)	203
	Eng.	The Storehouse of Sundry Valuables	
10-II	*Ch.*	Fa-chü-p'i-yü-ching (法句譬喩經)	211
	Eng.	The Scriptural Text: Verses of the Doctrine, with Parables	
11-I	*Ch.*	Hsiao-p'in-pan-jo-po-lo-mi-ching (小品般若波羅蜜經)	227
	Skt.	Aṣṭasāhasrikā-prajñāpāramitā-sūtra	
11-II	*Ch.*	Chin-kang-pan-jo-po-lo-mi-ching (金剛般若波羅蜜經)	235
	Skt.	Vajracchedikā-prajñāpāramitā-sūtra	

Vol. No.		Title	*T.* No.
11-III	*Ch.*	Jên-wang-pan-jo-po-lo-mi-ching (仁王般若波羅蜜經)	245
	Skt.	Kāruṇikārājā-prajñāpāramitā-sūtra (?)	
11-IV	*Ch.*	Pan-jo-po-lo-mi-to-hsing-ching (般若波羅蜜多心經)	251
	Skt.	Prajñāpāramitāhṛdaya-sūtra	
12-I	*Ch.*	Ta-lo-chin-kang-pu-k'ung-chên-shih-san-mo-yeh-ching (大樂金剛不空眞實三麼耶經)	243
	Skt.	Adhyardhaśatikā-prajñāpāramitā-sūtra	
12-II	*Ch.*	Wu-liang-shou-ching (無量壽經)	360
	Skt.	Sukhāvatīvyūha	
	Eng.	The Larger Sutra on Amitāyus (In The Three Pure Land Sutras)	
12-III	*Ch.*	Kuan-wu-liang-shou-fo-ching (觀無量壽佛經)	365
	Skt.	Amitāyurdhyāna-sūtra	
	Eng.	The Sutra on Contemplation of Amitāyus (In The Three Pure Land Sutras)	
12-IV	*Ch.*	A-mi-t'o-ching (阿彌陀經)	366
	Skt.	Sukhāvatīvyūha	
	Eng.	The Smaller Sutra on Amitāyus (In The Three Pure Land Sutras)	
12-V	*Ch.*	Ti-ts'ang-p'u-sa-pên-yüan-ching (地藏菩薩本願經)	412
	Skt.	Kṣitigarbhapraṇidhāna-sūtra (?)	
12-VI	*Ch.*	Yao-shih-liu-li-kuang-ju-lai-pên-yüan-kung-tê-ching (藥師琉璃光如來本願功德經)	450
	Skt.	Bhaiṣajyaguruvaiḍūryaprabhāsapūrva-praṇidhānaviśeṣavistara	
12-VII	*Ch.*	Mi-lê-hsia-shêng-ch'êng-fo-ching (彌勒下生成佛經)	454
	Skt.	Maitreyavyākaraṇa (?)	
12-VIII	*Ch.*	Wên-shu-shih-li-wên-ching (文殊師利問經)	468
	Skt.	Mañjuśrīparipṛcchā (?)	
13-I	*Ch.*	Miao-fa-lien-hua-ching (妙法蓮華經)	262
	Skt.	Saddharmapuṇḍarīka-sūtra	
	Eng.	The Lotus Sutra	
13-II	*Ch.*	Wu-liang-i-ching (無量義經)	276

Vol. No.		Title	T. No.
13-III	*Ch.*	Kuan-p‘u-hsien-p‘u-sa-hsing-fa-ching (觀普賢菩薩行法經)	277
14–19	*Ch.*	Ta-fang-kuang-fo-hua-yen-ching (大方廣佛華嚴經)	278
	Skt.	Avataṃsaka-sūtra	
20-I	*Ch.*	Shêng-man-shih-tzŭ-hou-i-ch‘eng-ta-fang-pien-fang-kuang-ching (勝鬘師子吼一乘大方便方廣經)	353
	Skt.	Śrīmālādevīsiṃhanāda-sūtra	
	Eng.	The Sutra of Queen Śrīmālā of the Lion’s Roar	
20-II	*Ch.*	Chin-kuang-ming-tsui-shêng-wang-ching (金光明最勝王經)	665
	Skt.	Suvarṇaprabhāsa-sūtra	
21–24	*Ch.*	Ta-pan-nieh-p‘an-ching (大般涅槃經)	374
	Skt.	Mahāparinirvāṇa-sūtra	
25-I	*Ch.*	Fo-ch‘ui-pan-nieh-p‘an-liao-shuo-chiao-chieh-ching (佛垂般涅槃略説教誡經)	389
	Eng.	The Bequeathed Teaching Sutra (In Apocryphal Scriptures)	
25-II	*Ch.*	Pan-chou-san-mei-ching (般舟三昧經)	418
	Skt.	Pratyutpannabuddhasammukhāvasthitasamādhi-sūtra	
	Eng.	The Pratyutpanna Samādhi Sutra	
25-III	*Ch.*	Shou-lêng-yen-san-mei-ching (首楞嚴三昧經)	642
	Skt.	Śūraṅgamasamādhi-sūtra	
	Eng.	The Śūraṅgama Samādhi Sutra	
25-IV	*Ch.*	Chieh-shên-mi-ching (解深密經)	676
	Skt.	Saṃdhinirmocana-sūtra	
	Eng.	The Scripture on the Explication of Underlying Meaning	
25-V	*Ch.*	Yü-lan-p‘ên-ching (盂蘭盆經)	685
	Skt.	Ullambana-sūtra (?)	
	Eng.	The Ullambana Sutra (In Apocryphal Scriptures)	

Vol. No.		Title	*T.* No.
25-VI	*Ch.*	Ssŭ-shih-êrh-chang-ching (四十二章經)	784
	Eng.	The Sutra of Forty-two Sections (In Apocryphal Scriptures)	
26-I	*Ch.*	Wei-mo-chieh-so-shuo-ching (維摩詰所説經)	475
	Skt.	Vimalakīrtinirdeśa-sūtra	
	Eng.	The Vimalakīrti Sutra	
26-II	*Ch.*	Yüeh-shang-nü-ching (月上女經)	480
	Skt.	Candrottarādārikāparipṛcchā	
26-III	*Ch.*	Tso-ch'an-san-mei-ching (坐禪三昧經)	614
26-IV	*Ch.*	Ta-mo-to-lo-ch'an-ching (達磨多羅禪經)	618
	Skt.	Yogācārabhūmi-sūtra (?)	
27	*Ch.*	Yüeh-têng-san-mei-ching (月燈三昧經)	639
	Skt.	Samādhirājacandrapradīpa-sūtra	
28	*Ch.*	Ju-lêng-ch'ieh-ching (入楞伽經)	671
	Skt.	Laṅkāvatāra-sūtra	
29-I	*Ch.*	Ta-fang-kuang-yüan-chio-hsiu-to-lo-liao-i-ching (大方廣圓覺修多羅了義經)	842
	Eng.	The Sutra of Perfect Enlightenment (In Apocryphal Scriptures)	
29-II	*Ch.*	Su-hsi-ti-chieh-lo-ching (蘇悉地羯囉經)	893
	Skt.	Susiddhikaramahātantrasādhanopāyika-paṭala	
	Eng.	The Susiddhikara Sutra (In Two Esoteric Sutras)	
29-III	*Ch.*	Mo-têng-ch'ieh-ching (摩登伽經)	1300
	Skt.	Mātaṅgī-sūtra (?)	
30-I	*Ch.*	Ta-p'i-lu-chê-na-chêng-fo-shên-pien-chia-ch'ih-ching (大毘盧遮那成佛神變加持經)	848
	Skt.	Mahāvairocanābhisambodhivikurvitādhiṣṭhāna-vaipulyasūtrendrarāja-nāma-dharmaparyāya	
30-II	*Ch.*	Ching-kang-ting-i-ch'ieh-ju-lai-chên-shih-shê-ta-ch'eng-hsien-chêng-ta-chiao-wang-ching (金剛頂一切如來眞實攝大乘現證大教王經)	865
	Skt.	Sarvatathāgatatattvasaṃgrahamahāyānābhi-samayamahākalparāja	
	Eng.	The Adamantine Pinnacle Sutra (In Two Esoteric Sutras)	

Vol. No.		Title	*T.* No.
31–35	*Ch.*	Mo-ho-sêng-ch'i-lü (摩訶僧祇律)	1425
	Skt.	Mahāsāṃghika-vinaya (?)	
36–42	*Ch.*	Ssŭ-fên-lü (四分律)	1428
	Skt.	Dharmaguptaka-vinaya (?)	
43, 44	*Ch.*	Shan-chien-lü-p'i-p'o-sha (善見律毘婆沙)	1462
	Pāli	Samantapāsādikā	
45-I	*Ch.*	Fan-wang-ching (梵網經)	1484
	Skt.	Brahmajāla-sūtra (?)	
45-II	*Ch.*	Yu-p'o-sai-chieh-ching (優婆塞戒經)	1488
	Skt.	Upāsakaśīla-sūtra (?)	
	Eng.	The Sutra on Upāsaka Precepts	
46-I	*Ch.*	Miao-fa-lien-hua-ching-yu-po-t'i-shê (妙法蓮華經憂波提舍)	1519
	Skt.	Saddharmapuṇḍarīka-upadeśa	
46-II	*Ch.*	Fo-ti-ching-lun (佛地經論)	1530
	Skt.	Buddhabhūmisūtra-śāstra (?)	
	Eng.	The Interpretation of the Buddha Land	
46-III	*Ch.*	Shê-ta-ch'eng-lun (攝大乘論)	1593
	Skt.	Mahāyānasaṃgraha	
	Eng.	The Summary of the Great Vehicle	
47	*Ch.*	Shih-chu-p'i-p'o-sha-lun (十住毘婆沙論)	1521
	Skt.	Daśabhūmika-vibhāṣā (?)	
48, 49	*Ch.*	A-p'i-ta-mo-chü-shê-lun (阿毘達磨倶舍論)	1558
	Skt.	Abhidharmakośa-bhāṣya	
50–59	*Ch.*	Yü-ch'ieh-shih-ti-lun (瑜伽師地論)	1579
	Skt.	Yogācārabhūmi	
60-I	*Ch.*	Ch'êng-wei-shih-lun (成唯識論)	1585
	Eng.	Demonstration of Consciousness Only (In Three Texts on Consciousness Only)	
60-II	*Ch.*	Wei-shih-san-shih-lun-sung (唯識三十論頌)	1586
	Skt.	Triṃśikā	
	Eng.	The Thirty Verses on Consciousness Only (In Three Texts on Consciousness Only)	

Vol. No.		Title	*T.* No.
60-III	*Ch.*	Wei-shih-êrh-shih-lun (唯識二十論)	1590
	Skt.	Viṃśatikā	
	Eng.	The Treatise in Twenty Verses on Consciousness Only (In Three Texts on Consciousness Only)	
61-I	*Ch.*	Chung-lun (中論)	1564
	Skt.	Madhyamaka-śāstra	
61-II	*Ch.*	Pien-chung-pien-lun (辯中邊論)	1600
	Skt.	Madhyāntavibhāga	
61-III	*Ch.*	Ta-ch'eng-ch'êng-yeh-lun (大乘成業論)	1609
	Skt.	Karmasiddhiprakaraṇa	
61-IV	*Ch.*	Yin-ming-ju-chêng-li-lun (因明入正理論)	1630
	Skt.	Nyāyapraveśa	
61-V	*Ch.*	Chin-kang-chên-lun (金剛針論)	1642
	Skt.	Vajrasūcī	
61-VI	*Ch.*	Chang-so-chih-lun (彰所知論)	1645
	Eng.	The Treatise on the Elucidation of the Knowable	
62	*Ch.*	Ta-ch'eng-chuang-yen-ching-lun (大乘莊嚴經論)	1604
	Skt.	Mahāyānasūtrālaṃkāra	
63-I	*Ch.*	Chiu-ching-i-ch'eng-pao-hsing-lun (究竟一乘寶性論)	1611
	Skt.	Ratnagotravibhāgamahāyānottaratantra-śāstra	
63-II	*Ch.*	P'u-t'i-hsing-ching (菩提行經)	1662
	Skt.	Bodhicaryāvatāra	
63-III	*Ch.*	Chin-kang-ting-yü-ch'ieh-chung-fa-a-nou-to-lo-san-miao-san-p'u-t'i-hsin-lun (金剛頂瑜伽中發阿耨多羅三藐三菩提心論)	1665
63-IV	*Ch.*	Ta-ch'eng-ch'i-hsin-lun (大乘起信論)	1666
	Skt.	Mahāyānaśraddhotpāda-śāstra (?)	
63-V	*Ch.*	Na-hsien-pi-ch'iu-ching (那先比丘經)	1670
	Pāli	Milindapañhā	
64	*Ch.*	Ta-ch'eng-chi-p'u-sa-hsüeh-lun (大乘集菩薩學論)	1636
	Skt.	Śikṣāsamuccaya	

Vol. No.		Title	T. No.
65	*Ch.*	Shih-mo-ho-yen-lun (釋摩訶衍論)	1688
66-I	*Ch.*	Pan-jo-po-lo-mi-to-hsin-ching-yu-tsan (般若波羅蜜多心經幽賛)	1710
	Eng.	A Comprehensive Commentary on the Heart Sutra (Prajñāpāramitā-hṛdaya-sūtra)	
66-II	*Ch.*	Kuan-wu-liang-shou-fo-ching-shu (觀無量壽佛經疏)	1753
66-III	*Ch.*	San-lun-hsüan-i (三論玄義)	1852
66-IV	*Ch.*	Chao-lun (肇論)	1858
67, 68	*Ch.*	Miao-fa-lien-hua-ching-hsüan-i (妙法蓮華經玄義)	1716
69	*Ch.*	Ta-ch'eng-hsüan-lun (大乘玄論)	1853
70-I	*Ch.*	Hua-yen-i-ch'eng-chiao-i-fên-ch'i-chang (華嚴一乘教義分齊章)	1866
70-II	*Ch.*	Yüan-jên-lun (原人論)	1886
70-III	*Ch.*	Hsiu-hsi-chih-kuan-tso-ch'an-fa-yao (修習止觀坐禪法要)	1915
70-IV	*Ch.*	T'ien-t'ai-ssŭ-chiao-i (天台四教儀)	1931
71, 72	*Ch.*	Mo-ho-chih-kuan (摩訶止觀)	1911
73-I	*Ch.*	Kuo-ch'ing-pai-lu (國清百録)	1934
73-II	*Ch.*	Liu-tsu-ta-shih-fa-pao-t'an-ching (六祖大師法寶壇經)	2008
	Eng.	The Platform Sutra of the Sixth Patriarch	
73-III	*Ch.*	Huang-po-shan-tuan-chi-ch'an-shih-ch'uan-hsin-fa-yao (黄檗山斷際禪師傳心法要)	2012A
	Eng.	Essentials of the Transmission of Mind (In Zen Texts)	
73-IV	*Ch.*	Yung-chia-chêng-tao-ko (永嘉證道歌)	2014

Vol. No.		Title	*T*. No.
74-I	*Ch.*	Chên-chou-lin-chi-hui-chao-ch'an-shih-wu-lu (鎮州臨濟慧照禪師語録)	1985
	Eng.	The Recorded Sayings of Linji (In Three Chan Classics)	
74-II	*Ch.*	Wu-mên-kuan (無門關)	2005
	Eng.	Wumen's Gate (In Three Chan Classics)	
74-III	*Ch.*	Hsin-hsin-ming (信心銘)	2010
	Eng.	The Faith-Mind Maxim (In Three Chan Classics)	
74-IV	*Ch.*	Ch'ih-hsiu-pai-chang-ch'ing-kuei (勅修百丈清規)	2025
75	*Ch.*	Fo-kuo-yüan-wu-ch'an-shih-pi-yen-lu (佛果圜悟禪師碧巖録)	2003
	Eng.	The Blue Cliff Record	
76-I	*Ch.*	I-pu-tsung-lun-lun (異部宗輪論)	2031
	Skt.	Samayabhedoparacanacakra	
	Eng.	The Cycle of the Formation of the Schismatic Doctrines	
76-II	*Ch.*	A-yü-wang-ching (阿育王經)	2043
	Skt.	Aśokarāja-sūtra (?)	
	Eng.	The Biographical Scripture of King Aśoka	
76-III	*Ch.*	Ma-ming-p'u-sa-ch'uan (馬鳴菩薩傳)	2046
	Eng.	The Life of Aśvaghoṣa Bodhisattva (In Lives of Great Monks and Nuns)	
76-IV	*Ch.*	Lung-shu-p'u-sa-ch'uan (龍樹菩薩傳)	2047
	Eng.	The Life of Nāgārjuna Bodhisattva (In Lives of Great Monks and Nuns)	
76-V	*Ch.*	P'o-sou-p'an-tou-fa-shih-ch'uan (婆藪槃豆法師傳)	2049
	Eng.	Biography of Dharma Master Vasubandhu (In Lives of Great Monks and Nuns)	
76-VI	*Ch.*	Pi-ch'iu-ni-ch'uan (比丘尼傳)	2063
	Eng.	Biographies of Buddhist Nuns (In Lives of Great Monks and Nuns)	

Vol. No.		Title	*T.* No.
76-VII	*Ch.*	Kao-sêng-fa-hsien-ch'uan (高僧法顯傳)	2085
	Eng.	The Journey of the Eminent Monk Faxian (In Lives of Great Monks and Nuns)	
76-VIII	*Ch.*	Yu-fang-chi-ch'ao: T'ang-ta-ho-shang-tung chêng-ch'uan (遊方記抄: 唐大和上東征傳)	2089-(7)
77	*Ch.*	Ta-t'ang-ta-tz'ŭ-ên-ssŭ-san-ts'ang-fa-shih-ch'uan (大唐大慈恩寺三藏法師傳)	2053
	Eng.	A Biography of the Tripiṭaka Master of the Great Ci'en Monastery of the Great Tang Dynasty	
78	*Ch.*	Kao-sêng-ch'uan (高僧傳)	2059
79	*Ch.*	Ta-t'ang-hsi-yü-chi (大唐西域記)	2087
	Eng.	The Great Tang Dynasty Record of the Western Regions	
80	*Ch.*	Hung-ming-chi (弘明集)	2102
81–92	*Ch.*	Fa-yüan-chu-lin (法苑珠林)	2122
93-I	*Ch.*	Nan-hai-chi-kuei-nei-fa-ch'uan (南海寄歸内法傳)	2125
	Eng.	Buddhist Monastic Traditions of Southern Asia	
93-II	*Ch.*	Fan-yü-tsa-ming (梵語雑名)	2135
94-I	*Jp.*	Shō-man-gyō-gi-sho (勝鬘經義疏)	2185
94-II	*Jp.*	Yui-ma-kyō-gi-sho (維摩經義疏)	2186
95	*Jp.*	Hok-ke-gi-sho (法華義疏)	2187
96-I	*Jp.*	Han-nya-shin-gyō-hi-ken (般若心經秘鍵)	2203
96-II	*Jp.*	Dai-jō-hos-sō-ken-jin-shō (大乘法相研神章)	2309
96-III	*Jp.*	Kan-jin-kaku-mu-shō (觀心覺夢鈔)	2312
97-I	*Jp.*	Ris-shū-kō-yō (律宗綱要)	2348
	Eng.	The Essentials of the Vinaya Tradition	
97-II	*Jp.*	Ten-dai-hok-ke-shū-gi-shū (天台法華宗義集)	2366
	Eng.	The Collected Teachings of the Tendai Lotus School	

Vol. No.		Title	*T.* No.
97-III	*Jp.*	Ken-kai-ron (顯戒論)	2376
97-IV	*Jp.*	San-ge-gaku-shō-shiki (山家學生式)	2377
98-I	*Jp.* *Eng.*	Hi-zō-hō-yaku (秘藏寶鑰) The Precious Key to the Secret Treasury (In Shingon Texts)	2426
98-II	*Jp.* *Eng.*	Ben-ken-mitsu-ni-kyō-ron (辨顯密二教論) On the Differences between the Exoteric and Esoteric Teachings (In Shingon Texts)	2427
98-III	*Jp.* *Eng.*	Soku-shin-jō-butsu-gi (即身成佛義) The Meaning of Becoming a Buddha in This Very Body (In Shingon Texts)	2428
98-IV	*Jp.* *Eng.*	Shō-ji-jis-sō-gi (聲字實相義) The Meanings of Sound, Sign, and Reality (In Shingon Texts)	2429
98-V	*Jp.* *Eng.*	Un-ji-gi (吽字義) The Meanings of the Word Hūṃ (In Shingon Texts)	2430
98-VI	*Jp.* *Eng.*	Go-rin-ku-ji-myō-hi-mitsu-shaku (五輪九字明秘密釋) The Illuminating Secret Commentary on the Five Cakras and the Nine Syllables (In Shingon Texts)	2514
98-VII	*Jp.* *Eng.*	Mitsu-gon-in-hotsu-ro-san-ge-mon (密嚴院發露懺悔文) The Mitsugonin Confession (In Shingon Texts)	2527
98-VIII	*Jp.* *Eng.*	Kō-zen-go-koku-ron (興禪護國論) A Treatise on Letting Zen Flourish to Protect the State (In Zen Texts)	2543
98-IX	*Jp.* *Eng.*	Fu-kan-za-zen-gi (普勧坐禪儀) A Universal Recommendation for True Zazen (In Zen Texts)	2580
99–103	*Jp.*	Shō-bō-gen-zō (正法眼藏)	2582

Vol. No.		Title	*T.* No.
104-I	*Jp.*	Za-zen-yō-jin-ki (坐禪用心記)	2586
	Eng.	Advice on the Practice of Zazen (In Zen Texts)	
104-II	*Jp.*	Sen-chaku-hon-gan-nen-butsu-shū (選擇本願念佛集)	2608
	Eng.	Senchaku Hongan Nembutsu Shū	
104-III	*Jp.*	Ris-shō-an-koku-ron (立正安國論)	2688
	Eng.	Risshōankokuron or The Treatise on the Establishment of the Orthodox Teaching and the Peace of the Nation (In Two Nichiren Texts)	
104-IV	*Jp.*	Kai-moku-shō (開目抄)	2689
	Eng.	Kaimokushō or Liberation from Blindness	
104-V	*Jp.*	Kan-jin-hon-zon-shō (觀心本尊抄)	2692
	Eng.	Kanjinhonzonsho or The Most Venerable One Revealed by Introspecting Our Minds for the First Time at the Beginning of the Fifth of the Five Five Hundred-year Ages (In Two Nichiren Texts)	
104-VI	*Ch.*	Fu-mu-ên-chung-ching (父母恩重經)	2887
	Eng.	The Sutra on the Profundity of Filial Love (In Apocryphal Scriptures)	
105-I	*Jp.*	Ken-jō-do-shin-jitsu-kyō-gyō-shō-mon-rui (顯淨土眞實教行証文類)	2646
	Eng.	Kyōgyōshinshō: On Teaching, Practice, Faith, and Enlightenment	
105-II	*Jp.*	Tan-ni-shō (歎異抄)	2661
	Eng.	Tannishō: Passages Deploring Deviations of Faith	
106-I	*Jp.*	Ren-nyo-shō-nin-o-fumi (蓮如上人御文)	2668
	Eng.	Rennyo Shōnin Ofumi: The Letters of Rennyo	
106-II	*Jp.*	Ō-jō-yō-shū (往生要集)	2682
107-I	*Jp.*	Has-shū-kō-yō (八宗綱要)	蔵外
	Eng.	The Essentials of the Eight Traditions	
107-II	*Jp.*	San-gō-shī-ki (三教指帰)	蔵外

Vol. No.	Title		*T*. No.
107-III	*Jp*.	Map-pō-tō-myō-ki (末法燈明記)	蔵外
	Eng.	The Candle of the Latter Dharma	
107-IV	*Jp*.	Jū-shichi-jō-ken-pō (十七條憲法)	蔵外